THE ETHICAL SEDUCTION OF
THE ANALYTIC SITUATION

PSYCHOANALYTIC IDEAS AND APPLICATIONS SERIES

Other titles in the Series include

THE ETHICAL SEDUCTION OF THE ANALYTIC SITUATION

The Feminine–Maternal Origins of Responsibility for the Other

Viviane Chetrit-Vatine

Psychoanalytic Ideas and Applications Series

Routledge
Taylor & Francis Group

LONDON AND NEW YORK

First published in French in 2012 as
La séduction éthique de la situation analytique by PUF

First published 2014 by Karnac Books Ltd.

Published 2018 by Routledge
2 Park Square, Milton Park, Abingdon, Oxon OX14 4RN
711 Third Avenue, New York, NY 10017, USA

Routledge is an imprint of the Taylor & Francis Group, an informa business

British Library Cataloguing in Publication Data

A C.I.P. for this book is available from the British Library

ISBN 9781782200543 (pbk)

Translation by Andrew Weller

This book is supported by the Institut français du Royaume Uni as part of the Burgess programme (www.frenchbooknews.com)

Edited, designed and produced by The Studio Publishing Services Ltd
www.publishingservicesuk.co.uk
e-mail: studio@publishingservicesuk.co.uk

CONTENTS

In memory of my father Jacques Vatine,
for my mother, Germaine Vatine,
my life companion, Marcel Chetrit,
our children and parents of our grandchildren,
Yonathan and Orit, Talia and Shahal, Yehuda and Tamar,
and our grandchildren,
Hillel, Nadav, Mika, Uriah, Michael, Libi, and Chira,
and to my patients.

ACKNOWLEDGEMENTS

Author

I should like to thank: Marcel Chetrit for his tenderness and his determination in the face of every ordeal; Sylvie and Georges Pragier for their hospitality and their committed presence; Danièle Brun, my doctoral thesis director, for her confidence, her support, and her generosity; Jacques André, François Villa, Daniel Widlöcher, Christophe Dejours, and Susann Heenen-Wolff, for having spontaneously accepted to form the jury of the thesis which was the basis of this book.

This is also an opportunity for me to thank Dominique Scarfone for accepting, at somewhat late notice, to write a preface for this book, and for the proximity of his inspiration in spite of the geographical distance; Bernard and Emmanuelle Chervet for their friendly support since the year 2000 in Montreal; Colette Chiland for her intellectual rigour; Paul Denis for his encouragement; Julia Kristeva for her creative passion and the richness of our exchanges during the preparation of the forum on the three monotheistic religions in Jerusalem in November 2008; Denys Ribas for enabling me to publish my first articles; Amos Squverer for helping me make a major choice of direction at the right moment; René Roussillon for our stimulating encounters; Henri Vermorel, who orientated me towards the choice of the theme of this thesis; Stella Ovadia for her long-standing faithfulness; and Eva Weill for her finesse and thoughtfulness.

I would also like to thank all those who in Israel who have participated in my training: Batya Friesel and Pinhas Noi, my analysts, and, in chronological order, Yolanda Gampel, Didier Weill, Raanan Kulka, Yossi Tamir, Nurit Hess, Ruth Sitton, Ygal Guinat, Beatrice Priel, Rivka Eiferman, Edith Mittrani, Abigail Golomb, Hezi Cohen, Rami Bar-Giora, Yael Ofarim, and Ruth Safrire.

I would also like to thank Pierre-Louis Fort and Annie Marné for finalising the presentation of this work in French, for their patience, and their encouragement, as well as Andrew Weller for his competent and careful translation of my book for this English edition.

Finally, I acknowledge the kind permission to reprint the extract from C. Stein's "L'enfant imaginaire" (2011) granted by the publisher, Éditions Flammarion.

Translator

I would like to thank Viviane Chetrit-Vatine for entrusting me with this translation and for the help she has given me in finalising it. A warm thank you, too, to Monique Zerbib, who has kindly given a lot of her time assisting me with this task.

ABOUT THE AUTHOR

Viviane Chetrit-Vatine, former President of the Israel Psychoanalytic Society and faculty member of the Israel Institute of Psychoanalysis, is a training analyst for adults and children. Her professional activity includes a private practice in Jerusalem and in Tel Aviv, teaching and training at the Israel Institute of Psychoanalysis and on other Israeli psychotherapeutic post-graduate programmes, and research activity in the laboratory run by François Villa at Paris VII Diderot University (CPRMS). She is a member of the international reading committee of the *Revue Française de Psychanalyse*, of the international scientific committee of *Monographies de Psychanalyse*, and of the reading committee of *Maarag*. She publishes articles in Israeli journals (*Sihot, Maarag*), in French journals (*RFP, Le Coq-héron*), as well as in the *International Journal of Psychoanalysis*.

SERIES EDITOR'S FOREWORD

The Publication Committee of the International Psychoanalytical Association continues, with this volume, the series "Psychoanalytic Ideas and Applications".

The aim of this series is to focus on the scientific production of significant authors whose works are outstanding contributions to the development of the psychoanalytic field and to set out relevant ideas and themes, generated during the history of psychoanalysis, that deserve to be known and discussed by present psychoanalysts.

The relationship between psychoanalytic ideas and their applications has to be put forward from the perspetive of theory, clinical practice, technique, and research, so as to maintain their validity for contemporary psychoanalysis.

The Publication Committee's objective is to share these ideas with the psychoanalytic community and with professionals in other related disciplines, in order to expand their knowledge and generate a productive interchange between the text and the reader.

Viviane Chetrit-Vatine's *The Ethical Seduction of the Analytic Situation* is an original and extremely interesting text, in which the author offers the readers a broad idea of her thoughts on what she understands about the psychoanalytic cure, envisaged as an interhuman relationship that reproduces the earliest moments of the development of the human being and its encounter with its environment. The author introduces and applies Levinas's philosophical contribution on ethics and his core idea about "responsibility for the other", articulated with Laplanche's hypothesis of "the primal seduction". The articulation is condensed in what she calls the "ethical seduction", with a particular stress on the asymmetry inherent in both the first moments of the newborn and the demands of psychoanalytic treatment.

I have no doubt that this brilliant volume will encounter the interest of psychoanalysts and psychotherapists worldwide.

Gennaro Saragnano
Series Editor
Chair, IPA Publications Committee

Dominique Scarfone

Astronomy started at the dawn of human history, the clear starry sky offering itself to the naked eye, but it became a more exact discipline with the invention of the telescope a few centuries ago. Microbiology also could not have existed in its rigorous form prior to the invesion of the microscope. All things being equal, the same could be said of psychoanalysis: that we are indebted to Freud, first and foremost, for his invention of a method with which to explore the unconscious, a domain that poets and philosophers had envisioned but could not study in any systematic way. A major difference, however, exists between psychoanalysis and the sciences I have mentioned, both of which are indebted to the creation of a specific instrument. Indeed, while in astronomy, microbiology, radiology, or any of many other similar fields, the tool or instrument is an *adjunct* to the sensory apparatus of the researcher, the psychoanalytic method does not operate independently of the subjects involved in the exploration. The psychoanalytic instrument cannot be employed without changing something in the people who are using it. In that sense, psychoanalysis is even more probabilistic than quantum physics, for while in quantum mechanics carrying out a measurement has a decisive impact on what is observed, it was never said that such observation changes the experimenter himself. This, however, is precisely what happens in psychoanalysis: there is simply no observation of unconscious facts without analyst and analysand both being subjected to changes in their very being.

This is my way of saying that, on the one hand, psychoanalysis is a science of sorts—a discipline whose claims in terms of cognitive mechanisms, for instance, are increasingly well documented by neuroscientists (see, for example, Carhart-Harris & Friston, 2010)—but that, at the same time, it is an inextricably ethical endeavour.

This second aspect needs to be expounded in more detail. Indeed, every form of human practice carries a form of ethical responsibility. Your plumber needs to observe his professional code of ethics when repairing the pipes in your home, lest your building suffer serious structural damage. If he has been doing a valuable professional job as a plumber, however, this fact has no necessary link to his intimate being. This cannot be the case in psychoanalysis, where ethics do not intervene only in terms of what one could call a "professional mantle", for example, ensuring the patient that the analyst was well trained and operates following certain standards. The ethical stance of the analyst is not merely a requirement at the professional level (this we would preferably call the analyst's deontology) because ethics are, indeed, inseparable from what psychoanalysis is all about. For if psychoanalysis as a whole can be seen as a scientific discipline of some kind, psychoanalytic practice does not rest only on the validity of its scientific claims: more fundamentally, it rests on the instantiation of an ethical position on the part of the analyst. Actually, you could say that without the implementation of such an ethical attitude, you would simply not obtain significant psychoanalytic facts. My way of putting this is that in psychoanalysis, our ethics and our epistemics are two sides of the same coin. If a neologism is allowed, I would say that psychoanalysis is a case of ethepistemics.

This assertion is most obvious when you look at analytic praxis with the aid of the authors to which Viviane Chétrit-Vatine refers most eminently in the present book: Jean Laplanche and Emmanuel Levinas. The ethical stance is fundamental in Laplanche's description of the analytic situation, seen as a reopening of the "fundamental anthropological situation" where a newborn is immersed in a very asymmetrical relationship, exposed to the enigmatic aspects of messages emanating from the caring adults. The enigmas here are enigmas in more ways than usual, since, under normal circumstances, the adults themselves are unaware of the sexual "contaminants" that operate a seduction in spite of their irreproachable ethical conduct: an implantation of the sexual with which the child will have to deal for the rest of his life. Such unavoidable seduction, therefore, normally operates within the framework where the infant's helplessness is taken into account and taken care of, thereby verifying Freud's dictum that "the initial helplessness of human beings is the primal source of all moral motives" (Freud, 1895, p. 318, original italics in the original), something that the author of this volume addresses on numerous occasions.

It is not the place here to enter into the detail of what important consequences are implied in the innumerable variations that can occur around the theme of the infant's helplessness. More important for the analyst is to be aware of what Laplanche has highlighted, which is that the analytic situation reinstates the asymmetry of the infant–adult relationship, and, therefore, calls for what one cannot but qualify as a strict, intrinsically ethical framework. For Laplanche, the ethics here require of the analyst that he be the "guardian of the enigma", and this is instantiated in the analyst's "refusal to know". Therefore, it looks like a prescribed stance that the analyst must adopt if the analytic situation is to be maintained as active. In other words, the analyst is called upon to acknowledge that what he reinstates is a situation of primal seduction, and yet he is required not to make any deliberate use whatsoever of the influence that such seductive framework affords. Thus, it is clearly reasonable to call for an "ethical seduction" in psychoanalysis, as Chétrit-Vatine aptly calls it.

Yet, Chétrit-Vatine's recourse to Emmanuel Levinas brings the issue of ethical seduction to another level of reflexion. The question of the analyst's ethical stance is not simply a question of prescribing the appropriate technical attitude, such as the active refusal to know on the part of the analyst. In fact, it is not at all clear that Laplanche thought of such refusal as simply a prescriptive strategy on the part of the analyst. I think I concur with Chétrit-Vatine if I say that the links between Laplanche's and Levinas's thinking are more profound than either of them, if asked, could have acknowledged. This is because if the seduction occurring in the analytic situation is to be ascribed to a reopening of a more fundamental anthropological situation, then we are clearly dealing with something that, for Laplanche himself, sits at the border of psychoanalysis proper. Laplanche is, thereby, making a more universal claim which goes beyond the strict analytical situation, just as Freud did in the passage cited above. This is what allows Chétrit-Vatine——and all of us——to make use of the extra-analytic treasure inherited from Levinas. Taking care of a newborn baby is then not simply an ethological instinctual endeavour; it is the very paradigm of our inescapable responsibility for the other. If this responsibility can be said to have a "feminine origin", as asserted here by Chétrit-Vatine, this should not surprise us if we consider that, for Levinas, the Other is really the feminine (Levinas, 1948). Not the woman, but the feminine, a concept which, in spite of major differences between Levinas and Freud, cannot but resonate with the Freudian version thereof. The feminine in Freud's bisexual conception of the subject is linked with passivity, a very Levinasian theme indeed, although Levinas seems to think of these two themes separately. In fact, the question here becomes extremely tangled, requiring that we distinguish between the concepts of feminine, femininity, the maternal, etc. In view of this, Viviane Chétrit-Vatine proposes to consider a matricial space, a term whose coinage could, if not solve, at least help to bypass the difficulties that arise from the differences between Levinasian and psychoanalytic conceptions regarding the locus and source of responsibility for the other. In my understanding, the matrix in question contains an inescapable "activity", in the sense of the emission of the compromised messages (Laplanche), but it is counterbalanced by the acknowledgement of our radical passivity as a foundation of the human condition. Such "radical passivity" is essential if we are to acknowledge our responsibility for the other, a responsibility which the subject can deny and try to avoid, of course, but a responsibility which, as analysts, we discover we have been accepting from the very moment we started listening analytically to another human.

Today's search for scientific respectability by psychoanalysts may sometimes make things look as if it is not so much a matter of being receptive any more; the "passive" origin of our sense of responsibility seems to be traded for an "active" one, in the sense of a scientifically motivated therapeutic strategy. The present book calls our attention to a more fundamental point of view, which in no way counters the efforts towards ensuring that science supports our central theoretical tenets, but nevertheless asks of us to think of the very *raison d'être* of our discipline and of its foundational instrument: listening to the other in the responsible way afforded by the Freudian method, which may prove to eminently incarnate Levinassian ethics.

Introduction

The question of ethics, defined by Emmanuel Levinas as responsibility for the other, is intrinsically linked to the contemporary conception of psychoanalytic treatment envisaged as an inter-human relationship. After the *Shoah* (and all the other crimes perpetrated by humanity against humanity), and one hundred years after Freud wrote his article "'Civilized' sexual morality and modern nervous illness" (1908d), humanity, wounded by the events through which it has passed and continues to pass, is still destabilised by the gap between its psychic means on the one hand and the increasingly rapid development of technologies and their impact on the modalities of "dying", of "giving life", and of "living" on the other (see Appendix 1).

Although God will not disappear (Newberg, d'Aquili, Rause, 2003), the concept of God must be conceived of in a manner that is unfettered by his omnipotence, even if he retains his attributes of goodness and intelligibility (Jonas, 1984). Thus, and in a way that is not unrelated to the impact psychoanalysis has had on the *socius*, or social fabric, family structures are being transformed. The forms of conception and parenting are diversifying. The organising myths of reference are no longer so obviously adequate. The analyses we conduct are intended for people, children or adults, who are profoundly discontented and sometimes struggling to survive at all.

Thus, "the fundamental anthropological situation" (Laplanche, 1987), that is, the situation of primary distress of the human infant and its absolute dependency, for its survival, on an adult environment that cares for it, remains the bedrock of humanisation.

This primal situation is doubly asymmetrical, owing to the seductive and ethical power of the adult environment.

It is asymmetrical and seductive in so far as it is based on an encounter between, on the one hand, an adult world endowed with a sexual unconscious and adult sexuality and, on the other, a human infant endowed with psycho-physiological montages that are both immature and susceptible to being affected by this adult world on which he or she is totally dependent. It is asymmetrical and ethical in so far as this adult world is responsible for him or her, and either assumes this responsibility or declines it.

This foundational, seductive, and ethical asymmetry will be reactualised in the transferences provoked by analysis and during it. For this double asymmetry of the analytic situation, I propose the term "ethical seduction".

Furthermore, it is my contention that meaning can no longer be considered as being always *already there*, deposited in some hidden recess of the subject's unconscious. In analysis, it will, in many cases, be gradually constructed, found, and created at the heart of the analytic process and with the help of what I call the analyst's "affected" participation (*participation affectée*).[1] The work of symbolisation, necessary for all forms of psychic life, far from being a solitary task, will prove to be one that is carried out by two people. The shadow of the analyst—and his or her seductive and responsible impact—has fallen on the analysis. The other subject—the analyst—is necessarily involved in the work. To the analysis of the transference must be added not only the analysis of the countertransference, but also the analysis of the ferment constituted by the analyst's "affected" (i.e., emotionally cathected) presence, listening, and saying (*dire*). At the source of the capacity of analysis to bring about transformation, at the origins of the formation of a capacity for subjective appropriation, which might be deficient, and at the origin of subjectivisation, we will have to consider the role played by the analyst.

Analysis is a practice. Because it involves a relationship between two subjects, the analyst's own analysis is not sufficient. The fact that the analyst is an ethical subject, in so far as he or she has asymmetrical responsibility for the other, and the fact that the analytic situation is a repository of ethical seduction, must, henceforth, be taken into account. These considerations, anchored in clinical practice, will open out on to a number of propositions concerning the origins of the human capacity for responsibility for the other and its connection with the maternal/feminine dimension.

In the first part of this book, I briefly consider Freud's views on ethics and its origins, and, though it might seem strange, the possible points of convergence between Freud and Levinas, and then Lacan and Levinas. I then consider the propositions of Hans Jonas, which allow me to posit "from the beginning" the existence, in the neonate, of an "ethical exigency (or requirement)" *vis-à-vis* its environment and, consequently, the existence of an unavoidable interpellation or convocation of the adult to take responsibility for him. Finally, I develop those aspects of Levinasian philosophy that provide us with food for thought regarding analytic practice.

In the second part, I situate myself at the beginning of life and in analytic treatment, at the heart of what Laplanche has designated as the "fundamental anthropological situation".

I take up some of his hypotheses and his theory of generalised seduction. However, I explore in greater depth the question of the primacy of affect in as much as, for me, it is the conscious manifestation of drive activity emanating from the primal seduction, and with it the question of ordinary maternal passion. This leads me to examine the question of the mother as a sublimatory agent, as formulated by Julia Kristeva. I introduce the question of the analyst's passion and its articulation with the question of primal seduction in analysis.

After clarifying what I mean by "an exigency (requirement) for ethics", an exigency for self-preservation that is present right at the beginning of life, I examine in detail its manifestations in analytic treatment. I take up Bollas's idea that the mother, and, therefore, the analyst, is a transformational object, and put forward the idea that, when everything goes as well as possible in life, ethical asymmetry, understood as responsibility for the other, combined from the outset with the asymmetry of primal seduction, is at the origin of subjectivisation and of the subjective appropriation of the order of symbolisation—as conceptualised by Roussillon—which underlies the transformational capacity of analysis.

In the third part, I develop this proposition of a double asymmetry of the analytic situation, along with its implications for the analytic situation. This leads me to propose the concept of "ethical seduction". The analyst's passion, the need for ethics in analysis, the processes of subjectivisation, and the ethical seduction of the analytic situation at the origins of subjective appropriation in analysis, are illustrated by clinical sequences from child and adult analyses. The following subjects are the focus of particular attention: the offer of analysis, the analytic process, and the analytic setting.

The fourth part of the book opens up other paths of exploration, envisaging, for instance, an alternative origin for ethics to that posed by Freud, and, consequently, a supplementary psychoanalytic status for the human capacity for responsibility for the other. I reflect on the feminine–maternal origins of this human capacity for responsibility for the other, especially as I consider that the maternal and the feminine belong together. I put forward the following proposition: the exigency or requirement for ethics (ethics conceived of here as responsibility for the other) is intrinsically bound up with the self-preservative needs of the human infant. Its aim is the constitution of its identity. However, this exigency destabilises the one who is interpellated by it, owing to the unavoidable violence of this interpellation, of this breach or intrusion (*effraction*). This destabilisation of the adult who is in charge of the infant takes effect retroactively (*après coup*). Indeed, the violence of the interpellation by the newborn infant awakens traces left in the adult's psyche, at the beginning of his or her own life, through the encounter with the adult world interpellated by his or her own arrival in the world. The traumatic effect of this interpellation will be inscribed, in turn, in the developing psyche of the little human being as traces resulting from enigmatic signifiers whose translation is impossible. This inscription will be at the origin in the human being of the feminine–maternal dimension and, therefore, of the potential capacity for responsibility for the other.

By way of conclusion, I recapitulate the propositions I have made while reaffirming the intrinsic role in contemporary analytic practice of an analyst who is a subject with responsibility for the other, the subject of an ethics without ingenuousness, and without cynicism.

Finally, reflecting retrospectively on my own personal development, I insist on the analyst's awakening and of its ethical dimension.

In the Appendices, the reader will find some considerations on new forms of parenting within the Israeli legal context, a digression on Margarete Neuman-Buber's book, *Milena*, and a commentary on Laplanche's personal questionings, in dialogue with Levinas, on . . . responsibility.

Translator's note

1. Normally affecté (par) means "affected by" something or someone. The author's use of the word here is a neologism in French meaning "emotionally cathected or invested", but it also plays on the ordinary meaning of being "affected by" (affecté par). I have preserved this neologism in English between inverted commas when it appears in the text.

The analysis of the psychoanalyst is his whole psychoanalytic work, and more particularly the fruit of the work he does with his patients; whether this product manifests itself simply in the progress of daily reflection or whether the psychoanalyst shares it with the public in the form of more or less elaborate works, it is only the reflection of the endless pursuit . . . of the construction of a past that has its roots in the most distant aspects of childhood by which it is nourished.
(C. Stein, 2011, p. 399)

PART I

ON A POSSIBLE CONTRIBUTION OF LEVINAS'S THOUGHT TO CONTEMPORARY PSYCHOANALYSIS

Introduction to Part I

I f the question of ethics is self-evident for the analyst (in so far as he or she respects the human person), it is perhaps less so to put Levinasian thought to the service of psychoanalytic thought and its practice (the latent risk being one of a confusion of genres and a lack of rigour with regard to the fields concerned, namely, philosophy and psychoanalysis) or to consider as clinically effective an intervention that is understood to be an expression of the analyst's ethics in action. The contiguous nature of these diverse positions might be the fruit of a hazardous patchwork that is not necessarily harmonious on a first reading; or, and this is my hope, of an encounter that is potentially creative and inspiring.

In *Ethics and Infinity* (1982b), Levinas posits "responsibility for the other" as defining ethics, and ethics as "first philosophy". He proposes a critique of the European philosophical tradition and, in particular, of philosophical reflections on totality (as it is presented, in his view, in the writings of Friedrich Hegel). He is interested in subjectivity and intersubjectivity from a non-psychological standpoint. For him, intersubjectivity is ethical and the structure of subjectivity is responsibility for the other. The human subject is "being for the other". And being for the other "is to address oneself to the other in the mode of the caress and not of mastery—*Begriff* (Kemp, 1977, pp. 66–67) or *Bemächtigung* in German (Freud, 1924c, p. 163)". Pontalis (2000) speaks of "the concept's clutch or grasp. It is a predator, a tyrant". After citing Nietzsche's remark that "the concept is formed by forgetting what differentiates one thing from another", he goes on to write, "When I say hysterical, obsessional, borderline, I am forgetting the person who is speaking to me" (pp. 18–20).

Now Levinas is the philosopher of singularity. Levinas's vision has been considered by some as romantic. In fact, if, for him, man is not a wolf for man, it is because man is a man for man. Here, he concurs with Laplanche (or rather Laplanche concurs with him) when the latter insists on the human particularity of the sexual unconscious and, with it, the specifically human capacity for committing the worst atrocities, but also for realising the most lofty creations. However, Levinas (1982a) writes, "The only absolute value is the human capacity to give priority to the other over oneself", and he continues, "I do not affirm human holiness; I say that man cannot question the supreme value of holiness" (p. 119). I shall return to this point later (see Part IV).

It has been pointed out that there are certain similarities between Levinas and Jacques Lacan (Assoun, 1993), Donald Woods Winnicott (Pisanté, 2002), and Heinz Kohut (Kulka, 2005). The latter two have advanced the hypothesis of a primary need to be loved and recognised, alongside the existence of the need to be capable of loving and of seeking truth. In this sense, they have a less pessimistic conception of the human being than Freud or Lacan, and, following in the footsteps of Ferenczi and Balint, they propose a transformative psychoanalysis based on the central role they give to the environment, with regard to both the origins of psychopathology and to its capacity for reparation. But Winnicott and Kohut both blunted considerably the sexual dimension as an organiser of the psyche. Although Meltzer, who was a neo-Kleinian but also influenced by Winnicott's thinking, attributes a role to seduction, for him it is symmetrical between the mother and the infant, and is sublimated from the outset into seduction of beauty (Meltzer, 1988).

For my part, I am interested in an encounter between Levinas and Laplanche. For each of them, primacy belongs to the other, and this primacy is a mark of the asymmetry of the encounter. In Laplanche's work, this encounter occurs between a newborn infant and an adult world in an asymmetrical relationship owing to the primal seduction coming from the messages of the adult world in charge of the infant's care. For Levinas, this encounter is the other person's face interpellating or summoning me, immediately making me aware of my asymmetrical responsibility for him.

That said, I begin by taking a brief look at Freud's views on ethics and its origins, without claiming to cover the question exhaustively. I explore some possible points of correspondence between Levinas and Freud, then between Levinas and Lacan, where, strangely enough, their reflections might coincide. As a first indication, I shall consider the propositions of Hans Jonas concerning the origins of responsibility for the other. These propositions allow me to posit the existence, "from the outset", of an ethical requirement in the newborn infant and a summons for the adult to take responsibility for him. Finally, I develop those aspects of Levinasian philosophy that offer food for thought concerning analytic practice.

CHAPTER ONE

Ethics and psychoanalysis

Freud and ethics: The Project, The Ego and the Id, Civilization and its Discontents

I n the *Project* (1895), Freud writes: "If the [child] screams . . . [it] will awaken the memory of the subject's own screaming and at the same time his own experiences of pain" (p. 331). Earlier, he had indicated that, at these early stages, the human organism is incapable of bringing about the "specific action" (p. 318) aimed at satisfying his needs of survival. Extraneous help, *fremde Hilfe*, is indispensable. It takes place, he writes,

> *when the attention of an experienced person is drawn to* the child's state by discharge along the path of internal change [by its screams, for example]. In this way, this path of discharge acquires a secondary function of the highest importance, that of *communication. The initial helplessness of human beings is the primal source of all moral motives* ["*die Urquelle aller moralischen Motive*"]. (p. 318)

In Schneider's terms, "it is this experience, which is not exempt from effects of interference and contagion, that Freud places at the foundations of ethics" (1993, p. 208).

It is worth noting that although at the beginning of life he places concern for the other at the origin of ethics, Freud uses a language that is devoid of all affect; when he speaks of the first object he calls it a *Nebenmensch*, a fellow human being, a neighbour. Schneider sees a link between this *Nebenmensch* and the Levinasian ethical subject. Indeed, for Levinas, the other who interpellates me with regard to my responsibility for him is approached through "proximity". In Levinas's work, as in Freud's *Project*, this *Nebenmensch*, this fellow human being, is thought of as asexual. As the centrality of sexuality is increasingly affirmed, Freud's interest turns not to responsibility but to guilt. Indeed, he soon posits that the origin of ethics lies in guilt. The question of responsibility is not given specific treatment, as he shifts from one conception to the other. It is perhaps due to this shift regarding the origin of ethics that the latter would be situated on the side of paternal and masculine filiation.

We might wonder what could have prevented Freud from re-examining his foundations prior to the Oedipus complex, even though he had touched on the subject in the *Project* and shown interest in the psychoanalytic origins of morality. Was it perhaps his fear of the maternal, his fear of the feminine, his fear of the maternal being too entangled with the feminine, his fear of matricidal tendencies in himself (see Brun, 1990a, pp. 198–200)? My hypothesis is that, in both Freud and Levinas, this asexualisation of the subject who is responsible for the other is connected with an "impossibility of thinking" (*in-pensabilité*) of the maternal in terms of sexualised femininity. Consequently, maternal and feminine are barred, and in their place the primal ethical subject is neutralised.

Schneider has made a very penetrating examination of Freud's thought concerning guilt and its function, with reference to *The Interpretation of Dreams* (1900a) and *Totem and Taboo* (1912–1913). I will just cite the last paragraph of her above-mentioned article:

> If the world of transgression, as it is articulated in oedipal conflicts, can serve as a gag to silence a woman's grievance [she is referring to Irma's dream], can one not detect a hidden complicity between the feminine [a feminine connected with the maternal] and that which has its origin in the "*Urquelle*" (primal source) of all moral motives, a source that disorients the separating [and I would add "defensive"] criteria? (Schneider, 1993, p. 208, translated for this edition)

The specific nature of the feminine position in relation to the superego thus calls for a re-examination.

Following this line of thinking, in the fourth part of the book I will put forward an alternative view of the origins of the capacity for responsibility for the other. What I want to draw attention to here is Freud's indication that the origin of ethics lies in the inescapable necessity for the survival of the little human being of a *Nebenmensch* who is capable of responding to his state of *Hilfslosigkeit*, or helplessness. We will come across the same idea further on in the work of the philosopher Hans Jonas, who is also interested in the question of responsibility.

In the *Project*, Freud touched, then, upon the self-preservative origin of ethics. The child, fearful of losing the object on which he depends for survival, will comply with the demands of the object in exchange for continued ministrations of care—compliance that is based on his capacity to recognise intuitively the demands or expectations of his objects. In the last instance, morality is associated with "helplessness". Assoun (1984) comments that Freud's formulation in the *Project* "is interesting insofar as it links the ideal to helplessness – to distress – or to *absence*" (p. 189, fn. 4, translated for this edition). I must say that I have doubts about an ethical position whose ends are self-preservative. Moreover, the child who is preoccupied with taking into account the adult in order to ensure his own survival makes me think of the individual functioning on the basis of a *false self*, as described by Winnicott. I want to call into question such foundations for ethics defined as responsibility for the other.

At the time of the *Project*, Freud's perspective was monadic. His interest was focused on intrapsychic functioning. After abandoning his *neurotica*, his Copernican revolution, the revelation of the other in oneself, that is to say, the recognition that the ego is not the master of its own house, would be based on an approach and research centred on the functioning of the human mind as such. Admittedly, Freud distanced himself from the positions in vogue with his masters, who had turned their attention to hereditary causes and constitutional predispositions in an attempt to understand mental pathologies, but the necessity of a mother providing attentive care was taken for granted. What was not envisaged, however, were the vagaries of this care, and the need to question the origins of the capacity of the adult to meet this responsibility for the other, for his survival and development.

When Freud refers to the origins of ethics in the *Project*, he mentions allusively what happens to the adult partner: "If he [the child] screams . . . [it] will awaken the memory of the subject's own screaming and at the same time his own experiences of pain" (1895, p. 331), but then this partner is, as it were, circumvented. It is true that we come across him—or rather her—again, in the form of the first seductress, in the *Three Essays* (1905d) and in his *Leonardo* (1910c). But it was not until Ferenczi, Klein, and, above all, Michael Balint in Hungary, and Winnicott and Bion in the UK, that full importance was given to the impact of the quality of the adult environment, as the first provider of care, on the formation of the human psyche.

Freud considered for a long time that "what is moral (or ethical) is self-evident" (Assoun, 1984, p. 230, fn. 2, translated for this edition, a formulation borrowed from Théodor Vischer in a letter to Putnam dated 8 July 1915). It was not necessary to construct a theory of it: what is ethical is always there and stands to reason; it refers to the factual nature of something. Yet, Assoun, as we have seen, links the status of ethics in Freud to the question of the ideal (1984, p. 195) and stresses the close relationship in Freud's work between the ideal and narcissism. He writes,

> The term 'ideal' made its appearance in Freud's work as an explicit category with the introduction of narcissism, and precisely as a predicate of the ego (ego-ideal). It was in the newly created humus of narcissism, around 1910, that the ideal was at the zenith of psychoanalytic theory, which means that its metapsychological credentials were solemnly recognised. (Assoun, 1984, p. 196, translated for this edition)

Now this ideal opens out to the question of ethics, when Freud links it to what he calls "moral conscience", "an instrument for measuring the ideal which informs the ego about the state of its relations with the ideal; it indicates to the subject the state of his relations with his ideal" (Assoun, 1984, p. 196. translated for this edition).

In *The Ego and the Id* (1923b), Freud writes, "Psycho-analysis has been reproached time after time with ignoring the higher, suprapersonal side of human nature" (p. 35). This reproach is unjust, he says, notably from the historical standpoint: "We have from the very beginning attributed the function of instigating repression to the moral and aesthetic trends in the ego" (1923b, p. 35). Psychoanalysis had hitherto concerned itself with the study of what was repressed in mental life but, he continues,

> ... now that we have embarked upon the analysis of the ego we can give an answer to all those whose moral sense has been shocked and who have complained that there must surely be a higher nature in man: 'Very true,' we can say, 'and here we have that higher nature, in this ego ideal or super-ego the representative of our relation to our parents. When we were little children, we knew these higher natures, we admired them and feared them; and later we took them into ourselves.'

> The ego ideal is therefore the heir of the Oedipus complex, and thus it is also the expression of the most powerful impulses and most important libidinal vicissitudes of the id. . . . Whereas the ego is essentially the representative of the external world, of reality, the super-ego stands in contrast to it as the representative of the internal world, of the id. Conflicts between the ego and the ideal will . . . ultimately reflect the contrast between what is real and what is psychical, between the external world and the internal world. (1923b, p. 36)

Here, Freud continues with his phylogenetic hypothesis rather than staying with "the very beginning" not only of the history of psychoanalysis, but of the history of the little human being. Throughout this book, I will be re-examining, in a latent manner, the notion of "the very beginning" of ethics. Laplanche (1999b) notes that Freud speaks of guilt and not of responsibility, "with the purpose", he says "of not subjectivising the problem too much" (p. 147). Is it a matter of not subjectivising the problem or is it that neither Freud nor Laplanche question the foundations of responsibility? "Freud", Laplanche continues, "refers to 'moral feelings' which call into question our responsibility" (differentiated here from guilt) for the immoral contents of our dreams. This "problem of moral responsibility for the contents of dreams" (Freud, 1925i, p. 131) is a late addition (Laplanche, 1999b, p. 151, cf. Appendix 3) to *The Interpretation of Dreams*. This was the period of the second topography, when the psychical apparatus was divided into ego, id, and superego.

Now, the condemnation of possible immoral contents can be just as sadistic as the id. Klein and Lacan are in complete agreement: the superego is ferocious. If there is nothing ethical about the id, how can we speak about the ethics of such a superego?

As for the ethics of the ego, Freud finally sweeps this notion aside as illusory, because it has its origin in "moral narcissism": "If anyone is dissatisfied with this and would like to be 'better' than he was created, let him see whether he can attain anything more in life than hypocrisy or inhibition" (Freud, 1925i, p. 134).

But in 1929—six years after *The Ego and the Id*—he was also able to write, in *Civilization and its Discontents* (1930a), that "Ethics is thus to be regarded as a therapeutic attempt – as an endeavour to achieve, by means of a command of the superego, something which so far has not been achieved by means of any other cultural activities" (p. 142). In fact, Freud no longer adhered to the views he had expressed a few years earlier. Further evidence of this may be found in an earlier passage:

> Men are not gentle creatures who want to be loved, and who at the most can defend themselves if they are attacked; they are, on the contrary, creatures among whose instinctual endowments is to be reckoned a powerful share of aggressiveness. (p. 111)

The neighbour, therefore, is not only a potential helper or sexual object, but also someone who incites man to violence and murder. Man is tempted

> to satisfy [his] aggressiveness on [his neighbour] to exploit his capacity for work without compensation, to use him sexually without his consent, to seize his possessions, to humiliate him, to cause him pain to torture and to kill him. *Homo homini lupus.* Who, in the face of all his experience of life and history, will have the courage to dispute this assertion? (Freud, 1930a, p. 111)

Further on, Freud asks, "What means does civilization employ to inhibit the aggressiveness which opposes it?" His answer to this is

> His aggression is introjected, internalised . . . directed towards his own ego. There it is taken over by a portion of the ego, which sets itself over against the rest of the ego as super-ego, and which now in the form of "conscience" is ready to put into action against the ego the same harsh aggressiveness that the ego would have liked to satisfy upon other, extraneous individuals. The tension between the harsh super-ego and the ego that is subjected to it, is called by us the sense of guilt . . . (Freud, 1930a, p. 123)

Freud rejects the principle of a natural capacity to distinguish goodness from evil. Thus, he assumes the existence of an "extraneous influence" that decides what is to be called good and bad. Evil, then, is what causes the child to be threatened with the loss of the love of another person on whom he is dependent. The next stage is the establishment of the superego, which is just as implacable as the first authority figure experienced by the infant. It should be noted that while, for Klein, the newborn infant arrives in the world with such a superego, for Laplanche, the superego is the product of an impossible translation of the categorical imperatives addressed to the child by its parents. These enigmatic messages are all the more untranslatable and non-metabolisable by the infant's psyche in that they are unjustifiable by definition (Laplanche, 1987, p. 139).

Freud also writes,

'Natural' ethics, as it is called, has nothing to offer here except the narcissistic satisfaction of being able to think oneself better than others . . . But so long as virtue is not rewarded here on earth, ethics will, I fancy, preach in vain. (1930a, p. 143)

According to Assoun (1984), Freud's position regarding ethics is "the moment of truth of his theory of the ideal" (p. 227). He continues,

Freud presents indifference to the ideal as both a technical requirement of analysis and a personal attitude . . . 'a constitutional incapacity'. Paradoxically, this position is combined with Freud's need to converse with James Putnam or the pastor Pfister, 'professionals of the ideal', who 'are a refreshing change for him from those who have silenced their superego too cheaply'. (p. 228, translated for this edition)

Assoun adds, "We know how contemptuous Freud was towards those who practise analysis with a 'perverse' disposition" (p. 228, fn. 1, translated for this edition), and in a letter to Oskar Pfister, Freud declared, "If we are to talk of ethics, I subscribe to a high ideal from which most of the human beings I have come across depart most lamentably" (Assoun, 1984, fn. 1, letter to Pfister of 9 October 1918 (Meng & E. L. Freud, 1963, p. 62)). Reflecting on this apparent paradox in Freud's positions, Assoun states, "The real ideal would be one that does without any consideration of the ideal" (translated for this edition. Ethics would, thus, dissociate itself from such a discourse.

For my part, I have found ethics, as defined by Levinas, and in Freud's own words, to be "a kind of highway code for traffic among mankind" (Assoun, 1984, n. 1, letter to Pfister, 24 February 1928, in Meng & E. L. Freud, 1963, p. 123). If the Freudian status of the ideal was the law itself, as Assoun proposes, I would say that a Levinasian code of ethics for the analyst would be based rather on a command, but that, in spite of their potential opposition, Freud and Levinas would agree on the following formulation by Freud in *The Ego and the Id*: "The normal man is not only far more immoral than he believes but also far more moral than he knows" (Assoun, p. 230, n. 4, translated for thuis edition, citing Freud, 1923b, p. 52). I can only agree with Assoun when he evokes the message addressed by psychoanalysis to humanity: "It is necessary to come to terms with narcissistic infatuation and to know that psychoanalysis not only has much less affinity with the ideal than it thinks, but many more aptitudes than it realises" (Assoun, 1984, p. 230, translated for this edition).

Freud and Levinas: desire and call

Continuing for the moment on this paradoxical note, I am going to introduce Chalier's (2002) proposition, showing how Freud's critical conceptions of the spiritual converge, curiously enough, with those of Levinas. For Levinas, the idea of a God—and, more broadly, of a metaphysical desire arising from a need, a lack, or a situation of distress—"entering the economic circuit" is sharply criticised. Levinas refutes this economic conception of religion based on the idea of a consoling or protective God who supposedly turns towards man in his distress in order to encourage, relieve, or compensate him. She suggests that in this sense Levinas shares the views of Freud, for whom the root of this illusion of belief in God lies in the state of distress or helplessness, which, from childhood onwards, places each human life under the stamp of anxiety and fear for one's own life. As we shall see further on, Levinas's views concerning the origin of belief in God go hand in hand with his insistence on the fact that the other who interpellates or summons me to responsibility for him disturbs me, violates me, and unsettles my state of well-being.

Whereas Freud's vision of religion is tragic, Chalier indicates that Levinas's thought on human needs, happiness, desire, and religion differs from this tragic vision. Levinas asks, "And what if religion does not depend only on economic factors? What if we were to imagine a man who has all he could wish for?" Levinas speaks of spiritual desire that is born of well-being—a state of well-being that is violated by another person's distress. In fact, there are unsatisfied people who have no idea of God. Many atheists calmly accept the finiteness of life. So, the spiritual is not a need. One can live and die without it. Chalier notes that for Levinas spiritual desire does not originate from pain, but "constitutes the trace in the human psyche of a reality that is not felt to be lacking, and therefore is not expected one day to offer fulfilment" (p. 17, translated for this edition). She continues, "the proximity of the Infinite in the finite occurs at the heart of the psyche in the form of a call that creates a dimension in oneself that cannot be reduced to that of a prior lack" (p. 18, translated for this edition). This proposition resonates very closely for me with the idea of the analyst envisaged as an ethical subject. So, ethics, regarded as a modality of transcendence, can be thought about in terms of the secularisation of the sacred. (Rolland, commenting on Levinas, writes, "Levinas may be read as a thinker of secularisation looking to grasp the opportunity provided to thought by the death of a certain God, tenant of the world-behind-the-world" (cited in Levinas, 1993, p. 275, n. 1).) As a matter of fact, Levinas is not, strictly speaking, a thinker of the sacred. To the sacred he opposes the saint, in the sense in which the word "saint" is the translation of the Hebraic word *Kadosh*, which, etymologically, means "separated". (In *Totality and Infinity* (1961), Levinas insists on the question of the separation between the ethical subject and the other for whom the subject is responsible. I share this insistence, for it resonates with a conception of the human being separated from birth from his environment. This separation is the pre-condition for the enriching experience, from the beginining of life, of co-presence, and in analysis, for non-alienating co-thinking (Widlöcher, 1995).)

Lacan and Levinas

Before returning to certain points emphasised by Assoun in his 1993 article concerning the encounter that never took place between Lacan and Levinas, I want to turn to Guyomard's *Désir d'éthique* (1998), in which he writes,

In 1973, Lacan sought to derive an 'ethics of *bien-dire* (saying well)' from clinical practice, thereby 'bringing ethics back into the foreground'. Lacan makes a Good (*un Bien*) of a saying . . . Saying (*le dire*) is speech. The saying of the analyst (Lacan in his practice), the saying (*le dire*) as distinct from the said (*le dit*) is a concept. (p. 185, translated for this edition)

Saying becomes style; it is style. And style "is the man whom we are addressing". I would just like to note here that while, for Levinas, saying is responsibility for the other man, for Lacan, it is restricted to style.

"Ethics essentially consists", Lacan (1986) writes, "in a judgement of our action, with the proviso that it is only significant if the action implied by it contains . . . a judgement, even if it is only implicit" (p. 311). For Lacan, ethics begins

at the moment when the subject . . . is led to discover the deep relationship as a result of which that which presents itself as a law is closely tied to the very structure of desire. If he does not discover right away the final desire that Freudian inquiry has discovered as the desire of incest, he discovers that which articulates his conduct so that the object of his desire is always maintained at a certain distance. But this distance is not complete; it is an intimate distance that is called proximity, which is not identical to the subject, which is literally close to it, in the way that one can say that the *Nebenmensch* that Freud speaks of as the foundation of the thing is his neighbor. (Lacan, 1986, p. 76)

Apropos of this *Nebenmensch*, Laplanche preferred to stick to a non-philosophical understanding of the term, insisting on the human aspect of the *Nebenmensch* more than on the aspect of proximity. Indeed, it was this situation that led him to propose the term "fundamental anthropological situation". For my part, I want to take up this notion of the neighbour, in dialogue with Laplanche, while at the same time drawing on Levinas.

First, though, I want to return to Lacan and the comparison with Levinas proposed by Assoun. It will help the reader to understand more clearly the foundations of the comparison I am proposing between Laplanche and Levinas.

On reading these authors, Assoun (1993) was struck, as I was, by "the insistent recurrence of the same theoretical signifiers": desire, subject, need, and demand. This insistence, "as equivocal as it is eloquent", might be said to indicate something of "a mysterious affinity". So, "it is through Levinas that the Other makes its entry into ethics, but through Lacan that the Other is promulgated within psychoanalysis". We know that Levinas had reservations about psychoanalysis and ignored Lacan, who in turn quietly ignored Levinas. Assoun notes in particular that Lacan's *Ecrits* were due to be published at roughly the same time as *Totality and Infinity*, which was first published in French in 1961, and that Lacan, in his seminar, was to give particular attention to the "Ethics of psychoanalysis" with, "in effigy . . . those two powerful emerging concepts associated with the names of their authors: the face, on the one hand (in Levinas), and the Name of the Father, on the other (in Lacan)" (Assoun, 1993, p. 125). Assoun shows how

> one of them organises his whole way of thinking on the basis of psychoanalysis, while the other leaves psychoanalysis out of his thinking, yet they meet, paradoxically, through the idea that the subject – *unconscious, ethical* – leads back to the question of the Other in respect of its "symbolic" function and also in respect of what it leaves outside itself [*the real*]. (Assoun, 1993, p. 127, translated for this edition)

While Lacan refers to anti-humanism with regard to the status of the subject of psychoanalysis, Levinas, in *L'humanisme de l'autre homme* (1972), defines "an original position in which the ethical reference to the Other finds the means to radically destabilise the beliefs that are central to the identity of traditional humanism" (Assoun, 1993, p. 127, translated for this edition). But, when he deals with the question of time in the work of Lacan and Levinas, Assoun insists on the "decoupling" in Levinas's work of the relations between desire and time, where a relationship with the other would only be "conditional" (as in Lacan), whereas, in fact, for Levinas, "the Other acquires meaning, throughout 'its manifestations', as a call, as mysterious as it is unconditional, inscribing a weakness at the heart of the 'powers' of the subject" (p. 131, translated for this edition). In addition, although Lacan found in Hegel (via Kojève)—in the dialectics of the master and slave—a reference for his theory of unconscious desire, Levinas situates himself in the "rupture" of a logic of recognition. According to Assoun, it is "the relation of 'the ethics of psychoanalysis' to ethics 'full stop'" which is at stake between Lacan and Levinas. Ethics, full stop! We know that it has assumed, and can assume, multiple forms: ethics of power, ethics of honour, ethics of worldly goods, ethics of the Good, etc. This form of ethics may be contrasted with the ethics of the caress and of proximity, an ethics signifying responsibility for the other person.

Although I cannot, for my part, speak of an ethics of psycho-analysis, I will be dwelling on what I conceive of as the *ethics of the psychoanalyst* and, consequently, of *ethics in psychoanalysis*.

Introduction to the question of an ethical exigency at the beginning of life: Hans Jonas's principle of responsibility

Before discussing those aspects of Levinas's ideas that make sense for me with respect to the way they can be articulated with analytic prac-tice, I want to make a brief detour in order to consider the proposi-tions Jonas (1979a) puts forward in his book *The Imperative of Respons-ibility*. Thinking along the same lines as Levinas, his contemporary, and inspired, too, by Edmund Husserl and Martin Heidegger, he insists on the radical dissymmetry that is characteristic of relations of responsibility wherever they appear. For Jonas, being responsible means *accepting* being taken hostage by that which is most fragile and most threatened, but he positions himself on the terrain of the philos-ophy of nature. Owing to the influence of technology, nature is less and less that power over which man has no control and which faces him with his limits. With the advance of technological progress, nature is increasingly open to manipulation and has become a fragile entity, almost without defence, and, thus, an object of responsibility. "Whether we like it or not," writes Greisch (1979b), who translated and prefaced the French edition of Jonas's work,

> we are the architects of society to come, for it is no longer within our grasp to curb technological progress, even if we wanted to. What is within our grasp, however, is to be aware that we are already hostages of this future that we are creating. (pp. 12–14, translated for this edition)

For Jonas, this responsibility implies a non-reciprocal, uncondi-tional relationship, which leads him to turn his attention to a form of

responsibility that is "instituted by nature", that is, parental responsibility. For him it is a natural responsibility which "is independent of
prior assent or choice, irrevocable and not given to alteration of its
terms by the participants" (1979a, pp. 94–95). This leads him to
consider the question of "The parent–child relation: the archetype of
responsibility", the title of Chapter Four, section VII in his book.

For me, this chapter was the catalyst for the rapprochements and
developments which will acquire clearer delineation throughout the
course of the present work. It was due to the influence of Jonas's ideas
in particular that I elaborated the psychoanalytical hypothesis of a
very early origin for the human capacity of responsibility for the other
(I give an account of this in Part IV).

For Jonas, the child is an elementary object of responsibility. With
the newborn "whose mere breathing uncontradictably addresses an
'ought' to the world around, namely, to take care of him", we have
"an *ontic* paradigm in which the plain factual 'is' evidently coincides
with an 'ought' which does not, therefore, admit for itself the concept
of a 'mere is' at all". The elementary "ought" is at the heart of the "is"
of the newborn. Jonas insists that this "ought" is uncontradictable,
which does not mean that it is irresistible. He writes,

> Its call can meet with deafness, or can be drowned by other calls and
> pressures, like sacrifice of the firstborn . . . It can even be drowned by
> bare self-preservation, but this fact takes nothing away from the claim
> being incontestable as such and immediately evident.

He continues,

> Nor do I say 'an entreaty' to the world ('please take care of me'), for
> the infant cannot entreat as yet, and anyway, an entreaty, be it ever so
> moving, does not oblige. Thus no mention also is made of sympathy,
> pity, or whichever of the emotions may come into play on our part,
> and not even of love. I mean strictly just this: that here the plain being
> of a de facto existent immanently and evidently contains an ought for
> others (a responsibility for others!).

And he adds, ". . . he would do so even if nature would not succour
this ought with powerful instincts or assume its job alone" (pp. 130–
131). For Jonas, the essence of responsibility is delineated in the arche-
typal evidence of the newborn. He says that the "always acute,

unequivocal, and choiceless responsibility which the newborn claims for himself stands out as utterly beyond comparison" (p. 134).

I will continue to quote Jonas extensively, because his ideas form a basis for my own elaboration as well as my concluding propositions at the end of this book, even though ultimately, and necessarily, I adopt a different position from his. Although I have the opportunity of coming back to it later on, I think it is important at this stage to consider the following proposition of Jonas, which has given me much food for thought:

> The radical insufficiency of the begotten as such carries with it the mandate to the begetters to avert its sinking back into nothing and to tend its further becoming. The pledge thereto was implicit in the act of generation. [This point is obviously open to discussion: at what level of consciousness and freedom of being is Jonas positioning himself?] Its observance (even by others) becomes an ineluctable duty toward *a being now existing in its own authentic right and in total dependence on such observance.* The immanent ought-to-be of the suckling, which his every breath proclaims, thus turns into the transitive *ought-to-do* of others who alone can help the claim continually to its right and make possible the gradual coming true of the teleological promise which it carries in itself from the first . . . Their power over the object of responsibility is here not only that of commission but also that of omission, which alone would be lethal . . . Thus the 'ought' manifest in the infant enjoys indubitable evidence, concreteness, and urgency. Utmost 'facticity' of 'thisness', utmost right thereto, and utmost fragility of being meet here together. In him it is paradigmatically evident that the locus of responsibility is the being that is immersed in becoming, surrendered to mortality, threatened by corruptibility. (1979a, pp. 134–135)

It is my contention that this is where the "germ" of the capacity of responsibility for the other lies. I shall suggest that this germ is created by the enigmatic messages coming from an adult world that is destabilised and violated by the interpellation of the newborn baby, by the injunction that he embodies as soon as he comes into the world, which is formulated in terms of a necessity to take responsibility for him. This destabilisation, this violence, cannot be circumvented, whether this responsibility is apparently immediately accepted or not.

The desire for ethics in Levinas results from the violence felt by the ethical subject in his encounter with the distress of the other. This desire will correspond (without being confused with it), in the patient and at the beginning of a child's life, to an "ethical exigency". One can speak of a desire for ethics that is solicited in the adult environment by the infant's distress, which is experienced by the adult as an ethical exigency or requirement of the newborn infant. This distress contains an ethical exigency within it. We could say that the infant requires its environment to feel interpellated and immediately responsible for him. This requirement is also evoked by the analytic situation. It convokes in the analyst a desire for ethics understood as responsibility for the other (see Part Two).

CHAPTER TWO

Asymmetrical responsibility for the other as the analyst's ethic

B efore proposing certain echoes between certain Levinasian texts and analytic practice and the analyst's position, as I see it, I shall trace in broad outline Levinas's philosophical journey with reference to a close reading of an interview with Levinas by Philippe Némo on Radio France in 1981, in which this journey was discussed. After this, rather than following a linear progression, I shall follow the thread of the evocations that have crystallised in the articles I have published in recent years. Linked to the question of responsibility for the other as the analyst's ethic, a certain number of Levinasian "non-concepts" will thus be emphasised. (In Levinas's work, there is the impossible utopian and ethical desire not to reduce the use of this or that term to the concepts that they seem to cover. It might be said, at the risk of a didactic reduction of his effort, that the terms used only have an evocative value. He explains this particularly when he speaks of the non-concept of the *face*; we see this later on.)

Some salient traits of Levinas's philosophical journey

If Emmanuel Levinas is the philosopher of ethics, this does not mean he is a specialist in ethics. For him, ethics is not a speciality but a "first philosophy", on the basis of which the other branches of philosophy take on meaning. On the one hand, the question of justice is that by which being is torn apart and the human established as "otherwise than being", as transcendence in the world; on the other hand, that without which, in return, "any other interrogation of thought is nothing more than vanity and chasing the wind" (Levinas, 1982b, p. viii).

The question of justice is that by which being is torn apart. For Levinas, thinking starts through "traumatisms or gropings to which one does not even know how to give a verbal form" and he instances "a separation, a violent scene, a sudden consciousness of the monotony of time. It is from the reading of books—not necessarily philosophical—that these initial shocks become questions and problems, giving one to think" (p. 21). For Levinas, books, and, in particular, the Book, that is, the Bible, are not tools or manuals; they are a "modality of our being". It is through respect for the Book and books as such that his philosophical approach takes shape. Thinking philosophically is to address oneself "to all men". In this sense, philosophy and biblical wisdom are not in contradiction with each other. As all philosophical thought is based on "pre-philosophical experiences", for Levinas, reading the Bible was one of the founding experiences of his thought.

At the same time as studying the Bible, he read the great Russian writers and it was only at the age of eighteen, when he embarked on his studies in philosophy in Strasbourg, that he became acquainted with Plato, Aristotle, Descartes, and Kant, and then Durkheim and Bergson. He tells Philippe Nemo: "In Durkheim [even though he was a sociologist], there is, in a sense, a theory of 'levels of being', of the irreducibility of these levels to one another, an idea which acquires its full meaning within the Husserlian and Heideggerian context" (p. 27). As for Bergson, he was indebted to him for reducing

> the fear of being in a world without novel possibilities, without a future of hope, a world where everything is regulated in advance ... it is Bergson who taught us the spirituality of the new, 'being' disengaged from the phenomenon in 'an otherwise than being'. (p. 28)

Then he came across the work of Husserl, who was concerned with the question: "Where are we?" ...

A radical reflection, obstinate about itself, a *cogito* which seeks . . . Phenomenology is the recall of these forgotten thoughts, of these forgotten intentions; full consciousness, return to the misunderstood implied intentions of thought in the world . . . It is the presence of the philosopher . . . not answering only the question of knowing 'What is?', but the question 'How *is* what is?' What does it mean that it is?' (pp. 30–31)

What interested Levinas particularly in Husserl's thought was his idea of "a specific attitude of consciousness, of a non-theoretical intentionality, from the outset irreducible to knowledge" (p. 32). Indeed, in the light of his reading of Husserl, he could say that "the relationship with the Other can be sought as an irreducible intentionality, even if one must end by seeing that it ruptures intentionality" (p. 32). (I will not enter into a discussion here of the possible relations between a philosopher rooted in the phenomenological perspective—even though he went beyond it in a singularly and thoroughly original way (see Appendix 3)—and a psychoanalyst such as Laplanche, who was vigorously opposed to it. I would refer the reader to the interesting remarks of Bernard Golse, who, through the interposition of the "baby-being" (*l'être-bébé*) and via Merleau Ponty and his particular views on phenomenology, proposes a possible articulation between these two perspectives. As for me, my point of view is twofold: while concurring at a certain level with the propositions of Golse (2006a, pp. 69–83, 307–310), I adopt what is finally the non-phenomenological perspective of Levinas. This will become clear in the course of this book.)

It was under Heidegger's influence that Levinas, during an early stage of his personal thinking, turned towards ontology, understood as the comprehension of "being" as a verb and not as a substantive. Heidegger "aims at describing man's being or existing—not his nature" (Levinas, 1982b, p. 40). Levinas was interested in the pages Heiddeger wrote about affectivity and particularly anxiety: "For Heidegger, one does not 'reach' nothingness through a series of theoretical steps but, in anxiety, from a direct and irreducible access" (1982b, p. 40). Likewise, he found in Heidegger

a new and direct way of conversing with philosophers and asking for absolutely current teachings from the great classics . . . But in this hermeneutic one does not manipulate outworn things, one brings back the unthought to thought and saying. (pp. 43–44)

We will see how for Levinas, the *said* (*le dit*) does not count as much as the *saying* (*le dire*). What matters to him is that the said is addressed.

In his first book expressing his personal thinking, *Existence and Existents* (1947), he discusses what he has called the "there is" (*il y a*). He defines it as "the phenomenon of impersonal being: it". In *Ethics and Infinity*, he explains, "I insist . . . on the impersonality of the *there is* . . . *Existence and Existents* tries to describe this horrible thing and, moreover, describes it as horror and panic" (pp. 48–49). He also analyses other phenomena such as insomnia, fatigue, indolence, and effort. "I showed a dread before being, an impotent recoil, an evasion, and, consequently, there too, the shadow of the 'there is'" (p. 51).

In this first book of 1947, as in that which followed it in 1948 under the title *Time and the Other*, "what is presented as exigency is an attempt to escape the *there is*, to escape the non-sense" (Levinas, 1982b), p. 51). What Levinas now proposes, in order to escape the non-sense, is the *dis-interested* relationship. "Responsibility for the Other, being-for-the-other, seemed to me, as early as that time, to stop the anonymous and senseless rumbling of being" (1982b, p. 52). Thereafter, Levinas no longer spoke about the *there is* for itself, but he continued to consider its shadow, the shadow of non-sense "as the very test of disinterestedness".

Time and the Other (1948) is "a study of the relationship with the Other insofar as its element is time" (Levinas, 1982b, p. 56). The book represents an attempt to escape from this isolation of existing, just as the preceding book was an attempt to escape from the *there is*. After trying a way of "exit" through knowledge, Levinas shows that there is "no rupture of the isolation of being in knowledge": "Being in direct relation with the Other", he says,

> is not to thematise the Other and to consider him in the same manner as one considers a known object, nor to communicate knowledge to him . . . existence is the sole thing I cannot communicate; I can tell about it, but I cannot share my existence . . . The social is beyond ontology. (pp. 57–58)

Here, Levinas insists on the inadequacy of the word "sharing", as existence is not of the order of having. (This echoes for me with the inadequacy, from an ethical point of view, of the term *sharing of affect*, suggested a few years ago by Catherine Parat, insisting, in so doing, on the symmetry of the feelings between the analyst and the analysand. I shall come back to this in Parts II and III.)

So, already in this little book, knowledge is always "an adequation between thought and what it thinks ... Knowledge has always been interpreted as assimilation ... [so we must keep in mind] all that there is of 'prehending' in 'comprehending'" (p. 60). Knowledge is finally always of the order of possession, of the same, of what is assimilated with myself. The relationship with the Other requires a dispossession. In this book,

> Time is not a simple experience of duration, but a dynamism which leads us elsewhere. It is as if in time there were a movement beyond what is equal to us. Time as relationship to unattainable alterity and, thus, interruption of rhythm and its returns. (p. 61)

In *Time and the Other*, Levinas characterises the feminine as that which "withdraws elsewhere, a movement opposed to the movement of consciousness ... mystery" (1982b, p. 68), and he defines Eros as "the relationship with alterity, with mystery, that is, with the future, with that which, in the world where there is everything, is never there" (p. 68). In his interview with Nemo, no doubt in reaction to the criticisms (see de Beauvoir, 1949, p. 18, n. 1) he encountered concerning his "archaic" conception of ontological differences between the masculine, "the subject's ego posited in its virility", and the feminine "described as the *of itself other*", he proposes that instead of dividing humanity into two species, these two ontological categories would signify the attribute of every human being. He recalls the verse in Genesis 1. 27: "Male and female created He them" (p. 69). (I shall come back to this idea of the feminine in the human being in Part IV, albeit in a modified form.)

He pursued his research by making an analysis of voluptuousness, thereby laying the initial foundations of his conception of the *caress*, the "not knowing" of the caress. I shall come back to this later. The last point touched on in this little book, related to the question of alterity, is that of filiation: "It is a relationship with the Other", he writes, "where the Other is radically other, and where nevertheless it is in some way me; the father's ego has to do with an alterity which is his, without being a possession or a property" (p. 69). Here, in my view, when, in spite of his reservations, he considers the specific relationship between father and son, Levinas is returning to a conception that was influenced by his "archaic" views. Yet, it is not impossible that these lines influenced Hans Jonas and his vision of the child as an *elementary object of responsibility*, while the question of alterity raised at the heart of filiation would lead to the more general question in Levinas's work of responsibility for the other.

Totality and Infinity was published in 1961. The very title of this essential work contains a critique of "the attempt at universal synthesis, a reduction of all experience, of all that is reasonable, to a totality wherein consciousness embraces the world . . . and thus becomes absolute thought" (Levinas, 1982b, p. 75. He continues, "One can see this nostalgia for totality everywhere in Western philosophy, where the spiritual and the reasonable always reside in knowledge" (p. 76).

Although the Freudian point of view exploded a certain notion of totality, owing to the decentring it proposes with the very existence of the unconscious, it was necessary to wait for Laplanche, after Lacan, and the primacy of the other in the constitution of the unconscious, to see the subversive movement initiated by Freud reinforced. Levinas, for his part, sets against this globalising Hegelian vision, which offers the possibility of totalising all meaning in a single body of knowledge,

> the irreducible and ultimate experience of relationships . . . in the face to face of humans . . . in its moral signification . . . The relationship between men is certainly the 'non-synthesizable' par excellence . . . One has always known this in speaking of the secrecy of subjectivity; but this secrecy has been ridiculed by Hegel: speaking thus was good for romantic thought. (Levinas, 1982b, pp. 77–78)

The Levinasian critique of totality was, in fact, developed after the experience of the Shoah. Instead of conceiving of politics as a means of internal regulation within a society, as in a society of bees or ants, a naturalistic and "totalitarian" conception, Levinas posits that politics must be susceptible to criticism by ethics:

> This second form of sociality would render justice to that secrecy which for each is his life, a secrecy which does not hold to a closure . . . but to the responsibility for the Other . . . a responsibility which is inaccessible in its ethical advent, from which one does not escape, and which, thus, is the principle of an absolute individuation. (p. 81)

In *Totality and Infinity*, Levinas speaks at great length of the face, a theme he returns to frequently in his other works or interventions.

With the elaboration of this theme, Levinas finally differentiates himself, and in the most open way, from phenomenology, even if it was the phenomenological approach that led him to it. Indeed, when he speaks of "access to the face", he does not describe what appears:

> The relation with the face can surely be dominated by perception [the colour of the eyes, the fineness of the skin, the very quality of the expression] but what is specifically the face is what cannot be reduced to that . . . The face is exposed, menaced, as if inviting us to an act of violence. (p. 86)

Levinas continues,

> At the same time the face is what forbids us to kill . . . Murder, it is true, is a banal fact: one can kill the Other; the ethical exigency is not an ontological necessity . . . the appearance in being of these 'ethical peculiarities' is a rupture of being. It is significant, even if being resumes and recovers itself. (p. 87)

This idea of a rupture of being in the encounter with the other is violence.

In this encounter, there is a breach or intrusion, a trauma, destabilising the subject and creating in him the possibility of opening himself towards the other. (I shall return in Part IV to this proposition, which resonates so well with Laplanche's hypotheses.)

It is in this same book that Levinas begins to elaborate in more depth the question of the difference between the said (*le dit*) and the saying (*le dire*), since, for him, face and discourse are linked. By "discourse" he means response, or rather, responsibility, a capacity to respond. He raises the question of justice. Justice emanates from the multiplicity of men:

> If I am alone with the other, I owe him everything; but there is someone else [a third party]. Do I know what my neighbour is in relation to someone else? Do I know if someone else has an understanding with him or his victim? (pp. 89–90)

It is here that the need for institutions guaranteeing justice appears. Thus, Levinas escapes from Heidegger's ontology, which is an ontology of the Neutral, an ontology without morals. However, he does not attempt to construct a code of ethics; he only tries to discover the meaning of ethics. He does not exclude the possibility, though, that this research might open on to a practice.

Finally, he emphasises that access to the face implies a non-completion of knowledge and, therefore, access to the idea of infinity. Here, the relation to infinity is not, as it is for Descartes, knowledge. This relationship is desire, "like a thought which thinks more than it thinks or more than what it thinks. It is a paradoxical structure, without doubt, but one which is no more so than this presence of the infinite in a finite act" (p. 92).

We saw earlier how, for Chalier, this Levinasian conception of desire allowed her to forge links with Freud and with psychoanalysis. As with Lacan, need is something that must be satisfied, whereas desire "feeds on its own hunger". This is what enables me to speak of ethical desire, on the analyst's part, and of a need for ethics on the part of our analysands.

If, in the very last part of *Totality and Infinity*, Levinas introduces the centrality of asymmetrical responsibility for the other by stating, "I am responsible for the Other without waiting for reciprocity" (p. 98), it is in *Otherwise than Being or Beyond Essence* (1974a) that he gives full scope to this responsibility, a responsibility defined as a fundamental structure of subjectivity, subjectivity itself defined in ethical terms. In fact, he supplements what he had advanced in *Totality and Infinity*: not only is the face not of the order of pure and simple perception or of intentionality which tends towards adequation, but "when the Other looks at me, I am responsible for him, without even having *taken* on responsibilities in his regard; his responsibility is *incumbent on me*" (1974a, p. 96). Subjectivity, in this sense, is not for itself, but for another, and "the proximity of the Other is presented as the fact that the Other is not simply close to me in space, or close like a parent, but he approaches me essentially insofar as I am responsible for him" (1974a, p. 96). From there, Levinas develops the idea of substitution, of taking hostage (a notion I shall come back to in order to emphasise the ethical dimension of the "use of the object" in Winnicott, or of projective identification in Bion's wider sense of the term), and of testimony (which I shall not develop here as it is discussed from time to time in the context of analytic practice (see Desche, 2008).

Levinas extends his meditation on responsibility for the other by a further meditation on responsibility for the death of others. "Fear for the death of the other is certainly at the basis of responsibility for him", he writes. He speaks of a dis-inter-ested fear which is not fear of sanction (1974a, p. 120) and he concludes his interview thus:

> A truly human life cannot remain life *satisfied* in its equality to being that is awakenened by the other; that is to say, it is always getting sobered up, being is never its own reason for being [and] the famous *conatus essendi* is not the source of all right and all meaning. (p. 122)

Ethics as responsibility for the other and analytic practice

After this swift overview of the development of Levinasian thought, I want to take up a certain number of his key words which were meaningful to me, and then to reflect on the way they echo in analytic practice.

The key words "asymmetry", "the caress", "the face", and "the saying" appear in a variety of ways throughout the four most important books by Levinas which I have just mentioned: *Existence and Existents, Time and the Other, Totality and Infinity, Otherwise than Being or Beyond Essence*.

Although, as we have seen, Levinas drew inspiration from the phenomenological sources of Husserl and Heidegger, his philosophy having opened out on to an "otherwise than being, a beyond essence", we are dealing with a philosophy before reason, beyond the phenomenon, even before the phenomenon, before being, and, in this sense, a philosophy that is non-phenomenological.

We know that Levinas did not feel at home with the psychoanalysis of the first Freud. He could not see eye to eye with a Freud who had made knowledge and the possibility of gaining access to knowledge his ultimate aim. However, we also know that Freud did not rest there. His thinking was constantly evolving and changing. In fact, he opened the door and showed the way forward to all the great figures of psychoanalysis such as Ferenczi, Klein, Fairbairn, Winnicott, Bion, and, subsequently, Lacan, Laplanche, and André Green. The latter, in particular, continued the movement of Copernican decentring that Freud had begun by positing that the human being was not master of his own house because he has an unconscious that continually eludes him.

For Levinas, responsibility for the other is not of the order of free-dom, of choice. It imposes itself, it summons us, and is stronger than us. To know the other is already to have sway over him. The other is not knowable; ethically speaking, he is an enigma to be respected. In *God, Death, and Time* (1993) he writes,

> The "for" (in the expression: responsibility for the other) is the way in which man approaches his neighbour, the way in which a relationship is established with the other that is no longer proportionate to the one. It is a relation of proximity where the responsibility of the one for the other is played out. In this relation, there is a non-thematizable intel-ligibility; this relation is intelligible by itself and not by virtue of the effect of a theme or a thematization. (p. 169)

Asymmetry of responsibility for the other and vulnerability

Levinas insists on the asymmetry of ethical intersubjectivity. In the very last part of *Totality and Infinity*, this asymmetry seems to emanate from a disequilibrium that, at first sight, might appear to be permuta-tional (1961, pp. 215–217). From my first reading, I retained the idea of a basic disequilibrium, a basic asymmetry of responsibility for the other. And it was this notion of asymmetry that Levinas was to develop in the writings that followed. Thus, commenting twenty years later on his first proposition, he said, "The intersubjective rela-tion is a non-symmetrical relation. In this sense, I am responsible for the other without waiting for reciprocity . . . Reciprocity is *his* affair" (Levinas, 1982b, p. 98).

It seems to me important, though, to take up in his own terms this first proposition, which I shall try to elaborate further by emphasising the centrality of the asymmetry of the analytic situation, while remod-elling it at the same time.

Levinas (1961) writes,

> The Other does not only appear in his face . . . infinitely distant from the very relation he enters; he presents himself there from the first as an absolute. The I [he means the subject] disengages itself from the relationship, but does so within the relationship with a being absolutely separated. The face which the other turns to me is not reab-sorbed in a representation of the face. To hear his destitution which

cries out for justice is not to represent an image to oneself, but is to posit oneself as responsible, both as more and as less than the being that presents itself in the face. Less, for the face summons me to my obligations and judges me. The being that presents himself the face comes from a dimension of height, a dimension of transcendence whereby he can present himself as a stranger, without opposing me as obstacle or enemy. More, for my position as *I* (of subject) consists in being able to respond to this essential destitution of the other, finding resources for myself. (p. 215)

Listening to the distress of the other who cries out for justice is the position adopted by the one who listens as if he or she is responsible. It is a matter of positioning myself as more than the other and at the same time as less than him. As less than him or her, how? His or her face, through which the other aims at me, reminds me of my duties and judges me. It is an order that comes from above. As more than him or her, how? My positioning, as a human subject, and I read here, as a psychoanalyst, requires me to respond to his or her distress and fragility, in other words, to find resources in myself.

Hearing the distress of the other . . . Our patients address themselves to us because they are suffering. In our positioning as analysts there is a conscious/unconscious desire for "justice to be done", justice *vis-à-vis* our own former suffering, and justice *vis-à-vis* the suffering of our parents, of those who have taken care of us. Is this masochistic positioning or an encounter between two life masochisms (Rosenberg, 1991)? "Two human beings will encounter the suffering of the other", Guillaumin (1999) writes, and

through this encounter they will trap the death drives; two human beings will side for a while with the life drive and rebel – one by placing his voice in the hollow of the setting, the other by listening to this voice – against this fundamental injustice, namely, the suffering of the human being. (p. 75, translated for this edition)

For Guillaumin, the analytic encounter is a shared and symmetrical undertaking. For my part, I want to emphasise the ethical asymmetry of this encounter. Just as I am responsible for the analytic situation, so, too, am I responsible for the analysand.

Thou shall not kill are the first words of the face; it is an order. It is an order that comes from on high and concerns alterity, the menace presented by the very fact of encountering the other: this encounter connects me with the other in myself. It points me to the stranger in myself, to what is menacing, and so it disturbs me. At the same time, as we have seen, the face of the other is denuded and fragile, and, in this respect, it is lower than me. It is up to me to find (within myself) the resources to respond to his distress. The intersubjective relationship is an asymmetrical relationship. I am responsible for the other without expecting reciprocity. The face of the other interpellates me; it commands me. It is potentially menacing violence and, at the same time, it is fragility, exposure, and vulnerability.

The bell rings; I open the door. It is a first and asymmetrical encounter, even if the sense of unease is shared. In this face, inscribed in black and white, are the words: "Thou shall not kill".

This is the first commandment coming from the face. Encountering the other takes me out of my dwelling place. This stranger brings me back to what is unknowable in myself, unknown and strange, strange and potentially menacing; the strange alterity of the other. I am touching here on the death drives of the patient as much as of the analyst, and on the expectation, the mutual hope, of finding in the analytic setting, in the situation that the analyst offers to this patient, the means to "overwhelm them, hinder them, deflect them, thwart them and combat them" (Guillaumin, 1999, translated for this edition), to transform them into life drives, to make the transition from a situation of survival (*une survie*) to a life (*une vie*), for the period of a lifetime. Levinasian philosophy is not soothing. The relation to the other is violent from the first. Exciting my anxiety, it excites my own violence. The encounter with the other is at once violence and interpellation (see Derrida, 1967).

Responsibility for the other and face

The anti-concept "face", already proposed in *Time and the Other*, a text written when Levinas was a prisoner in Germany, would be developed and elaborated, as we have seen, in *Totality and Infinity*.

At the beginning of the Levinasian inspiration, we find an expression that appears many times in the Bible: *pnei elohim*—faces of God. The face, in Hebrew, is plural (*panim*); the root of the word that qualifies it, *pan*, means "versatility". On two counts, then, this implies something of the versatility of the face. Each one of us necessarily possesses several faces . . . Yet, in the address to the other, when God addresses Adam, it is not a plural address but, rather, an incisive address. God questions Adam with the cutting words, "Where are you?" Adam had just touched the prohibited fruit of the tree of the knowledge of good and evil. It should be noted that, for Adam, the question, "Where are you?" is posed once the transgression imposed, and, I would say, implanted, through the intermediary of the serpent, has been committed. (We shall see in Part II how Laplanche uses the terms *implantation* and *intromission* when he speaks of enigmatic, traumatic messages that are more or less metabolisable by the infantile psyche. For a Laplanchian allusion to the foundational seduction in the Bible, see Laplanche, 1995, p. 190.) Without any possibility of translation or elaboration, Adam is able, eventually, with the help of the Other (*l'Autre*), to ask himself questions about the place that he occupies. (This is a primordial example, if ever there was one, of the weaving of primal seduction and responsibility for the other; in other words, of ethical seduction.)

It is interesting to note that the formula "faces of God" appears in the episode where Abraham himself takes responsibility for the sins of Sodom and prays for Divine clemency, and, once again, when God speaks to Moses from the burning bush. Here, the question does not concern the nature of the place that he occupies, his private and singular place, as in the case of Adam, but rather Abraham's, and then Moses', tendency not to want to confine themselves to it any longer. They will have to take responsibility for their people upon themselves, and, in Moses' case, to work to bring about the collective deliverance from their exodus and slavery in Egypt, and to set them on the path again towards the promised land. Thus, for Levinas, the interpellation in the address of the other man's face, eliciting my sense of responsibility for him, is just as incisive and free of all versatility.

In the other's face, there is, then, for Levinas, the faceless-face of God. For him, access to the other's face is ethical from the outset. The face triggers my responsibility for the other. Levinas makes it clear that it is not a perceptible face, in the order of the perceived, or pertaining solely to this order. Although the relation to the face can be dominated by perception (the colour of his or her eyes, the softness of his or her skin, the expression of his or her smile, etc.), face, ethically speaking, is what cannot be reduced to that (Levinas, 1982b, p. 86).

I shall quote a passage remarked on by Rolland, which will give any analyst cause for thought:

> To signify is to signify one person for the other. There is a priority in this *one*; it is the priority of immediate exposure to the other, a first person exposure which is not even protected by the concept of the ego [*moi*] [as it exists in legal society] . . . the *I* [*Je*] *is outside the ego* [*hors du moi*]. (Levinas, 1993, p. 150)

For Rolland, the difference between *Totality and Infinity* and *Otherwise than Being* is concentrated in this opposition. In *Totality and Infinity*, the ego is in a world where it encounters the other who disrupts and calls into question its primary innocence. In *Otherwise than Being* (1974a), Levinas carries out an archaeology of the ego. He discovers the ego, already altered by alterity: "Infinity does not signal itself to a subjectivity, a unity already formed, by its order to turn toward the neighbour. In its being, subjectivity undoes *essence* by substituting itself for the other" (p. 13). Again, he writes,

> The *I* (Je) is already thought of as *me*, and yet it remains unique in the impossibility of eluding the other man. The other man in his demand, in his face, which is extreme, immediate exposure, total nudity, and as such entrusted to me. (Levinas, 1993, p. 138)

How can one fail to think once again of the mother–infant encounter? It should be noted that here the exposure is that of the other's face in the nudity of its fragility; the exposure is just as much a feature of the ethical subject himself, who, more than nude, is exposed in all his vulnerability of I (*Je*), dispossessed of all me/ego (moi).

According to the classical metapsychological model, this two-way process of asymmetrical intrusion can only be symmetrical at the unconscious level. Yet, its intrinsic asymmetry is posited at the foundations of the unconscious and of the drives in Laplanche's hypothesis of primal seduction, which I shall be discussing later. It remains to be seen what the fate of ethical asymmetry will be once it has traversed the psyche of the infant.

The time of the other, proximity, the caress

As early as 1941, Levinas had proposed to consider time "not as the achievement of the isolated and lone subject, but as the very relationship of the subject with the other" (1948, p. 39). For him, "time signifies this *always* of non-coincidence, but also the *always* of the relationship, of aspiration and an awaiting" (p. 32), and he asks, "Is time the very limitation of finite being or the relation of finite being . . . to God?" (p. 30). As for the future, Levinas continues,

> Anticipation of the future and projection of the future . . . are but the present of the future, and not the authentic future; the future is what is not grasped, what befalls us and lays hold of us, the future is the other. The relationship with the future is the very relationship with the other. (pp. 76–77)

The analyst should be without desire, that is, without expectation, Bion suggested. Did he appreciate the ethical implications of this suggestion?

Levinas's reflection on the time of the other would lead him to another anti-concept: the caress. "The caress", he writes, "is the way in which I approach the other". This relationship is a proximity which is *responsibility* for the other. He writes,

> The caress . . . which brushes lightly in pain does not promise the end of suffering; it does not announce any compensation . . . it is tied to the very instant of pain, which is then no longer condemned to itself, and which, carried elsewhere by the movement of the caress, and is freed from the vice-grip of 'itself', finds 'fresh air' . . . a dimension and a future. (1948, p. 156)

The caress is not there to compensate or repair. It allows pain to free itself of itself. It allows a window to be opened. It emphasises, it points towards the existence of a future, a future which is forgotten in the instant of pain; pain is then nothing more than this instant, this entire instant.

The position of the caress, listening (or the saying of the analyst), his presence as an ethical subject, does not have a reparative aim. This presence frees the subject who is suffering from the sway this suffering has over him or her, from the anxiety that is linked to it, anxiety that nullifies both the past and the future. This presence in the form of a caress brushes lightly and takes the suffering upon itself. At once presence and withdrawal, it makes room for the other. It is active in its apparent passivity. Levinas also writes, "The caress is a mode of the subject's being [I propose that we read this as "a mode of the analyst's being"] where the subject, in contact with the other, goes beyond that contact". The caress seeks:

> This seeking of the caress constitutes its essence, in that the caress does not know what it is seeking . . . it is like a game with something slipping away, a game absolutely without purpose or plan, always still to come [à venir]. The caress is awaiting this pure future with no content. (1948, p. 89).

"The caress is not knowledge", Ouaknin (1992) writes, "but . . . an encounter. The caress is not knowledge of the other but respect for him. It is neither force nor violence but tenderness. It is not fusion but relation, the enigma of a relation without a relation" (pp. 132–123). Once again, the caress, as the approach of the analyst as an ethical subject, is not in the order of compensation or reparation, but, rather, of testimony, of compassion. Upon contact with the caress, the intolerable pain traced in the body of the subject in his or her exacerbated isolation seeks to soothe itself, wants to believe in the reparative seduction of analytic treatment. This involves, though, an impossible mourning process with regard to what should have been but did not take place, while opening, perhaps, a window towards a shared mourning of this impossible mourning. This is reminiscent of Ferenczi, who ended his 1931 article "Some thoughts on trauma", published posthumously, with these words:

> Although we cannot offer him everything which he as a child should have had the mere fact that we can or may be helpful to him gives the necessary impetus towards a new life, in which the pages of the irretrievable are closed and where the first step will be made towards acquiescence in what life yet can offer instead of throwing away what may still be put to good use. (p. 238)

The caress is both the unknowability of the other and non-indifference.

Singularity and unknowability

Levinas puts knowledge in the dock. For him, knowledge of the other, the quest or belief that one can know the other, confines him, for it categorises him, generalises him, and necessarily eradicates his singularity. For Levinas, knowledge of the other is aim, and, consequently, capture, mastery. The analyst's listening to the other must be "affected" (see n. 1 in the Introduction) and singular, but also open, "ignorant", uneasy, and alert to what it is going to elicit or to what is going to come. The other is not knowable. He is encountered through proximity.

So, Levinas comes back to the term "neighbour" (*prochain*), while stressing the contingent character of this relationship with the neighbour. The other, the neighbour, is always newly arrived, unforeseen, and unpredictable.

> The neighbour qua other is not preceded by any precursor who depicts or announces his silhouette. He does not appear . . . Absolving himself from all essence, from every genus, all resemblance, the neighbour, the *first come*, concerns me for the first time. (Levinas, 1974a, p. 86): even if he were an old acquaintance, an old friend, and old love [a longstanding patient] in a *contingency that excludes the a priori*, the excess of a before the a priori. (Rolland, in Levinas, 1993, p. 276, n. 1)

The analyst, a subjective object for Winnicott, a self-object for Kohut, a malleable medium for Roussillon, with "sufficient distance" for Kristeva, presence–absence–presence, is, in accordance with his (or her) patient's associations and affects, tossed about, aggressed, loved too much, detested. Serving as a buoy, as a lifeline, in the flow of this process in which he is equally engaged, he is, none the less, careful not to let himself be thrown up on to an inaccessible shore, with the risk of colluding with the death drives which are always on the watch. Caress, presence, then, in this responsibility to the other, proximity, sensibility, and vulnerability. The caress of the analyst, of the analyst who offers to let him or herself be "used" (in Winnicott's sense of the term) is the caress of "someone who . . . accepts to attenuate the reminder of his (or her) alterity so that a space for symbolising can be created" (Roussillon, 2001b). His passion transpires through this acceptance that is incumbent upon him ethically. When Bion speaks of the analyst's disposition–availability, in each new session, in each moment of the analysis, without desire or memory, there is certainly something of the caress. This approach "without desire (as expectation) or memory", is combined with passion. (I shall develop this point in Part II.) Roussillon, who is more reserved, refers to the centrality of affect in the analyst, following Green, and the detour via the other. If Fédida has often alluded to presence in absence, he also emphasises the necessity of human presence when considering his "new" patients (2002, pp. 59–68). Alvarez (1992), who has suggested the idea of interventions functioning like an "ethical grammar", has proposed the term of "living presence". For my part, I would like to put forward the idea of a matricial space, imbued with *ethical* passion.

Roussillon (2000) has an intuition of this:

> If the problem of absence is at the centre of a psychoanalysis centred on the act of gaining new awareness (*prise de conscience*) and the analysis of the intrapsychic, if the question of the mode of presence is at the centre of a psychoanalysis centred on intersubjectivity and the work of symbolisation, the reference to experiences of the "capacity for being alone in the object's presence" [and, thereafter, of being alone in enriched and fertile solitude] that is to say, to intermediate and transitional experiences, is at the heart of a psychoanalysis—or moments of analysis—centred on the question of subjective appropriation. (p. 45, translated for this edition)

These transitional experiences pertain to what I shall later designate (see Part III) as "subjectal experiences", because they consist of the simultaneous appropriation of a matricial space that is always ready to be "used", at the ethical foundation of subjective appropriation.

The "saying" (le dire) and the "said" (le dit) of the analyst

Responding without giving a literal response, saying without said, or barely. Levinas distinguishes between the saying and the said. In all saying, there is the said, but

> the saying is the fact that before the face I do not simply remain there contemplating it; I respond to it. The saying is a way of greeting the other, but to greet the other is already to answer for him [*répondre de lui*]. (1985, p. 88)

Again, I can recall the following approximate citation, without being able to localise it, which I found striking: man is the only being that I cannot encounter without expressing this very encounter to him. This obviously does not mean that, in daily life, I cannot refuse this encounter, but that, whatever I do, it is imposed on me from the outset.

Let us consider for a moment the commonplace situation of waiting in a queue or at a bus stop or a railway station. In the analytic situation, to refuse this encounter would be in the order of a perversion of practice; answering for it, and sometimes responding to it, is of the order of ethics.

There was a time when being an analyst, in France in particular, meant keeping silent for most of the time. When the analyst's task is one of separating things out, of analysis, in the primary sense of the term, it is a question of finding the words that will help to get the patient's associations going again and, at best, to create a new opening. At a certain period, there was a great fear of an iatrogenic countertransferential impact. Yet, what is said by the analyst (*le dit analytique*) has taken on various forms under diverse theoretical influences, and especially when the indications for analysis were extended. Interpretations, which for some might be longer and more incisive (e.g., Klein, Segal), and for others more complex, more constructed (e.g., Kernberg), can be encountered in clinical vignettes just as much as others that are based closely on experience, which are more accompanying and supportive (e.g., Ferenczi, Balint, Winnicott, Kohut, Ogden). (I would like to refer the reader to my recently published commentary on this subject (Chetrit-Vatine, 2008a.)

My little patient Hen would often put her hands over her ears, saying, "Stop, stop" whenever I tried to reflect the situation to her that was being played out between us. I understood that, in those moments, she was communicating to me the fact that what I said (*mon dit*) went right through her, disconnected her from herself, instead of helping her to constitute herself. It made her feel trapped once again in her confused identity, which a moment before had been more or less stable, anguished as she was to find herself now in bits, with the risk of inducing an outright psychotic episode. Yet, session after session, month after month, a process gradually took shape. In the things I said (*mes dits*), which were often clumsy, there was this saying (*dire*), this greeting of her presence, my iterated welcome.

Saying precedes the language that communicates propositions and messages; it is a sign given by one person to the other about proximity, through proximity, before the construction of any system of signs (Levinas, 1974b, p. 148). So I have proposed (Chetrit-Vatine, 2007) that the analyst's speech should also be seen as "fraternity and responsibility, as proximity which does not refer to my freedom" (p. 1500). Its transformative effect is linked to this. The analysand is also, and first and foremost, my neighbour, the one who is close, "the person who has a meaning immediately before we attribute it to him" (Chetrit-Vatine, 2007). Levinas (1974b) writes, "His saying, in being said, would rupture at each moment the definition of what he says, and would thus shatter the totality that it encompasses at that moment" (p. 236). Thus,

> the relationship with the other is a relationship that is never finished with the other; it is a difference that is a non-intervention and which goes beyond all duty; a difference that is not reduced to a debt that one can discharge (we are a long way from the idea of the third party which thematizes what happens between the one and the other) . . . In other words, the relationship of responsibility with the other signifies itself as saying . . . The saying is not held in consciousness or in engagement, and does not trace a connection with the one to whom it is addressed. It is a way of being completely exposed, of exposing oneself without limits. (Levinas, 1993, pp. 161–162)

If, as Laurence Khan maintains, the analysand's speech "takes shape in the body" (see Chetrit-Vatine, 2007) of the addressee, at the same time it signifies to me *my* responsibility for *him*. It interpellates me, whether I like it or not. As for the analyst's speech, in his or her address and saying, it influences and also takes shape in the patient's body; equally, it signifies *my* responsibility for *him*.

Matricial space or the analyst's person

As I indicated at the beginning, for Levinas (1987, p. 61), contrary to Buber, the intersubjective relationship is asymmetrical. Levinas speaks of "ethical inequality". Although this aspiration may seem utopian in our daily encounters, in the caring/curing relationship (and for me, the psychoanalytic relationship is indeed a caring/curing relationship), this aspiration becomes an exigency and is part of the analyst's ethics. How many times have I felt in much better shape at the end of a working day than in the morning? Inevitable pleasure? Masochistic pleasure? Successful sublimation? The pleasure in creating together and asymmetrically; the pleasure of an encounter that sometimes leads to a greater sense of well-being or to a particularly enlightening dream, an unforeseen opening, tears at last . . . a secondary gain, one that must only be secondary. We are all too familiar with the unfortunate vicissitudes of analytic encounters that compensate for the analyst's lacks and narcissistic wounds of life outside the consulting room / off the couch. Yet, how many times do I find myself, once the door of my consulting room is closed again, vacillating and disorientated by the passion . . . the rage . . . the tears . . . the deadly silences, the invectives, and the violence that is sometimes completely unrestrained.

"All the forms of excess . . . touched, wounded, demolished in my inner being", Pontalis writes on this subject, and he continues,

> Staying in the dark, dreaming, if possible in this darkness traversed briefly by rays of light . . . trying to get as close as possible to that which is radically foreign to me, to that which the other feels is foreign to him, and from which he cannot escape. (Pontalis, 2000, p. 28, translated for this edition)

Pontalis's words make me think of Sartre's *La Nausée* (1938) and his conception of the other. What I am proposing, precisely, is to consider that analysis and its transformative capacity permits the transition from a Sartrian conception of the relation to the other to the Levinasian conception of this relation, a transition from equivocation, from turning one's back, to an encounter with the face.

Levinas suggests,

> In the present-day crisis of morality only responsibility for the other remains, responsibility without measure, which does not resemble a debt that one could always discharge, for we are never quits. This responsibility goes to the point of fission, to the de-nucleation of the "me" (*moi*). And therein lies the subjectivity of the "me". (Levinas, 2000[1993], p. 138)

It is in this sense that I think of the analyst as an "ethical subject".

As such, the analyst will have left room within him or herself for what I have called "matricial space" (Chetrit-Vatine, 2004b).

Lichtenberg-Ettinger (1997a) had already proposed the very similar concept of "matrixial space". Inspired by Levinas, she developed the idea of a mother–foetus, intrauterine encounter, sharedness without fusion, relation without relating.

My own use of the concept of matricial space is limited to characterising the ethical position of responsibility for the other that is incumbent on the mother/adult care-taker at the beginning of life, and on the analyst at the beginning of the analysis.

At the 2003 Congress of the European Psychoanalytic Federation, the theme of which was "The person of the analyst", I suggested that the person of the analyst is precisely that part of him or her that is capable of being responsible for the other (Chetrit-Vatine, 2002). The matricial space refers to the analyst's capacity to make a place for the other. It is a space for a relation with someone other than myself, at the risk of my own being, at the price of this other occupying a place "in my body and in my entrails".

For Levinas (1981[1974a], p. 75), maternity is "responsibility for the other to the point of substitution for the other". It is vulnerability, proximity, contact, and sensibility. It metaphorises "ethical passion" (Meir, 1994). This passion respects the alterity of the other; it does not seek to satisfy itself, and hates totalising. It is hospitality, that is to say, the ethical situation in which the host, allowing the other to enter his world, is responsible for him.

I saw in this matricial metaphor the idea of enabling the other to come to him or herself, the idea of a continuous listening, at once intentional and unintentional. There are also all those fantasies and wishes linked to this "pregnancy", our cathexis or investment of this other, from the very first encounter and sometimes even before. There are life wishes and sometimes death wishes, there is "objective hate" and "objective love" (Winnicott, 1947). There is also the danger that he or she shows his or her persecuting, disturbing aspect to us, which might make us "vacillate" owing to the injunction from the "face" which challenges us with the message, "Thou shall not kill". Finally, in this metaphor there is the expression of the sexual life drives. Levinas (1972, p. 122, n. 6) reminds us that in Hebrew the word "uterus" is translated by the term *rehem*, from which the term *rahamim* is derived, meaning compassion, mercy, and generosity (Chetrit-Vatine, 2004a).

In the Old Testament, when the world was created, God was designated by the word *Elohim*. According to the Midrash, he is the god of the forces of nature. When God creates man, he is designated by the word *Rahamim*, god of compassion. According to the Cabbalah, to create the world, God withdraws partially from the space he had occupied entirely hitherto, thereby leaving room for man to find his own space. Thus, the Zohar speaks of the *tsimtsum*, of God's withdrawal. The same "movement" is found, more or less consciously, in pregnancy. This withdrawal, this *tsimtsum*, can be approved, desired, refused, avoided, or denied; if the future mother does not abort, the foetus develops inside the matrix and will encroach on the mother's body, possibly causing it distress. In certain cases, it can be experienced as invasive, cruel, "shameless and unscrupulous", and persecuting. Here, Levinas's words resonate once again:

> The I [*Je*] or "me" [*moi*], approached as responsibility, is stripped bare, exposed to being affected, more open than any opening, that is, not open to the world that is always proportionate to consciousness, but open to the other that it does not contain. (2000[1993], p. 159)

Laplanche uses, does he not, the same terms to describe the way the adult intrudes on the child by proffering enigmatic signifiers?

I propose to take up these terms with regard to the mother who is open to her child—a child, ethically speaking, whom she cannot contain. (In the Levinasian sense of the term, obviously, and not in the Bionian sense.)

Ora, the mother of two children, was pregnant for the third time. She had begun an analysis two years earlier because she had the feeling that "she was missing out on things, and was sad or exasperated without knowing quite why". It was the first time that she had been in touch with what was happening to her . . . She was fantasising, with horror, that a sort of Dracula, a monster of unspeakable violence, was growing in her. My "affected", that is, emotionally engaged, presence (see Part II) during the months of her pregnancy, bearing her violence and her hatred towards a terrifying mother that she had long denied, helped her to put words to this "new" experience. "On the previous occasions, I felt nothing; it was afterwards that it was difficult . . . How am I going to manage? It's awful, why did I want another child, things are already difficult enough as they are!" After each session, I myself felt "touched" (*entamée*) (an expression used by Bokanowski (2004) and taken up in Chetrit-Vatine, 2004b), overwhelmed, and worried.

It is clear that Ora was prey to a repetition of the rejection of which she had been a victim when she found herself in her mother's entrails. The place that she found in me not only allowed her to elaborate her prenatal anxieties, projected on to the child to come, but also to experience in the transference what she had not been able to experience at this archaic stage: what I call a "non-linear transference of matricial space" (see Part III).

She finally gave birth to a little boy whom she breast-fed with pleasure and satisfaction for ten months, and who continued to develop peacefully with a loving mother who was attentive to his needs.

For Laplanche, the analytic process consists of making room for the life drives where the death drives were in action or enacted. In other words, and in my opinion, the analyst as an ethical subject is a *passeur*, a transformer, in himself and for the other, of the sexual death drives into sexual life drives. He continues, "No doubt investigation or the quest, like creation, comes from the individual . . . but what calls it forth and orients it is a vector that comes from the other" (1999c, p. 47). A few pages earlier, he wrote, "Sublimation, the mutation of the drive as regards its aims and its objects would in fact appear to be the transference or transposition of the sexual energy of the death drive into the sexual energy of the life drive" (1999c, p. 36). Last, concerning the desexualisation involved in sublimation which finally culminates in Eros, he notes, "Where the sexual death drives (of the order of destruction) were, there Eros (the sexual life drives) shall be" (p. 36).

I can now move on directly to the second part of my study.

PART II

AT THE BEGINNING OF LIFE: PRIMAL SEDUCTION, PASSION, AND ETHICAL EXIGENCY

Who are you, you who were born of me, you whom I do not know?
What do you have to do with the little one that I had imagined?
Other than me, you are strange for me, a stranger
If I do not nourish you, you will die.
If I do not hold you back, you will be crushed.
Dependent on me, totally I have full responsibibilty for your life, for
    your existence, whether good or bad.
I am a woman, an adult . . .
and I feel so helpless!
But you are tender,
what a pleasure it is to caress you, to touch you, to breathe you.
You have hair as soft as silk,
a little round mouth, well-formed shoulders,
a perfect body, a small sex organ.
There is even a drop of blood like a pearl on your vagina.
But you cry, you scream, you worry me.
Don't you want my milk? I don't know how to suckle you.
My breasts are burning. What do you want from me?
I am tired, I want to sleep.
You don't even look at me. Why?
Are you running away from me? Your gaze is empty.
Can you see me or not?
Can you hear me or not?
Do you know that I am your mother?
Do you know that you were born from my body? Do you know that I
    was torn because of you?
You're suckling a little, how good it is, how sweet!
Oh! You are almost looking at me[1]

CHAPTER THREE

The asymmetry of the primal situation: primal seduction and some elements of the Laplanchian theory of generalised seduction

Whereas, for Levinas, the demand for asymmetry comes from the call of the other's face (owing to the very fact of his fragility, his distress), for Laplanche, asymmetry has its origin in the parent, and, more precisely, in the mother, who proffers enigmatic signifiers to the newborn infant. Laplanche would subsequently prefer to qualify them as compromised signifiers, as messages compromised by the parental unconscious, a sexual unconscious according to him. These signifiers, these messages, are indicators of *primal seduction*. "The basis of the relation to the primal other," Laplanche (1987) writes, "is primal seduction; and the relationship with the analyst re-actualises this relationship, even taking it to its absolute limit" (p. 156). Thus, for Laplanche, the very offer of analysis creates its force of impulsion; it incites the transference.

I want to insist on the asymmetry of the relationship with the primordial other, and I should like to stress right away that it is initiated by the adult. The primordial other is first the parent, the adult

---

* This poem took shape while I was working on my presentation in view of obtaining membership of the Israeli Psychoanalytic Society. It first appeared in English in the *International Journal of Psychoanalysis*, 2004, 85: 841–856, and is reprinted with kind permission of John Wiley & Sons. It has been slightly revised for this book.

who is in charge of the infant. What is reactualised in analysis is the encounter with this primordial other of birth, and what permits this reactualisation is the presence of an analyst who offers to be there and be used as such.

This offer is not innocent. It is compromised from the outset by the analyst's unconscious, at the basis of his/her desire to be an analyst. I propose to call this reactualisation, the *transference of primal seduction*, which Laplanche designates by the term "hollowed-out transference" (*transfert en creux*).

Caretaking adults (the mother, paradigmatically), without whom the newborn infant could not develop, are, therefore, at the heart of this "fundamental anthropological situation". In his book *Freud and the Sexual*, Laplanche (2007b) asks: "Why not speak of a fundamental familial, even oedipal situation?" (p. 205). His answer is that a fundamental anthropological situation would exist "between an infant without a family and an absolutely non-familial educational environment" (2007b, p. 205). In this situation, the important terms are: "communication" and "message". Furthermore, he adds, "All messages are produced on the conscious–preconscious level". The messages coming from the adult world are not unconscious, but they are compromised by the adult's unconscious.

Adults are endowed with adult sexuality, mixed with unconscious infantile sexuality. This mother and/or that father are endowed with an unconscious. The mother's breasts, used for feeding her infant, are a source of sexual pleasure for her. The physical contact that she necessarily has with him, when everything goes well, is a source of great satisfaction for her, and this contact is sexually cathected whether she is aware of it or not. So, the maternal breast is not only a good or bad object. It wants something from the infant, who does not understand what this breast wants from him: "What does this breast want from me apart from wanting to suckle me and, come to that, why does it want to suckle me?" (Laplanche, 1987, p. 126). Primal seduction is inherent to the relationship between mother (father, other adults) and infant. It presides over the structuring of the human psyche and is at the origin of the unconscious.

Laplanche recognises the mutual dimension of parent–infant relations. Recent investigations based on the observation of early parent–infant relations (see Stern et al., 1998) have strongly emphasised this mutuality. Reference to this dimension can be found in certain quarters of contemporary psychoanalytic literature, drawing particularly on the contributions of Ferenczi. It is true that other authors, such as Mitchell (1997), Hoffman (1998), Aron (1996), Benjamin (1988) in the USA, or Stein (1997) in Israel, drawing on relational theory, stress the fact that the mother (the father/care-taking adult) is intrinsically in possession of adult sexuality. However, they do not emphasise sufficiently the asymmetry implied by the existence of this sexuality in the adult in relation to the child's sexuality. Admittedly, a degree of reciprocity, even on the sexual level, is established quickly, but "what counts, finally, in this situation is in fact what the recipient does with the message, that is to say, precisely the attempt at translation and the necessary failure of that attempt" (Laplanche, 2007b, p. 205).

While the mother is taking care of her infant, she emits messages that are enigmatic for him and, to a large extent, for her, too, since these messages are infiltrated by her own unconscious: in other words, by her infantile sexuality. The enigmatic quality of these messages has its origin in the asymmetry between the two partners: on the one hand, an adult endowed with mature sexuality and, on the other, a newborn baby, then a child, who will have to wait until puberty to acquire adult sexuality. Neurobiology has shown that the human infant does not come into the world with an endogenous sexuality; he only possesses preformed psychophysiological montages allowing him to be receptive to affects originating in the human environment. I agree here with Dejours (2003[2001]) who, in proposing a third topography, insists on the centrality of the body, the site from which the first work of translating the messages will take place.

Sexual life drives, sexual death drives

For Laplanche, they are constituted in the child as a consequence of primal seduction. There is no direct transmission to the child, however, of the parental unconscious (comprising sexual life drives, sexual death drives): a process of translation specific to each infantile psyche has to take place and this process will continue throughout the child's development. It is this process of translation of the parental messages that permits the constitution of the infantile unconscious. This capacity for translating messages, for Laplanche, is linked to the innate, and, at the beginning of life, potential capacity of self-theorisation.

I think that when the conditions of care are good enough, this potential can be realised via the adults themselves, who are permeated by their cultural and artistic environment, etc. However, in some of our patients, this potential of self-theorisation, which is directly linked to the capacity for symbolisation, has to be developed. This development might eventually be achieved with the help of analysis and an analyst who is able to accept his or her own affects.

At any rate, if we come back to an initial situation that is as favourable as possible, owing precisely to the enigmatic aspect of the messages, certain elements will not be translatable. These untranslated elements will be repressed. This is where the formation of the unconscious, that is, infantile sexuality as described by Freud in the *Three Essays on the Theory of Sexuality* (1905d), begins. This infantile sexuality is characterised as perverse and polymorphous. It affects both the subject's body and that of the object. It not only affects the person of the object, but also parts of the object. It gives flesh to fantasies that are the product of the residues constituting the unconscious. Infantile sexuality, for Laplanche, is the fruit of the child–parent encounter, which necessarily has a seductive quality.

Traumatic seduction, precocious seduction, and primal seduction

I think it is important to establish a clear distinction between different forms of seduction.

Laplanche developed his theory of generalised seduction from Freud's first theory of the seduction lying at the origin of hysteria, which he subsequently neglected. After the famous letter to Wilhelm Fliess and his renunciation of his "*neurotica*", Freud seems to have abandoned this first theory. Yet, the question of seduction never really ceases to appear in his writings. Thus, Scarfone's (1997) reflections seem particularly relevant here. "It seems essential," he writes,

> to note the following fact: when Freud explains to his friend Fliess that he is abandoning the theory of infantile seduction, he does not say that such a seduction does not exist or that it is without consequences. He merely points out that there are no criteria in the unconscious that allow us to distinguish fact from fantasy; fantasy can carry conviction just as much as an actual fact. It can be just as pathogenic. (p. 145)

Laplanche has given seduction its full place once again, proposing to go beyond the radical opposition between fantasy and reality, between internal and external causes, and between internal and external objects.

Although for Laplanche primal seduction is definitely factual and of parental origin, it is not pathogenic. Indeed, he differentiates between primal seduction, infantile seduction (which I propose to call "traumatic seduction"), and precocious seduction.

Traumatic seduction

This implies an adult exploiting a child sexually. It is the seduction that Freud speaks about in his first theory of the origins of hysteria, and to which Ferenczi refers in his text "The confusion of tongues between adults and the child" (1932). For me, it is also this seduction that permeates both the physical or verbal violence and the lack of interest of the parental and / or adult environment in charge of the child, which in turn results in the child feeling physically and / or psychically abandoned. When the environment is incapable of "meeting the child's needs", to use Winnicott's expression, or when deficiencies or damage exist in the child's constitution, most of the messages coming from the adult world will be experienced by the child as traumatic messages. In such cases, Laplanche (1987, p. 355) has spoken of the *intromission* of messages. Such messages cannot be translated. They will become embedded in the psyche and remain close to consciousness like foreign bodies that are incapable of metabolisation. The essential defence will be splitting and not repression (Laplanche, 2007b). This will be the case with those patients who invade the analyst with overwhelming material and affects that they themselves are unable to contain, making the analyst share the experience. Such patients suffer from insurmountable difficulties in creating close relationships while, at the same time, in order to get rid of their pain, they make use of intense projective identification with their analysts and their immediate environment alike. They are also prone, very often in alternation, to be victims of grave somatic disorders. These individuals often lack the feeling of having a creative inner life and suffer from an absence of a stable sense of identity as well as of a responsible "I" that is the agent of their own life. Their self-esteem is always very low.

Precocious seduction

This is the seduction Laplanche has in mind when he refers to the bodily ministrations and physical contact that are so important in the relations between children and their parents. It includes caresses, kisses, hugging, massages, carrying, fights for fun and laughter, and so on; and, for infants, breast-feeding, baths, washing and dressing, etc. As Freud wrote in the *Three Essays* (1905d),

> If the mother understood more of the high importance of the part played by instincts [drives] in mental life as a whole – in all its ethical and psychical achievements – she would spare herself any self-reproaches even after her enlightenment. [While she takes care of his physical needs] she . . . is teaching the child to love. (p. 223)

Freud's positioning of the mother as the first seducer in the *Three Essays*, as well as in his study on *Leonardo* (1910c), tended to be repressed, in fits and starts, by Freud himself, at the same time as he repressed the theory of infantile seduction (Laplanche, 1987, p. 116). Right up to the present time, this tendency has been iterated in the international psychoanalytic community of Anglo-Saxon influence in general, and in the Israeli psychoanalytic community in particular. In 1964, Jacobson, one of the respected figures of the movement of ego psychology, wrote,

> In fact, when a mother turns the infant on his belly, takes him out of his crib, diapers him, sits him up in her arms and on her lap, rocks him, strokes him, kisses him, feeds him, smiles at him, talks and sings to him, she offers him not only all kinds of libidinal gratifications [note that the libidinal gratifications belong to the infant; the mother's are not mentioned here] but simultaneously stimulates and prepares the child's sitting, standing, crawling, walking, talking, and so on, i.e. the development of functional ego activity. (1964, p. 37)

With the insistence on ego functioning in the USA and in the wake of Anna Freud, with the development of object relations theory, in spite of the importance that would soon be accorded to the quality of the environment, and, later, with attachment theories and the subsequent insistence on the question of mentalization, there was an increasing tendency for the centrality of infantile sexuality as an organising

factor of the human psyche, and, what is more, the seductive dimension of the environment (see Part III), to disappear from psychoanalytic theorisations that were outside the influence of the "French
school".

Primal seduction

For Laplanche, as for me, primal seduction is inherent to the relationship between the mother/father (or any other care-taking adult) and
the child. In health, that is to say, in cases of "good enough" parenting, coupled with a good enough constitution of the child, most of the
messages coming from the adult world will be *implanted*. These
messages will to a large extent be translated and this process of translation will permit the structuring of the developing psyche.

Primal seduction, for Laplanche, is the basis of the two other types
of seduction. It is necessarily re-evoked or, more precisely, provoked
by the offer of analysis, and it remains active throughout the analytic
process until it ends. It is the only seduction pertaining to psychotherapeutic or psychoanalytic practice. The two other types of seduction
would be a perversion of practice.

I am touching here on the theoretical and ethical necessity of there
being no physical contact between analyst and patient (an issue
recently raised in Israeli psychoanalytic circles). Laplanche (1987)
writes,

> Precocious seduction and infantile seduction are obviously not
> enacted in psychoanalysis, unless its practice becomes perverted. It is
> *primal seduction alone* which comes into play here, and it does so in a
> much purer and more essential form than it does in childhood
> because, in childhood situations, it was always to some extent medi-
> ated by sexual gestures or sexual behaviour [necessarily infiltrating
> physical contact]. (p. 157)

If primal seduction and its re-evocation by the offer of analysis is
an active and activating presence of the analytic process, and if it is at
the foundations of the sexual active in the analytic tub (*baquet*) (this
is how Laplanche designates the analytic setting, 1987, p. 156), respect
for the rule of analytic abstinence serves both to consolidate the
closure of the tub and to lay bare the material that is thereby brought

to light. Failure to respect it, by definition accidental, can only precipitate the analytic situation, the analysis, and the patient into the pit of the traumatic experiences of early childhood, experiences that have not been metabolised. In my terms, it results from an erasure of the matricial space in the analyst, from an obliteration of the ethical asymmetrical dimension of the analytic situation.

Implantation and intromission

The adult proffers enigmatic messages. This primal proffering will only become destabilising later on (Laplanche insists on these two stages, two stages that are necessary to produce an effect of "afterwardsness" (Laplanche's proposed term in English for Freud's *Nachträglichkeit*, translated by Strachey as "deferred action"). This means that the child's psyche will be grappling with a necessity for translation that his innate capacity for self-theorisation will enable him to realise. (I shall be questioning the innateness of this capacity, already mentioned above, further on; although I consider that this capacity undoubtedly corresponds to a potentiality, I see the realisation of this potentiality as an acquisition linked to a structuring, symbol-generating, adult environment.) However, a complete translation is impossible. Part of the message will not be translated.

It is clear that for Laplanche the unconscious has nothing to do with phylogenesis (1987, pp. 29–37). The little human being comes into the world without an unconscious. His unconscious will be the product of his encounter with the adult world. As I have already said, the child's unconscious will be constituted by a work of translation carried out by its own psyche. So, these untranslated messages, these partial, fragmented, sexual contents, will be the very matter of the unconscious. If, for Freud, primal fantasies, polymorphous infantile sexuality, and drive functioning are rooted in the biological and/or the phylogenetic domains, for Laplanche, the little human being is endowed with preformed motor and perceptual schema, but not with instinctual sexuality. He is constituted of supple matter and open to all the winds and influences coming from the world that takes care of him. Susceptible to impact, he is touched by the enigmatic nature of the messages that are addressed to him; he is subsequently disturbed by the compromised nature of the messages—compromised by the unconscious sexual signifiers that they contain. It would seem that he is able to separate the wheat from the chaff, since part of the message is translated while the other part is repressed; therefore, he participates in the constitution of his unconscious. He is, thus, endowed with a primary capacity for selection or sorting. This supposes that he comes into the world with an innate sense of what is translatable and what is untranslatable, of what is "good enough" or "not too bad". Does this mean that for Laplanche the capacity for translation and selection belongs to the self-preservative order? This impossibility of complete translation, which is, in fact, inherent to all translation, results from the excess implied by the very gap between the infant's psyche and the adult's.

Laplanche (1992c) distinguishes between structuring and destructuring enigmatic messages. The first allow the child to make this selection, while the second overwhelm his capacities for translation. It is these structuring messages, then, that he designates as "implanted messages", while the destructuring messages are denoted as "intromitted messages".

By insisting on this distinction, Laplanche has opened up a new perspective regarding our understanding of borderline states or states characterised by difficulties of identity (see Scarfone, 1997, p. 74).

The three meanings of the term "unconscious"

In his last book, Laplanche (2007b) proposes three meanings of the term "unconscious".

1.   The unconscious, in the Freudian sense, that is to say, the repressed, is, in Laplanche's terms, "the residue of what is always an imperfect translation of the message". It stands opposed to a preconscious ego in which the personality is constituted in temporality, "historicising itself". The personality is infiltrated by this unconscious. This unconscious results, then, from the work of translation imposed on the psyche by the so-called "implanted", compromised messages coming from the adult world.
2.   The enclaved unconscious, which Laplanche proposes to call "subconscious", is very close to consciousness. It comprises

untranslated messages. These messages are those that have suffered a failure of translation owing to their quality as "intromitted" messages. However, these messages can be de-translated elements, awaiting a new translation. In this sense, the enclaved unconscious is as much a zone of stagnation as a zone of passage or transition. I shall be using the term "enclaved unconscious" in a broader way to include traces of messages without representation, traces of affect *deposited* in the infantile psyche at a very early stage of development (see Part IV).

3.   The pseudo-unconscious of the mytho-symbolic order. Laplanche qualifies this pseudo-unconscious as "implicit" rather than "collective". What is important, he emphasises, is its psychic function: it supplies "an aid to translation" (p. 217).

It may be surmised that in psychoses and borderline states greater consideration will have to be given to the part played by the enclaved unconscious. Dejours (2001, p. 170) has proposed the concept of the proscribed unconscious. In so doing, he seeks to underline the effects of arrested thinking in the child, which can be caused by intromitted messages (in the case of parental violence, for instance).

Whatever the enigmatic messages are, whether they are implanted or intromitted, it is important to reiterate that under no circumstances is a direct transmission from the adult's unconscious to the child involved. The messages are subject to a translation. This translation will depend equally on the infant's capacities. Thus, in the case of unmetabolisable messages comprising the enclaved or proscribed unconscious, it is important to take into account the psycho-physiological state of the infant in conjunction with the role that is played "objectively" by the adult environment.

CHAPTER FOUR

Maternal passion, the analyst's passion, or the primacy of affect

Although speaking of the drives and their constitution implies referring to what constitutes the unconscious (or, in terms of the second topography, the id), I shall turn now to their manifestation at the preconscious and conscious level (or, in second topography terms, the ego). In other words, I am going to address the manifestation of these drives at the level of subjective experience. Widlöcher's (1999) proposition is particularly relevant here to what I want to say: "If, clinically, affect presents itself with all the complexity of a subjective experience involving multiple registers of expression, metapsychologically it can be defined as the quantitative expression of the drive (a movement towards others)" (p. 174).

Furthermore, I would add that "ordinary" (André, 2006) parental passion, with its weighty mixture of hate and love, is the affective manifestation of parental drive functioning. To be sure, the term "passion" evokes multiple significations (see André, 1999; Gori, 2002).

Is it not pure embodied maternal madness (and, therefore, countertransferential madness), in terms of the analyst's function, to evoke the parental passion at the foundations of the generative power of parenting and, on this basis, to speak of the analyst's passion and of the transformational power of analysis? (See the critique by Adam Phillips, below.)

From Ferenczi to Bion, via Winnicott

As we have seen, Ferenczi (1932) put forward the idea of a confusion of tongues between the adult's language and the child's language. This confusion is held to be at the origin of the psychical trauma caused by an adult's sexual abuse of a child. For Ferenczi, the child speaks the language of tenderness, whereas the perverse adult speaks the language of passion.

In fact, Ferenczi took up Freud's "repressed" theory of infantile seduction or, in my terms, traumatic seduction. In so doing, and notwithstanding the fact that his writings were effectively banned by the psychoanalytic community for a long time, we are indebted to him for having insisted on the importance of the role played by the adult environment and for having drawn attention to the role played by seduction in the formation of the psyche. Thereby, he supplied Laplanche with additional backing for his theory of generalised seduction.

Although I emphasised earlier—in agreement with Laplanche—the need to differentiate between different forms of seduction, I propose, in distinction to both Ferenczi and Laplanche, to retain the term "parental passion" as expressing the affective manifestation of the parental sexual drives: in other words, of the parental unconscious, at the conscious and preconscious level. This term is evocative of a potential excess, the mark of intensity, and I would say that it is this passion that affects the messages coming from the adult.

For Bion, the "analyst's passion" is what corresponds to his affective or emotional participation. He considers the analyst's emotional participation as the central organiser of meaning. He situates it at the heart of the analytic encounter. He emphasised the primordial importance of the analyst's emotional participation, beyond the countertransference. Bion posits the existence of a central existential conflict in each human being in the form of a tension between the need for knowledge—knowing in the sense of having an "emotional" experience—and the human tendency to avoid this knowledge. Indeed, any emotionally connected insight is often accompanied by a painful realisation. Lacan went as far as positioning the desire for ignorance radically alongside hate and love.

Bion's ideas concerning the analyst's emotional/affective participation were forged in his work with groups. He would, thus, share with the group, by way of an analytic intervention, the feelings that he was experiencing at this or that particular moment. Bion (1962a) was one of the continuators of Klein who, after Winnicott (1947), Heimann (1950) and Racker (1953), modified the conception of the countertransference.

For him, the countertransference is more than the manifestation, in analytic work with this or that patient, of difficulties inherent to the analyst's resistances and unresolved conflicts that impede its smooth progress. Becoming aware of this countertransference becomes a tool for the analyst's understanding of the current emotions of his patient. It becomes a path towards a realisation of his affects and of their eventual representation. Projective identification, in turn, was increasingly understood as a means of preconscious communication aimed at informing the analyst of the affects (and eventually the representations associated with them) of his patient.

Yet, no doubt to avoid participating in the erasure of the first sense of the countertransference, Bion (1963) differentiated between the countertransference and the analyst's passion. He writes, "Passion must be clearly distinguished from countertransference, the latter being evidence of repression" (p. 13). He qualified this passion as "optimal emotional position". It consists of three primordial emotions, which I would prefer to call "primordial affects": Love, Hate, and Knowledge as curiosity (L, H, K). He stated,

> By 'passion' or the lack of it, I . . . mean the term to represent an emotion experienced with intensity and warmth though without any suggestion of violence: the sense of violence is not to be conveyed by the term 'passion' unless it is associated with the term 'greed'. (pp. 12–13)

Thus meaning, without any trace of violence, and without any association with the term "greed". Bion's insistence on this point seems to me particularly important. He has, thus, described three dimensions of affective experience. These dimensions, L, H, and K can only be realised through experience.

It is true that speaking of experience harks back to a level of reflection of a phenomenological type. Here, Bion's anticipates Golse's (2006a) point of view, which I share. As Golse points out, while we are concerned today with archaic states,

> our means of recourse, whether proclaimed or not, is of a phenomenological order. This is true, for example, concerning the utilisation of the phenomenon that is subjectively felt or experienced by the analyst in order to understand the patient's subjective experience. (p. 71)

Thus, Golse envisages "a complex but potentially enriching articulation between psychoanalysis and phenomenology . . . centred on the transference and the counter-transference" (2006a, p. 71).

In his famous article, "Hate in the counter-transference", Winnicott (1947) enumerated more than fifteen reasons why a mother can hate-objectively—her baby. I construe this "objective hate" as the manifestation of the sublimation of the sexual death drives—in other words, as the manifestation of the sexual life drives. However, Winnicott does not seem to have been interested in the love in the countertransference, in the seduction inherent to the maternal function and to the analytic function. By the same token, he paid little attention to the passionate manifestations of his patients. In 1954, he undertook the analysis of Margaret Little (see Little, 1991). How are we to understand Little's explosive behaviour, or those moments when she is crying uncontrollably under her blanket, if no reference is made to the passion of which her analyst was quite clearly the object? Likewise, Winnicott does not seem to take into consideration the seductive aspect of the "good enough mother". As Kristeva pointed out to me during our discussions when she was visiting Jerusalem in 2006, "Winnicott's notion of the 'good enough mother' lacks a fair amount of salt!!! And maternal passion? Where has that gone?"

In Winnicott's last works, the mother seems to have come into the world as an asexual and naturally devoted being. Bleichmar (1985), a disciple of Laplanche, has also remarked on this lack of consideration for the sexual and the sensual in Winnicott's work, even though he is interested in the infantile psyche. She writes,

> Winnicott locates an intermediate area of illusion between the mother and the child, which will subsequently be occupied by the transitional

object. This area of illusion is the effect of the maternal capacity to adapt to the baby's needs. It is a question of constituting an interme- diate area of experience born of the exchanges established in the inter- subjective relationship which constitutes primary infant care . . . but Winnicott remains a prisoner of a theoretical question that has not been elucidated by the English school, namely, the reduction of the maternal relationship to the level of self-preservation, the initial fail- ure to clarify the role of sexuality in the constitution of the psyche. However, if the transitional object functions, it is precisely because it recovers from the relationship with the mother residues of reality, a shared odour, a certain texture. (p. 144, translated for this edition)

I concur with Bleichmar's critique concerning "the initial failure to clarify the role of sexuality in the constitution of the psyche" in Winnicott's work. Where I disagree with her, just as I disagree with Laplanche for the same reason, is that she aligns herself with Winni- cott in considering the maternal relationship as belonging to the self- preservative order. If the infant functions at the beginning of life at a level of self-preservation, the mother, the helpful parent, functions fundamentally, as an ethical subject, at a level which could be said to transcend the level of self-preservation (see Part IV).

So, for me, the good enough mother is at once seductive and ethi- cal. Consequently, since I consider that the analyst forms an integral part of the analytic setting, I shall refer to the ethical seduction of the setting and of the analytic situation (see Part III).

Affect, feeling, emotion

In order to clarify the differences between affect, feeling, and emotion, I will refer to Danon-Boileau's (1999) paper. Overlappings of meaning can, of course, be found in psychoanalytic and non-psychoanalytic literature, but there are also constructed differences between these different terms.

- The notion of "affect" is linked to the notion of representation. This conjunction is to be envisaged as an effect of the drive.
- The term "feeling" (*éprouvé*) could be said to characterise the psychic tonality of the material brought by the patient or of a quality that has emerged in the countertransference. As soon as

the analysis can be continued, as soon as a later characterisation of what is perhaps involved succeeds in linking up this feeling with the internal movements of the session, and then with the qualitative shifts in the object relationship in the transference, the term must give way to the term "affect". "What allows us to speak of affect and not just of feeling is the fact that what is experienced psychically can be envisaged as awaiting a representation to which this felt experience can temporarily attach itself" (Danon-Boileau, 1999, p. 10). So, it is the potential for linking up with what is representable, a process that has not yet taken place, that makes it possible to distinguish between feeling and affect.

● The notion of "emotion" seems to me to be adequate in respect of the child, when one considers the first exchanges between a mother and her infant. The nursling infant's emotion appears to be a movement in response to an event in the outside world. The source of the emotion is linked to the here-and-now of the situation. Danon-Boileau insists on the current quality of emotion, whereas affect is related to the subject's history. He suggests that what is felt or experienced by the subject during the session and localised in the present instant should be called "transference emotion" (and not transference affect). The term "emotion", thus, has a connotation of discharge through action and, in this sense, it also different from affect. One could speak of countertransferential emotion, of countertransferential feelings, and one could speak of maternal madness as a madness of feelings.

To return to Bion (1963) and his definition of passion, it is worth noting his insistence on the necessity of "two minds" for passion to exist: "Awareness of passion is not dependent on sense. For senses to be active only one mind is necessary; passion is evidence that two minds are linked ..." (p. 13). In other words, we can only speak of maternal passion (the analyst's passion) when we consider two separate minds, the mother's and the infant's (the patient's and the analyst's). This mind, this apparatus for thinking, and this passion, will enable the analyst to contain and to transform *beta* elements into *alpha* elements; or, in terms of Laplanche's conceptualisation, they will permit the transformation of the sexual death drives into sexual life drives. As for Green (1986), he writes,

Instinctual action, [which, he has said, is *'nothing but passion'*] itself active, 'passivates' the subject who is submitted to it . . . the child who is passivated by maternal care must be able to count on the mother . . . Now the psychoanalytic cure is not possible without this confident passivation, where the analysand gives himself up to the analyst's care. (pp. 247–248, my italics)

For my part, I want to insist on the asymmetry of the analyst's passion and its ethical character, and it seems more appropriate to me to speak of three primordial affects originating in the mother and the analyst, and not of primordial emotions, particularly where the analyst is concerned.

Maternal passion, the analyst's passion

In her book, *Seule, une femme*, Kristeva (2007) turns her attention to maternal passion. I am going to draw on her arguments to develop my own elaboration of the question of the analyst's passion.

"Female fertility and pregnancy", she writes, in "Cet incroyable besoin de croire" (2008), "not only continue to fascinate our collective imagination but also serve as a sanctuary for the sacred" (p. 170, translated for this edition). She is referring to the mothers of disabled children who feel demoralised, undermined, and narcissistically wounded by having to face the fact that they have given birth to a damaged child. Generally speaking, these mothers are fighters and are preoccupied first and foremost with the future of their child "after their own death". Levinas, who has enabled me to metaphorise responsibility for the other as a matricial position, laid equal emphasis, in my view, on the violence implied by this interpellation of the "face" which issues me with the command: "Thou shall not kill".

This other to whom I offer, whether I want to or not, a place in my uterus and then in my life, and in life in general, is a reflection as much of his fragility as of my potential violence, especially if he or she is born with a disability. His or her feared/desired death cannot fail to obsess me. Yet, the central value to which these women adhere is that of life, notwithstanding their ambivalence. The question of maternal passion has not been given sufficient consideration. We have seen that although Winnicott took an interest in the maternal function, he seems only to have skimmed over the question of "the passionate violence of the maternal experience" (Kristeva, 2008, p. 171). Kristeva makes a correlation between maternal passion and its violence and the ties of love. For my part, I want to liken it to "the analyst's being" woven with "analytic doing".

The analyst's passion, like maternal passion, is complex. To employ Kristeva's terms, I would say that analysts undoubtedly partake in the occultation of this passion, for it comprises as many benefits as it does risks, not only for the analyst, but also for his or her patients, colleagues, and immediate entourage. As is the case with the mother, it no doubt evokes our fears of incest, our fears of deadly violence; it touches on our infantile and polymorphous sexuality, as well as on the ever-present possibility of transgression.

How are the ambiguities of this passion to be dealt with?

Maternity is not instinct; neither is the desire to have a child. By what complex ways does this desire become a reality in the human being, even if at the beginning it is potentially part of our physiological and preformed structures? Being an analyst is obviously not of an instinctual order. Certainly, the faculty, the capacity for empathy, which, in my view, is an intrinsic quality of the "analyst's being" seems to be an innate gift (see Noy, 1984). But the fact of having transformed (sublimated?) this capacity that might, in the infantile history of the majority of analysts, have been abused by the parental environment, into a means of earning one's living raises some difficult questions, notwithstanding the analyst's experience of personal analysis, however "almost complete" it might have been.

Much has been said about the analyst's desire, about the desire to be an analyst, and about an ethical principle consisting of not yielding to one's desire, but were we speaking about the same "analyst's being", defined, as I have proposed above, as an ethical subject who is responsible for the other?

According to Kristeva (2008), we can speak of passion when the emotions of attachment and aggressivity towards the foetus/baby/child "are transformed into love (idealisation, future life project, devotion), with its correlate of more or less attenuated hate" (p. 172, translated for this edition). In my view, when things go as well as is possible, as the philosopher Hans Jonas argues, this transformation occurs from the outset: this devotion, which is responsibility for the other, appears immediately. Just as, at the beginning, the narcissistic dimension is prevalent for the "mother-to-be", so, too, it is prevalent in the desire to become an analyst. An analyst's training involves a destabilisation and a reinforcement of this narcissism. With his or her first case, the analyst in training experiences a loss of identity: he or she is at once analyst, analysand, and student. However, I would say, with Kristeva, that although his passion is dominated, as is the case for the future mother, by narcissism, it is, none the less, triangular. It has been said of the pregnant woman that she looks at the outside world without seeing it, that she is elsewhere. How many analysts in training hear that again and again from those around them? But, with "the first case", this passion that had hitherto been turned towards the inside is now turned towards the patient himself. The task is a complex one: it involves letting oneself be touched, letting oneself be transformed, accepting being taken hostage by the play of projective identifications which are quick to manifest themselves. It is a matter of letting oneself be controlled and possessed, without losing one's contours, without losing the relationship with oneself. It is a question of investing the patient with a living presence, a human presence, bathed in a passion, which, taking itself into account, takes the patient into account all the more.

Guillaumin (1999) writes,

> The analyst and the analysand play and suffer together, knowing it without knowing it. In this abyss where psychic experience and bodily experience are intertwined, powerful mutations of meaning and humour originate or are nourished from which psychoanalytic change is finally engendered, contained as they are by a belt, a uterus, the armature of the setting including the two partners. (p. 75, translated for this edition)

Admittedly, Guillaumin presents the analytic encounter more in symmetrical terms. I would like once again to insist on its asymmetry. I agree with him, though, that it is a matter of responding to the patient's fragility within a setting—in which I myself am included— that is supposed to trap his death wish and the untiring activity of the death drive. It is a question of "controlling and enrolling the death drive by compromising it in a new alliance with the life drives, giving fresh impetus to the original alliance" (Guillaumin, 1999, p. 75, translated for this edition).

For Donnet (1987), in order to have an effect an interpretation must communicate something of the analyst's engagement in the situation. He writes, "The foundational dysymmetry is corrected to some degree by the manifestation of a certain reciprocity" (p. 166, translated for this edition). I do not think that it is a matter here of reciprocity, but, rather, of the manifestation of ethical seduction which, by definition, is asymmetrical.

He continues,

> The analyst's subjectivity – leaving aside the elements of the setting and also the elements of his person which necessarily manifest themselves – or rather, what he reveals to his patient of his own personal implication, is precisely the implication present in the act of dis-implication. (p. 166, translated for this edition)

And again,

> The good oedipal parent is one who proffers the prohibition of incest in such a way that he or she reveals a mode of psychic functioning in which well-tempered negation permits him or her to *recognise* the child's desire [in him or herself too] – while prohibiting it. (pp. 166–167, translated for this edition)

The same may be said of moderate, positive countertransference love, which is also "a love between generations and permits the patient to feel loved by and in the analytic situation"—which is another way of speaking of the analyst's passion.

Freud was convinced that to love one's neighbour as oneself was a pious wish, and quite impossible to realise; and Lacan made a mockery of it. Kristeva, whose position I share, puts forward the following idea: "Loving one's neighbour as oneself returns us to the enigma of the good enough mother who allows the *infans* to create the transitional space allowing him or her to think" (2008, p. 174, translated for this edition). We find this living enigma again in the "good enough analyst".

Kristeva has noted that "feminine genius shows the presence of a tie with the object right from the start of psychic life" (2008, p. 174, translated for this edition). Through her in-depth studies of Arendt, Klein, and Colette, she has arrived at the Laplanchian conclusion that there can be no narcissism without an object first or, rather, that narcissism could not develop without a first other who cathects the newborn subject affectively, through his or her narcissism. And, I would add, narcissism tempered by responsibility for the other; narcissism tempered by the mother's matricial position.

If this primordial presence of the mother is foundational for the constitution of the infant's psyche, a presence of the same order is equally foundational for transformative analytic work. For the analyst and the mother alike, Kristeva writes,

> love and hate, wonder and frustration, pleasure and pain, a desire for closeness and a need for space, tranquillity and disquiet, pride and disappointment, interest and boredom, curiosity and detachment, cheerfulness and irritation alternate. . . . Passion may enable the mother to elaborate a potential bond with the other, to elaborate the passionate destructiveness underlying all kinds of bonds that the maternal experience allows us to get deeply in touch with. (2008, p. 175, translated for this edition)

While, as analysts, we are confronted with patients suffering increasingly from problems of identity, the question of this living presence, the importance of the "affected" (*affectée*) or emotionally cathected part of the analyst needs to be stressed more and more. For Kristeva, it is maternal sublimation that makes the elaboration of maternal passion possible. She speaks of the mother as a "sublimatory agent". She even goes so far as to say, "It is because it is a continuous sublimation that maternal passion makes the child's creativity possible" (2008, p. 179, translated for this edition). In other words, I would say that what permits this sublimation, this transformation of the sexual death drives into the sexual life drives, as Laplanche (1999b) defines sublimation, is the mother's capacity to be responsible for this other, her child. This responsibility, woven with a living, "affected" presence, and, thus, an ethically seductive presence, will be the source of the child's creativity. In analysis, it is a matter of the analyst's capacity to be responsible for the other, his or her patient, and to be responsible for the analysis itself. This responsibility for the other is intrinsically linked to the analysis of this other (Denis, 2007).

Kristeva continues,

> Maternal passion effects a transformation of the libido so that sexualisation is postponed by virtue of tenderness, whereas narcissistic

exaltation ... yields to a *sublimatory cycle* in which the mother constitutes herself by differentiating herself from her newborn baby. (2008,
p. 179, translated for this edition)

Ethically speaking, I would add that at the moment of this transformation of the libido, enacted by the maternal passion to which
Kristeva refers, mastery becomes caress. Like Kristeva, who refers to
the mother differentiating herself from her newborn baby, Levinas, as
we have seen, insists on separation. For him, separation-differentia-
tion—is inherent to the capacity for responsibility for the other. This
separation allows for a "caress position", the position of a subject/
analyst who is seeking without knowing what he or she is looking for,
knowing without claiming to have knowledge. The good enough
analyst is not invested in his or her own message, but in that of the
patient. By listening to the patient's message, the analyst approaches
the patient's psychic space. "The good enough mother", writes Kristeva, "is one who can go away, making room for the child to have the
pleasure of thinking about her" (2008, p. 181, translated for this
edition). Likewise, the good enough analyst is one who knows how to
keep silent, to allow the patient to be alone in his or her presence, in
order to allow the patient to have the space to find pleasure in thinking about the analyst ... in thinking, and in being. The analyst's
passion, then, is situated between mastery and caress.

Kristeva has alluded to the enjoyment (*jouissance*) derived by the
mother from her child's messages. We analysts can experience something of this enjoyment when a patient brings, for example, a series of
associations or relates a dream. This is a form of "sublimatory perver-
sity", suggests Kristeva. For my part, I prefer to speak of "ethical
seduction", and will try to show, however complex it may be, how
indispensable it is for any form of subjective appropriation (see Part
III).

CHAPTER FIVE

The ethical exigency at the beginning of life and the need for ethics in analysis

I remember my astonishment, many years ago now, when I realised that the constitution of varied forms of psychopathology often resulted from an encounter, at the beginning of life, and during the formative years, between a little human being who is developing and an adult world that is barely capable of satisfying what I later referred to as his ethical exigency. Kristeva has defined the mother as a sublimatory agent. Winnicott, for his part, referred to the importance of "meeting the infant's needs", and Bion emphasised the mother's holding capacity in this task. Bollas (1987), as we shall see, has stressed the transformational role of the maternal function, and I shall be looking at the links between this and my own propositions. In fact, none of these authors has formulated in terms of an ethical exigency the primary needs to which these maternal functions and, consequently, the contemporary analytic function, attempt to respond. For Hans Jonas (see Part One), (as for Bion and post-Bionion analysts) the little human being comes into the world with an innate search for truth. In my view, this innate search for truth should be linked with this ethical need, as I have described it, from the point of view of the toddler, of the human being, and, thus, of our patients.

If Freud, in the *Project* (1895), stated that the primary situation at the beginning of life—the situation of distress, of helplessness—was at the origin of our moral motivations, it seems, as we saw earlier, that he made the assumption that human beings have a capacity to show concern for others. This capacity, he claims, is motivated and rooted in the need for self-preservation. It is as if this same adult, who, at the beginning of life, was himself a little human being in distress, potentially lacking a helping adult, had taken this function upon himself and had directed it towards the adult in order to ensure the continuity of care which he could not have done without. In fact, as I have indicated, for Freud, ethics has its source in an essentially narcissistic motivation. Winnicott formulated the hypothesis, in certain subjects, of a *false-self* organisation, and before him Ferenczi proposed the notion of the "wise baby". Each of them described a psychopathological organisation characterised precisely by the infant's premature capacity for taking care of himself while "parenting" his own parents. It is assumed that this prematurity results from the experience of a traumatic or narcissistic seduction. Such an experience is antithetical to the child's ethical requirement of encountering, in this adult world, a matricial space, interwoven with primal seduction and maternal passion.

After taking up the propositions of Bollas, who has developed the idea of the maternal function, and, consequently, the idea of the analyst as a transformational function, I take up the suggestions of Roussillon, backed up by the ideas of Salman Akhtar, an American analyst of Hindu origin, who is also inspired by the Winnicottian current and today belongs to the post-Kohutian intersubjective current. This allows me to give shape to the second aspect of the asymmetry of the analytical situation, which I have qualified as ethical responsibility for the other, considered from the analysand's point of view.

The mother, the analyst: a transformational object

In his article, "L'esprit de l'objet et l'épiphanie du sacré", Bollas (1978) presented his concept of the transformational object to the French-speaking public. The *Nouvelle Revue de Psychanalyse* had chosen "Belief" as its theme. The text in question evokes the belief in the transformational capacity of our objects which underlies our existence and without which we would share the anxiety, if not the certitude, of the other's madness. This is a necessary and shared belief. Against this backdrop, Bollas is interested in another form of belief, which, for me, is connected with what I call "subjectal moments" (*moments subjectaux*) in analysis (see Part III). For Bollas, such moments are aesthetic. He might have qualified them as transformational moments. He writes,

> It is an intimate and deep belief which stops ordinary perception and places the subject in a space that is no longer mediated by metaphor . . . a moment in which the person feels chosen and maintained in a solitary clasp by the subjectivity of the object. (Bollas, 1978, p. 253, translated for this edition)

Bollas associates such a moment with experiences such as Christian conversion, the poet's reverie, the listener's ecstasy, the reader's captivation, or that of the art lover encountering this or that work of art: "Experiences of this kind crystallise time in a space where subject and object seem to achieve an encounter marked by a deep relationship" (Bollas, 1978, p. 253, translated for this edition). These moments, he adds, can be subjected to interpretation, but they "basically constitute a verbal event that is remarkable in terms of the density of the subject's affect (of felt experience!) and insight, independent of any representation of being held by the aesthetic object" (Bollas, 1978, p. 254, translated for this edition). There is a sense of both surprise and fusion—I would say encounter. There is a sort of induction by the object. "The strange relation with this object, the intense illusion of being chosen by the environment for an affective experience imbued with respect" evokes for Bollas, in conjunction with the associated feeling of being held, the psychosomatic memory of what Winnicott called "the holding environment". What is involved here, he posits, is a pre-representational re-evocation. The infant, by virtue of the ministrations of its mother, experiences a process of transformation, of mini-metamorphoses, in its internal and external environment, but he or she does not know that this transformation "is in part cautioned by the mother" (Bollas, 1978, p. 254). Experience of the object precedes knowledge of the object. Bollas writes,

> Before identifying her as an object, the infant uses the mother as a projective space for localising the deeply enigmatic psychosomatic registers of his being, thereby anticipating the future discovery that he

will make of her as an object that takes care of him. (Bollas, 1978, p. 256, translated for this edition)

The following question may be raised here: who projects on to whom, and what is the origin of the enigma in the infant, or else in the mother, who is an enigma for him because she proffers compromised messages permeated by her unconscious sexuality? This dimension escaped Winnicott and also Bollas at that time.

I continue my reading:

In the first months of life [the mother] supplies the infant with an experience of the sacred in which he is cradled by the sprit of the place – and gradually she will be identified with the spiritual, with the transformational process. (Bollas, 1978, p 256, translated for this edition).

Laplanche's propositions, as he develops them in his article "Séduction, persecution, révélation" (1995), allow us, in my view, to understand more clearly the reasons for this identification of the mother with the spiritual. I would say that it is the mother who, owing to the very fact of her passion and of the seduction that she exerts over her infant, arouses in him the bedrock of the experience of revelation and of the sacred, an experience that is linked to her care. Bollas proposes that the aesthetic moment, as a subjective experience, is directly linked to the fact of having been held by an object, and, thus, "has its roots in human ontology". The mother is a transformational object in so far as she is identified in the infant's experience with the process of the alteration of self-experience. The quest for the object is a quest for a transformational object. This object will never be found; its absence constitutes the radiance of its presence and its capacity to stimulate the subject to make personal changes. Its fundamental function is to be the object that will be identified by the subject throughout his life, with the changes that are continually occurring within him.

The offer of psychoanalysis might be said to evoke in analysands the buried memory of this object relation. Beyond a stable setting, with filtered light, protected from overly intrusive noises, the analyst proposes to his or her patient an extraordinary commitment. Each day, for a certain period of time, he or she will be there for the patient as totally and as unconditionally as possible. The patient can remain silent, collapse, get angry, fall in love, confess horrible thoughts, forget the analyst's presence, and so on: the analyst, meanwhile, will remain attentive and present. The analyst's function is that of a person who facilitates the deep process leading the patient to the micro metamorphoses of his or her moods, memories, and desires, everything that leads him or her to identify the analyst with the transformational object. From this point of view, the patient's expectation of a personal metamorphosis constitutes neither a resistance nor a magic expectation of the analyst; rather, it involves an evoked memory, provoked by the analytic situation, which must then be analysed as such. For the analyst, it is

> one thing not to respond to the identification with the transformational object; it is quite another to refuse to admit that, consciously or unconsciously, we know that the very nature of the setting and of our technique awakens a mnemic perception of this kind. (Bollas, 1978, p. 260, translated for this edition)

So, drawing on Laplanche and Bollas, I want to propose that what creates the transference, the motor of the analysis and its transformational capacities, is indeed the offer of analysis, that is, the setting of the analytical situation and the presence of the analyst as an integral part of this setting—a setting understood as space–time of ethical seduction.

Although the mother/analyst analogy is tempting, and although I myself make use of it again and again, I think it is, none the less, very important to express some restraint with regard to reducing the analyst's function to that of the maternal function in an overly simplistic way.

In his essay, "Playing mothers", Phillips (1993) has rightly offered a critique of the English psychoanalytic school for whom, he says, the analyst is concerned with "playing mothers". He quotes the following lines from Bion (1962b):

> Normal development follows if the relationship between infant and breast permits the infant to project a feeling, say, that it is dying, into the mother, and to reintroject it after its sojourn [for Phillips, "sojourn" refers to a "process of difficult hospitality"] in the breast has made it tolerable for the infant psyche. (p. 183)

Bion also writes that "the mother's capacity for reverie is the receptor organ for the infant's harvest of self-sensations gained by its conscious" (Bion, 1962b, p. 116), and Phillips comments,

> Like the analyst, the mother has to sow what she reaps. To be able to learn from experience in analysis is to be able to tolerate hearing the transference interpreted; and this depends on the analyst's having made it tolerable through what is effectively re-description. One can learn from experience, but one cannot be taught by it . . . This organ of reception is a state of mind as an act of faith; just as for Winnicott—in a paradox that can easily become a mystification—there can be learning in psychoanalysis but there must not be teaching. (1993, p. 106)

He notes that "those analysts influenced by Bion and Winicott [and I will not deny that I am one!] are poised, in their writings, between extreme authoritativeness and absolute scepticism, between 'having nothing to teach' and 'only being supposed to know'" (p. 106). On the one hand, there is the practice of the mother's *holding* of the baby, a practice on which so many things depend, but which cannot be taught, while, on the other hand, *holding* is a virtual definition of the analytic process, whether the process takes place thanks to the analyst maintaining the reliability and resilience of the setting or through interpretation, or both. For Phillips, there are two temptations for the analyst: "Identification either as caricature, playing mother, or as the willing victim of an open transference" (p. 107). We have two extremes, then, which, for him, involve either being a guru or a blank page.

As for my own personal options, they take into consideration—starting from the offer of a classical setting that is doubly asymmetrical (both seductively and ethically)—the psychic organisation of this or that patient at a given moment of the analysis or analytic session. While simultaneously taking into account the patient's associative contents, I am attentive to the affects/feelings evoked in me by those that have permeated the patient's own words or discourse. I also attach great importance to the impact on the patient and on the analytic process of my own affects (sustained by my own psychic organisation). They will permeate and qualify my own words and formulations, whether they are clarifications, interpretations, or constructions. The associations evoked by the patient, in response to my own formulations, will provide me with indications of this impact. Hence, neither a guru, nor a blank page.

My question here is: which anxieties—anxieties that are the common lot of all of us analysts—is Phillips referring to? Are they anxieties about taking oneself for God on earth, or, conversely, anxieties about being thrown into the great void of the unknown, about coming face-to-face with ourselves, directly in touch with the distress of the beginnings? It is not a coincidence that he concludes his article with these words: "There is, I think, an inevitable connection, between the analyst already in position as the mother—especially as the pre-oedipal mother—and psychoanalysis as the coercion or simulation of normality" (p. 108). He adds, "And this is the situation, traditionally, when Dionysos arrives, defined as 'an autonomous power whose natural energy erupts suddenly and remains incomprehensible'". The mother with whom he certainly does not wish to identify and on whose couch he is terrified of lying then makes her appearance: the mother who is too much of a woman, the seductive and perverse mother of Leonardo, the mother of Freud, the mother who is unaccompanied at her final resting place, *la bacchante* (see C. Stein, 1987b). That is to say, "the mother who, because she knows what's best for us, has nothing to offer" (p. 108).

Phillips accounts for the avatars, in certain contemporary psychoanalytic trends, of neglecting, repressing, if not denying, the *sexual* dimension present in the very first encounter between infant and adult, which, consequently, characterises as much the mother, and the so-called pre-oedipal period, as the oedipal and post-oedipal periods.

I would add that a mother who *knows* what is good for us is not a responsible mother for us. She is not taking into account our fundamental need to be differentiated and recognised in our singular identity, even though this identity cannot be known to the other. Caught between sky and sea/mother (*mer(e)*), how can we finally give up wandering and trembling with the aim of trying, one day, to come down to earth?

The analyst: malleable medium

Roussillon (1995b), a lover of paradox, has employed the term "malleable medium" to define the qualities of an inaminate object, thereby designating for me the qualities of the human/adult/parental object, who, in a matricial position, is responsible for the other. I want to recall the qualities that are required of the object, as Roussillon describes them, and to make them resonate with those synthesised by Akhtar, who has researched the needs of patients "met" by a wide variety of contemporary analysts representing different currents of thought—needs that had not been taken into account, however, as factors of transformation. In my view, these needs articulate what might be considered, at the beginning of life, as an ethical exigency, and then later, in analysis, as a need for matricial space. In this context, I shall envisage the analyst's function, which I consider to be an intrinsic part of the setting and, therefore, of the analytic situation.

Roussillon describes the qualities of the object as a malleable medium thus: "It is *graspable*, lets itself be handled . . . It represents *nothing* in itself". The analyst is space, a space of projection, a space of gestation.

"It is always *available*, always ready to be used." Think of the analytic situation, the constancy of the time of the sessions and of the place of those same sessions; think of the appointments, the days and times of which are as regular as possible. This facilitates the analyst's availability and, in turn, allows for the experience that he or she is "always ready to be used".

"It is indestructible." Roussillon is referring to the use of the object as Winnicott defined it: the child, through his spontaneous movements, can hit the object, just as he can destroy it. However, when the object survives this destruction, the child then discovers the object and at the same time discovers himself as subject.

Jumping ahead a bit, what Roussillon had in mind here was an object of the modelling clay sort:

> It is *reliable*. It is *faithful*; it *conserves* the form given by the subject's activity. It seems to have its own life; it lends itself to *animism*, to projecting the warm character of animated and living objects. It thereby ensures a stable interlocutor (*répondant*). (pp. 1487–1488)

Conserving the form given by the subject's activity, that is, his identity, it acknowledges and at the same time affirms the subject's spontaneous movement, along with the impact of this movement and, thus, the impact of the subject. "It lends itself to the exploration of the primary forms of freedom. It is *transforming*, the quantitative becomes qualitative; forces becomes meaning" (p. 1488). Here, we can see the link between Roussillon's ideas and Bollas's idea of the analyst as a transformational object.

As Roussillon has shown very well, the different inanimate objects given to the child to be used as he wishes in the context of an analysis or psychotherapy have a value that is highly indicative of the parental qualities and messages, and of their "filled-in" (*en plein*) or "hollowed-out" (*en creux*) impact on the infantile psyche. Hen's analysis, from which I will report long passages further on (see Part III), could also serve as the object of an in-depth study of these objects and of what they indicate with regard to the formation or distortion of her psyche. These "found" objects—the paintings, the paper, the glue, the water, and, above all, the modelling clay which our little patients find in our consultation rooms—have been put at their disposal by an adult psyche, by a responding, responsible, investing and "affected" (*affecté*) object which will allow a subjective appropriation to occur.

The needs "met" by contemporary psychoanalysts or the need for ethics as responsibility for the other in analysis, the need for matricial space

If I take up certain qualities of the malleable medium and apply them to a living object, I find that I am globally in agreement with the proposition of Akhtar (1999) who, after taking all the Anglo-Saxon theoretical currents in the psychoanalytic literature into account, has summarised six principal needs that the analyst "encounters" in the analysand. He notes that these needs are generally satisfied without any deliberate effort on the analyst's part. It is worth remembering here that this absence of deliberate effort is absolutely central when I qualify the analyst as an ethical subject, as Levinas defines the subject (see Part IV).

I propose, then, to recapitulate these needs in terms of a need for ethics, an exigency for matricial space (as far as the newborn is concerned, I think it is more adequate to speak of exigency rather than need. The term "exigency" refers at once to the intensity of a fundamental need in the infant, and to what happens in the adult who is interpellated by the newborn's state of helplessness. On the other hand, as far as our patients are concerned, from the patient's point of view, I think it is justified to speak of need, a need for ethics on the part of his or her analyst):

- a need to have his physical needs recognised as legitimate;
- a need to be identified, recognised, affirmed;
- a need for interpersonal and intrapsychic limits;
- a need to understand the causality of events;
- a need for optimal emotional availability from the object. (See above, "Always ready to be used, reliable, faithful" (Roussillon), and note how the emotionally cathected part of the analyst plays not only a psychological role but also, and no less, at another level, a direct role in the ethical dimension of the analytic encounter.);
- a need for the object to act continuously as a surety.

These needs correspond to what we call ego-needs. Akhtar distinguishes between needs and wishes. He points out, after Winnicott, that a need cannot be subject to repression. Although a wish can be replaced by another wish, a need cannot be replaced by another need. On the other hand, an unsatisfied wish can induce movements of transformation. I would add that this could be the case during the analysis of neurotic subjects or at certain moments in the analyses of non-neurotic subjects.

However, in many cases, the non-satisfaction of needs can lead to destructuration because it produces and reproduces a traumatic experience. If, for some patients, the "meeting" of these needs is not a subject for exploration, for others, and in particular those suffering from identity related narcissistic difficulties, the question of meeting these needs will be at the centre of the preoccupations of the analytic dyad for a long time.

For Laplanche, respecting these needs makes analysis possible, but it does not play a part in the transformations that might occur there. Respecting these needs corresponds for him to the dimension of self-preservation. For Laplanche, this is tangential in relation to the analytic tub. For me, striving to reduce the role of the primary environment to the ethological categories of attachment, however complex they might be, does not seem to be sufficient. Admittedly, Laplanche's point of view, which considers respecting the analysand's needs as tangential to the analytic situation, is coherent with his definition of analysis and his insistence on establishing a marked difference between psychoanalysis and psychotherapy.

Yet, his position is more moderate when he speaks of clinical facts. He writes,

> Psychoanalysis gives itself with the means of dissociating, of unbinding the ties that uphold conscious discourse, our personality (our ego), our symptoms, the ideologies that orient how we tell ourselves our own histories. This allows something to manifest itself, something we repress and which to a large extent governs our lives: the repressed sexual unconscious. Conversely, psychotherapy, the psychotherapies that have existed as long as man has been man, seeks to rebind, to reassemble, to synthesize whatever, arising from our unconscious fantasies, makes dominant within us the unbinding whose most extreme form is the death drive. (2007b, p. 230)

However, he adds,

> Psychoanalytic practice does not consist of analysis alone. The movement of unbinding and the ineluctable tendency towards rebinding coexist within it side by side . . . The tendency towards binding is the work of the analysands . . . But the situation is in fact more complex still, for there are cases in which the analyst has no choice but to make binding interventions: for instance, if the patient is, as they say, "completely unhinged" (*fou à lier*) [Translator's note: the colloquial term *fou à lier* literally means 'mad enough to need binding or tying up'.] . . . These are "two dimensions that may exist within a single practice. (pp. 230–231)

Here, I concur with Laplanche. In my view, both these dimensions exist in every analytic practice.

My interest for the transformative aspect of analysis and for the function of the analyst who is seen as playing a part in this process of binding—not always automatically, as Freud, before Laplanche, had suggested—is obviously connected with my own training. This training is itself connected with the problems of the patients we encounter more and more frequently in our practice. These problems are characterised by the prevalence of unbinding or, in Freudian terms, by a weakness of the ego and, consequently, a weakness of its "natural synthesising capacities". I attribute an important role to the phenomena of asymmetrically "shared associativity", involving the countertransference in the broad sense of the term—that is to say, its preconscious and conscious aspects. Laplanche rightly questions the use of the term "countertransference" defined as coming from the analyst's unconscious; by definition, this unconscious is a "register to which the analyst can only gain access with great difficulty" (Laplanche, 2007b, p. 231).

The analyst's accompaniment can take the form of underlining or accentuating what the patient has a tendency to leave out of the picture, thereby participating from time to time in a desired process of unbinding. But it can equally well take the form of a construction, thereby participating in a process of binding. "Interpreting the transference", Sechaud (1999) writes, "excites and liberates the sexual and seduction, whereas construction has a more soothing effect" (p. 147, translated for this edition). Interpretation facilitates the emergence of meaning, whereas construction leads to understanding. For Sechaud, interpretation is in the service of the sexual, whereas construction is in the service of life and love in its function of integration.

As far as I am concerned, like Laplanche, I am preoccupied by the sexual, whether it is a matter of the sexual life drives or the sexual death drives.

Even if interpretation evokes the manifestations of the death drive, and if construction tends to favour binding, which facilitates the transformation of the sexual death drives into sexual life drives, the very fact of the analyst's intervention has a binding function. This binding function results from his or her presence, from his or her capacities for empathy, and, thus, from his or her assiduous attention to the affective/emotional state of the patient. By choosing to say nothing or to intervene, to interpret or construct, the analyst underwrites his responsibility for his patient. This signification, this address, this saying towards his patient, has an intrinsic binding function.

As Smirnoff (1969) (cited by Sechaud, 1999, p. 149) writes,

Interpretations – whether they are long or allusive, whether they are transference interpretations or not, signalling or constructing – are all marked by a certain style that is the stamp of the analyst. On one side of the coin it is a message of meaning communicated to the other, and, on the other, it is the stamp of the analyst's unconscious, as it is revealed by the style of his or her enunciation.

"The style," Sechaud adds, "not only concerns aspects of language; it includes the voice, intonation, and rhythm" (Sechaud, 1999, p. 149, translated for this edition). I would add, the "flesh of the language" (Kristeva, 2005, p. 311). Freud writes,

> We believe that in general we are free to choose what words we shall use for clothing our thoughts or what images for disguising them. Closer observation shows that other considerations determine this choice, and that behind the form in which the thought is expressed a glimpse may be had of a deeper meaning – often one that is not intended. (1901b, p. 216)

Here, I would like to quote Widlöcher (1995), who points out that although listening is first of all access to a level of meaning, "it is without controlled intention that the mind advances into this network – an advance that depends on whether the thought that is expressed gives access more easily to what is masked or what is unmasked" (p. 1758, translated for this edition). Interpretation of the transference must be made at the point of urgency, Sechaud suggests, "at the moment when a drive-loaded representation (*représentation pulsionnelle*) is cathected" (Sechaud, 1999, p. 145, translated for this edition).

My question, then, is: *by whom* must such a drive-loaded representation be cathected? By the patient, obviously, but certainly not only by the patient; and a further question is: *for whom*?

The analyst's positioning, that is to say, the place from which he listens, intervenes, keeps silent, his place as someone who is responsible for the other, also comes into play and without intentionality.

I want to return now to the analyst's respect for the varied manifestations of the patient's need for ethics. It is this capacity for such a respect which manifests the existence of a matricial space in the analyst.

1. *The need for physical needs to be recognised as legitimate.* Does this go without saying today after years of abstinence and refusal, often practised in an arbitrary and ridiculous manner? Is the patient's need to use the toilets or for a drink due to an onset of anxiety that is impossible to contain with words, resisting any form of transformation at that moment in the treatment, or to the air that is getting drier and drier as the temperature outside reaches 40°?

Is the need for a warm blanket due to the fact that the body has cooled down after the evocation of icy material or to the fact that one tends to get cold after a while in the lying position? A suitable cushion and a clean and agreeable environment are all "trivial" elements that have their importance in the transference. All these elements have an effect on the analysis. Ogden (1989), after Bick (1968), Anzieu (1974), and Tustin (1984), has taken interest in the concrete effects of the analytic situation. He has suggested adding a third position to those proposed by Klein (paranoid–schizoid and depressive positions). He has posited the existence of a position of autistic proximity, the *autistic–contiguous position*. In this position, the patient is particularly sensitive to the messages proffered by the concreteness of the situation proposed, in fact, by the analyst.

2. *The need for identity (for identification), recognition, and affirmation.* Authors such as Killingmo (1995) or Benjamin (1988), each with different theoretical perspectives (the first, a neo-Freudian, influenced at the beginning of his training by the ego psychology movement; the second, one of the leaders of the "relational" movement) have both worked on the implications of these needs and on the way of meeting them during analysis. A painful fragment of one of Ora's dreams (see Part I), a patient I followed notably during her third and difficult pregnancy, illustrates this barely satisfied need during her childhood. In the transference, I was a negligent and absorbed mother: "We met in the street and you didn't recognise me; you were looking elsewhere . . . I was shattered." After she had brought associations connected with her history, I intervened, justifying her childhood need to be recognised by her objects in the past and reflecting her pain at not having been sufficiently recognised, while wondering, silently at first, then out loud with her, about her feelings regarding the quality of my attention and listening during the session before her dream.

3. *The need for interpersonal and intrapsychic limits.* This need is related to those childhood situations where limits have not been respected by the adult world, to traumatically seductive or narcissistically seductive situations. This *unmet* need for interpersonal and intrapsychic limits was the result of the proffering of intromitted messages by the adult world. It is very likely that the

failure to satisfy this need will be iterated in the analytic setting. I am thinking here of the deviations or lapses encountered from time to time in ethics committees and of those (less serious, but all too common) committed by some analysts or psychotherapists who, forgetful of their function, allow themselves to deviate from their mandate and are "led", for instance, to use information emerging from their patient's flow of associations as objects for their own consumption.

4. *The need to understand the reason for events as opposed to being subjected to an arbitrary decision.* The analysand might need to understand the reason for events that are outside his or her control, for instance, decisions concerning changes in the setting. This does not prevent him or her initially from having fantasies as to the possible reasons for these changes. Here, I am thinking of dysfunctionings on the analyst's part, such as making decisions about holidays and announcing them to the patient without prior warning or without any elaboration of this announcement and its implications. I am thinking of unplanned changes of setting, linked to sudden illness, and of the importance of understanding, when the analysis resumes, what the patient might have relived in the meantime, while informing the patient in a discreet manner as to the analyst's current state of health. I am also thinking of cases in which the analyst is suffering from a progressively evolving illness, a situation about which the patient has not been sufficiently informed in advance to allow for the future destabilisation of the setting to be elaborated.

5. *The need for maximum emotional availability.* The analysand needs a psychic and "affected" (*affectée*) presence from the analyst. If the analyst is depressed, this will certainly be noticed by the patient and its impact might be denied by the analyst. Now, this same depression might evoke the past depression of the mother, and, perhaps worse, denial of the analysand's feelings might reactivate past denials and reinforce iatrogenically the patient's doubts about the adequacy of his judgement *vis-à-vis* reality.

6. *The need to respond to . . . in certain circumstances (wars, explosions, earthquakes, etc.).* I will not go further into this subject here, as it has already been the object of many studies in our regions and necessarily raises important questions. (I will just report the question of a candidate who, having begun her training in Europe

before continuing it in Israel, was faced with the fact that some Israeli analysts, in response to a patient's unforeseen absence or late arrival, found it appropriate to telephone them, and the answer she received: "Perhaps something has happened!")

I suggest, then, bringing these needs together under the term "need for ethics" as responsibility for the other.

I am speaking here of need on the patient's part. Why am I opposing the self-preservative axis to which Laplanche, following Freud prior to the second topography, refers? What I want to stress is that although this need, considered more precisely as an ethical exigency from the point of view of the nursling infant, is undoubtedly self-preservative for him, although the presence of an adult who is capable of satisfying his vital needs is absolutely necessary, although communicating the existence of this necessity involves an exchange in which each of the protagonists, in a fundamentally asymmetrical situation, is busy "orientating" the other, and, although the child is "occupied" with satisfying his self-preservative needs, the mother, the adult, and the analyst are in another register. I will come back to the origins of this other register in Part IV.

PART III

THE ORIGINS OF SUBJECTIVE APPROPRIATION IN ANALYSIS, THE ANALYST'S PASSION, AND THE ETHICAL SEDUCTION OF THE ANALYTIC SITUATION

CHAPTER SIX

Subjective appropriation in analysis

The little human being comes into the world with trust. If this trust is betrayed, the enigmatic messages coming from the adult world that has turned its back on the interpellation of this new face will not be metabolised. They will either remain just beneath consciousness, or they will be encysted, or, alternatively, they will be proscribed and pursue their work of disuniting the subject's own psyche and, later on, that of his "objects", of his life partners. There will be no real possibility of choice. The transgression will be in the order of an imposition. The subject, like Adam, will take refuge—in the best of cases—in shame. His capacity for responsibility will not be realised. The task of the analysis, then, will be to try and help the subject re-establish this first trust and, to use Roussillon's terms, to facilitate a subjective appropriation of the order of symbolisation along with a process of subjectivisation.

This third part will contain several clinical illustrations, organised around the questions of the offer of analysis, the analytic process, and the setting as such. In order to render the commentaries that will accompany them more comprehensible, I shall first define what I understand by subjective appropriation of the order of symbolisation and then propose—taking into account the theory of generalised seduction and the emphasis placed on both the seductive asymmetry of the analytic situation and the ethical asymmetry of this same situation—three sorts of transference. I shall return briefly to the question of the analyst's passion and its articulation regarding both the seduction of the analytic situation and its ethical dimension.

Roussillon and subjective appropriation

Roussillon (1995b) has defined subjective appropriation as the little human being's acquired capacity to experience himself as a subject, that is to say, in his terms: first, the capacity to *sense himself*, to sense or feel what affects him, what moves him, what takes hold of him, as well as how he is affected by it and, thus, plans to transform it; next, the way in which the human being is capable of *seeing himself*; then, the way in which he *understands himself*; finally, the way in which he *represents himself* and, I would say, how he represents to himself his objects and the world in which he is living. Roussillon writes,

> This capacity to inform oneself or represent oneself ... theorise oneself, Laplanche would say – depends on the subject's history, on how the subject has been sensed, seen, and heard by his libidinally cathected objects and/or the objects on which the subject was or is objectively dependent ... all of which are decisive elements in the historical and current narcissistic regulation. (1995b, p. 104)

Roussillon speaks, then, of analytic practice centred on subjective appropriation. I want to emphasise, with him, that it is a

> subjective appropriation provided it is based on the work of symbolising subjective experience, symbolisation being understood as the process whereby the 'primary matter' of psychic experience will be transformed and integrated into the web of psychic life. (2006, p. 73, translated for this edition)

The double asymmetry of the analytic situation and the transference it arouses

According to Laplanche (1989, p. 160), in inaugurating the analysis, the analyst establishes the conditions for eliciting two sorts of transference:

the "filled-in" transference and the "hollowed-out" transference. Laplanche emphasises the fact that the transference is provoked by the analyst. In *Le primat de l'autre* (1992c) he writes:

> This offer of the analyst, the offer of analysis, does not create the analysis but its essential dimension, the transference (filled-in trans-ference, hollowed-out transference), perhaps not the whole transfer-ence, but what is the basis, the soul, the motor of it, that is to say the reopening of a relation, of the originary relation to the other, in which the other is first in relation to the subject (hollowed-out transference). (p. 430, translated for this edition)

We have seen that for Laplanche, the primacy of infancy takes us back to a situation which is not one of self-centring, not even one of reciprocity, but a situation that is essentially asymmetrical, where the infant is passive and helpless in relation to the message of the other.

As the analyst is the one who provokes the transference, he or she is responsible for it as a consequence. What is more, I want to suggest that, owing to this transference, which "re-opens" the primal relation to the other, the patient will, at the same time, elicit the analyst's res-ponsibility for him or her, the analyst being defined as ethical subject. So, we have three sorts of transference.

Filled-in transference

This is transference in its classical sense, repetition of the pain and the wounds of the past, the actualisation of parental imagos and of inter-nalised self-object relations, the actualisation in analysis of the con-scious and unconscious relations, real and phantasised, of early childhood.

Transference of primal seduction

For Laplanche, this hollowed-out transference (*en creux*) designates the re-opening in the analytic situation, by the analyst, of the primal seduction. The relation to the enigma of the other is renewed here, too. It is a question of the transference of something very early that has no possibility of being represented, resulting from enigmatic messages compromised by the mother's unconscious, and proffered by her. These messages have left their imprint, a sort of inscription under the skin, which cannot be elaborated and, as I have pointed out, come into existence through the first encounter with the mother, the adult world, and, thus, result from primal seduction. It should be noted that the messages that are the object of the first translations are not essentially verbal or intellectual. They include in large part "signifiers of affect" (Laplanche, 1999a, p. 108), which can either be translated or repressed: a smile, a pout, an angry gesture, a wink, a loss of visual or bodily contact, a grimace, and so on.

We have seen that Laplanche imagines a baby suckling at his mother's breast and asking himself: "What does this breast want from me?" This question is repeated, in my view, in the analytic situation, when the patient asks, "What does the analyst expect of me? Why did she choose to be an analyst? Why did he accept to see me? Was it for money? What does he get out of all this? Is it enjoyable for her? Is it curiosity that incites her? What, does he love me?" The experience is not persecutory, albeit a bit disturbing. "The transference," Laplanche writes, "is transference to the enigma". The transference is provoked by the analyst and the analytic situation. Here, Laplanche follows Lagache, and especially Macalpine, who, as early as 1951, insisted on this origin of the transferential manifestations which had hitherto received little attention, even if Freud had alluded to it at the outset in "Observations on transference-love" (1915a).

It is the offer of analysis, the offer of the analyst, and, I would say, the very fact that he or she is there presenting him or herself as an analyst, that creates the motor dimension of the analysis: the transference. As I have already pointed out, this offer permits the re-opening of a relationship, the relationship in which the other is first in relation to the subject. This offer provokes the hollowed-out transference, the transference of primal or originary seduction. "The transference and its interpretation," Sechaud (1999) writes, "puts the intrapsychic and the intersubjective in tension" (p. 132. translated for this edition). The intrapsychic conflicts, arising from real and phantasised infantile intersubjective relations, will find a site on the stage of the transference, or, rather, on the stage of the analysis or of the analytic situation, where they will once again be played out within a relationship, especially as this relationship is first and foremost the feat of the analyst. For without the analyst, no analytic situation can exist. The transference is movement, movement within the psyche, movement from self to the other—because, in the first place, it is movement from the other to self. The patient, however, finds himself faced with an enigma, one that is no less enigmatic for the analyst himself. While we know the extent to which the adult–child relationship is conducive to the reliving of conflicts and desires arising from the unconscious, are we sufficiently aware of this process of reliving in ourselves, as analysts, during this repeated encounter with our patients? Laplanche does not refer here to an unconscious that is capable of being made conscious, but of an unconscious that will always remain unconscious and which, from the outset, will compromise the parental messages. There are, thus, good grounds for reconsidering the question as to what sort of unconscious message exists in the analytic situation, and in the fact of positing oneself as an analyst. All these questions could be formulated with regard to the impact of these unconscious messages as they are activated in the analyst in his or her encounter with the patient's infantile experience.

The analyst is an inciting object, as was the source object of the drive. Mi-Kyung Yi (2007) writes,

> The question of the countertransference, treated classically in terms of a reaction induced by the patient, must also be regarded as prior to the transference and examined at the very source of analytic experience. But if there is indeed a "primal countertransference" (Pontalis, 1997, p. 238) which motivates and nourishes the analyst's practice, there is also a primal countertransference in its structural dimension, a founding dimension of transferences . . . By emphasising the precedence of the transference in the analyst, at the source and at the heart of the analytic enterprise, it is the seductive valency of the constitutive dissymmetry (asymmetry) of the analytic situation that emerges. (pp. 126–127)

To return specifically to the transference, I would say, with André (2009), that the transference is a movement that combines the present and the past with a view to recomposing it differently. However, I would add that this movement could bring into existence that which has not taken place or has not taken place sufficiently. Hence, I propose a third type of transference: the matricial space transference.

Matricial space transference

Matricial space, a term akin to the one employed by Lichtenberg-Ettinger (1997a), originates in the parent and is "required" by the

human neonate right at the beginning of his life as an ethical manifestation understood as responsibility for the other. Matricial space is
to do with the mother, with the father, and with the adult world, occupying a position of ethical asymmetry in relation to the child. Now,
this matricial space is created by the very fact of the offer of analysis,
right up until the end of the analysis, by the very existence of the
analyst's person defined as that in him (or her) which allows him to
position himself as responsible for the other, as the one who has
within him, and who is, this matricial space for the other: the ethical
subject. It is a matter of the analyst being in a position of ethical asymmetry in relation to his patient. By matricial space, I mean the
space–time that evolves into a matricial position and situates the
analyst as a person, as an ethical subject, as a subject in a position of
asymmetrical responsibility for his or her patient. The patient needs
to encounter in his or her analyst not only a psychic space, but also
the very offer of this space. I have formulated this offer in the following way: "It is the saying [le dire] in the said [le dit], it is an address to
the patient in the form of a caress and not in the form of control
[emprise]" (Chetrit-Vatine, 2005, translated for this edition). This position of the analyst provokes a matricial space transference in the
patient. It is a non-linear transference that corresponds to what met
(i.e., satisfied), or should have met, the fundamental ethical exigency
of the newborn baby and of the child that this patient was.

We have seen on several occasions that Laplanche touches on this
space, but that he links it to self-preservation. He speaks of the analyst
as a guardian of constancy, as benevolently neutral. This benevolence
positions him as wanting the best for the other without ever claiming
to know what it is. If, as far as the neonate—and later, the patient—is
concerned, we can understand this exigency as being linked to self-
preservation, I have often been led to ask the question as to whether,
with regard to the mother/adult, we can content ourselves with the
idea of natural benevolence. Is it merely tangential? I noted earlier
that, for Laplanche, the respect of self-preservative needs makes the
analysis possible, but he does not seem to consider them as factors of
transformation. In my view, and here I diverge from Laplanche, the
person of the analyst, as an ethical subject, is essential to the analytic
process and conditions its transformative power. More specifically, I
would argue that it is necessary so that primal seduction, manifested
by the hollowed-out transference, can be realised as a source of

creativity. Of course, for me, responsibility for the other is a matter of benevolence, but, clearly, not a natural benevolence, in the animal sense of the term. Neither is it motivated by a narcissistic need or unconscious guilt. It is not a matter of feminine, or even moral, erogenous masochism, and even if it might appear to be sacrificial, it is not a quest for sacrifice. (I will come back to these last points in Part IV.)

The matricial space transference is a non-linear transference. It is not reproduction. It refers not so much to what has taken place or what has partially taken place, but to what ought to have taken place. When everything goes as well as possible, the newborn baby finds a matricial space in the adult world, a space ready to be "used", a space imbued with "ethical passion" in which, and through which, he is felt to be a subject and approached as one. When things do not go so well, that is, when the adult environment was unable to procure for the infant the matricial space that he or she needed, the recognition by the analyst of the trauma engendered not only by what did take place, but by what should not have taken place, and also by what did not take place but should have taken place, will be the indispensable condition for the patient to accept the necessity of going through a process of mourning and, consequently, of freeing him or herself from alienating identifications "with the shadow of his objects" (Roussillon, 2006). The matricial space transference can be evoked or, so to speak, created at the beginning of each analysis, through the very existence of the person of the analyst, defined as an ethical subject, that is to say, a person who is capable of "finding resources in himself" (Levinas, 1961, p. 215) capable of answering for (*répondre de*) the other without necessarily having to answer him (*lui répondre*).

The ethical seduction of the analytic situation

L aplanche (1999a) sums up his project thus: "It consists in bringing that which is foundational in the practice of psychoanalysis into relation with the foundational process of the human being insofar as this is characterised by the creation of an unconscious" (p. 84). Further on, he adds, "The unconscious . . . is the other thing [*das Andere*] in me, the repressed residue of the other person [*der Andere*]. It affects me, as the other person affected me long ago" (p. 108). For Stein (1986), what is "primal" is "the present or the actuality of the analytic situation" (cited in Laplanche, 1987, p. 157). But Laplanche insists on the effective power of the infantile primal situation, the primal not being essentially that which comes first, but that which is fundamental. Hence, there is nothing surprising about the hypothesis that the primal dimension is present in every beginning, and that a situation such as the offer of analysis brings this primal experience into play once again in its very essence. For me, the effective power of the infantile primal situation and the process of "afterwardsness" (*Nachträglichkeit*) of the analytic situation are combined dialectically—and without this dialectic having to be resolved—with the present act of the analytic situation in the actuality of this situation.

The infant needs a mother and an adult environment that is capable of asymmetrical responsibility for him, capable of satisfying his ethical exigency. This condition is necessary so that the enigmatic messages can be translated by the infantile psyche, and so that this same adult environment can be a source of assistance and recourse with this translation. In analysis, the analyst's passion presupposes, if it is to be transformative and, thus, at the origin of a subjective appropriation based on a process of symbolisation, the existence within him or her of a matricial space, a space–time of asymmetrical responsibility for the other, containing and detoxifying his or her own possible excesses. It is on this condition that the analytic situation, and, specifically, the setting with the analyst as part of it, become repositories of ethical seduction. It is as repositories of ethical seduction that they provoke the transference of primal seduction and the transference of matricial space. Just as the asymmetry of primal seduction is reactualised from the outset in the first analytic encounter, in the first interview, by the analyst and the setting of the analysis, by the same logic, the ethical asymmetry—defined from the outset as interpellation, and no less violent—exerted by the encounter between the adult world and the newborn baby will be reactualised, or actualised at last, in the analyst by virtue of the presence of the patient, this stranger seeking an analysis, who appeared at the door of his or her consulting-room. It is this double asymmetry that I have qualified as ethical seduction. It is the feat of the analyst and of the analytic situation.

The ethical seduction of the analytic situation and its asymmetry

The primal situation, at the beginning of life, is doubly asymmetrical. Laplanche has insisted on the asymmetry of what he has called "primal seduction". The primal situation is one of an encounter between an adult world endowed with a sexual unconscious and adult sexuality on the one hand and, on the other, a newborn infant endowed with a particular bio-neurophysiological organisation that is capable of being affected by this adult world and also capable of affecting it, but who is not as yet endowed with a sexual unconscious or with a world of phantasy which has its source in this unconscious or, of course, with adult sexuality.

However, the primal situation is equally asymmetrical in so far as this adult world is responsible for this infant, responsible for it at a time when it is in a state of primary distress and absolutely dependent on the adult world for its physical and psychic survival. The asymmetry of the responsibility for the other has been emphasised many times by Levinas. Like the majority of philosophers, his perspectives are eminently adult-centred. Yet, in my view, in the mother–infant relationship and, consequently, in the psychoanalyst–patient relationship, we find ourselves at the very foundations of this ethical asymmetry. Jonas's principle of responsibility and his idea of primal responsibility have been useful to me (see Part I).

Following on from this double asymmetry of the primal situation, I have developed elsewhere (Chetrit-Vatine, 2004a) the idea of a double asymmetry of the analytic encounter. At once seductive and ethical, this foundational asymmetry is reactualised in the transferences incited by and in analysis, and, by extension, in all situations of psychic care. This double asymmetry characterises the analytic situation and its setting, understood as actively including the analyst. Thus, it makes them repositories of ethical seduction.

Nicole, a middle-aged woman, told me during the last session, without any apparent signs of emotion, how in her research work she had once carried out futile "operations" on laboratory rabbits. At this moment in the analysis, her husband was abroad on business. Nicole was vacillating: her mother, she said, "was excited by the idea that she could arrange a date for her with an old flame", an idea she found disgusting. After a moment of silence, she said, "with my husband, I'm in an impasse!"

At the next session the following morning, she said, "Yesterday, after the session I went to the bookshop; I felt the need to fill myself up." She told me that she had eagerly bought a number of books, on brain functioning, Japanese gardens, and the secrets of productive creativity: "It makes sense these days", she said, "to create gardens again, to offer a bit of nature to an over-urbanised population." She added that she had fallen flat on her face on her doorstep. I pointed out to her that on several occasions she had had a minor accident during her husband's absence. She went back to speaking about her new books and her new/old project.

I said, "Yesterday, you had a sense of being in an impasse—here too—and I am wondering if your feelings of disgust at your mother's suggestion have anything to do with your sense of being in an impasse."

"Today, I'm feeling thoroughly revolted by my mother's behaviour towards me. I could sense my mother's excitement. She was living my experiences as if they were her own . . . In fact, instead of protecting me— the majority of my lovers have been dangerous characters (a hard drug user, a high-risk alpinist, an alcoholic)—she would urge me, as on this occasion, to take pointless risks."

After wondering whether her mother was perhaps spiteful, Nicole changed track: "No, she would've enjoyed taking this kind of risk herself. But she couldn't see me; it was as if I was an extension of herself. In fact, she was completely closed to what I was going through."

My own associations, which I kept to myself, were connected with the "experiments on rabbits" she had mentioned the week before. At the time I had felt the terrible violence of the situation as she recalled and spoke about her experience of "operating" on live rabbits, and I suggested there was a link between her experience of impasse, her disgust, and her fall after leaving my consulting room, and I added, "Instead of screaming with rage."

She said, "I have just realised that it was the terrible screams of that rabbit in absolute distress that were inscribed in me." Nicole was visibly very moved.

In this sequence, she elaborated in the transference what she had experienced as a traumatic/narcissistic seduction by her mother. Her husband's absence reminded her of the absence of her mother "who could not see her", to her vicarious excitement, and to her own sadism towards the rabbits. In the transference, in the classical sense of the term, in the *filled-in* transference, I was her husband who dropped her (after each session), her mother who enjoyed the dangerous situations in which she put herself, no doubt excited by her sadistic tales, and who was, perhaps, "closed to what she was going through". Thanks to the transference of primal seduction, Nicole's interest was maintained, allowing a work of elaboration to take place.

As for the matricial space transference, it was sustained here by the fact of my being "taken hostage" (Chetrit-Vatine (2004b) and by my sense of the violence of her denied distress as well as her own violence towards the rabbits. It was this experience of being taken hostage, along with my own feelings, transmitted necessarily in the "saying" of my intervention, which allowed Nicole to get in touch at last with her own "absolute distress", stemming originally from the traumatic seduction to which she had been exposed during her childhood and adolescence.

This traumatic/narcissistic seduction was the product of enigmatic messages that were impossible to elaborate, and that had remained split off, just beneath consciousness, robbed of their affect.

The ethical seduction of the analytic situation permitted the beginnings of translation, and, thus, of elaboration.

The offer of analysis

On the analyst's side

Coincidence
Request for help, pain, dreams, encounter,
  A life,
  The other, menacing, close, stranger, facing me, in me
  His face aims at me.
  He is addressing me,
  He is suffering. She wonders:
  Who is she?
  Alone, she can't stand it any more; she has tried everything,
  He can't see a way out of his situation
  I am there
  I am ready to accept responsibility for it
   I answer,
    He will have to pay, pay me,
    He will protest that it is unjust,
    Or not,
    I will be there to underline the fact.

Chabert (1999) relates how she had hesitated to take Sarah into analysis with her. This patient seemed determined but distant, not very pleasant, and dry. During the fourth meeting, Sarah looked at her for the first time and Chabert "found herself agreeing to take her on". Chabert needed to establish eye contact with her to be able to decide to commit herself and to commit herself fully. If, psychologically, she needed to be recognised in the sense that Benjamin (1988) gives the word, I would like to suggest that she already been interpellated. Consciously, this appeal had to be supported by the eye contact that was finally exchanged, the result of her unconscious or, to be more exact, "subconscious" ethical presence. (I shall return in Part IV to the question of the psychoanalytic status of an "ethical presence".)

When I saw Hen for the first time, it was behind a one-way mirror. She was a little eight-year-old girl, the youngest in a family of three children, and had been referred for a consultation because she had been using the masculine gender ever since she had begun to speak. So, I took some notes: *I was impressed by how skinny she was; by her long and blank face, her dark skinned complexion, and the darkness of her eyes. Her hair was cut short; she was wearing a tracksuit and trainers. Her movements were tense, giving an impression of violent and pent-up resolve. When the consultant spoke to her, she responded with a blank stare. During the Squiggle, she used only a few halting, barely audible words and, spontaneously, with quick movements, as if wanting to be done with it, she scribbled a figure in a skirt, which she immediately obliterated with blank ink. Then she suddenly got up impatiently and disappeared behind the puppet-theatre. She then made a fluffy grey mouse appear, and placed it, folded up, on the curtain rail.* In that position, the mouse made me think of a corpse. The silence in the room was deafening. I was overwhelmed with sadness, while at the same time sensing that she was calling for help.

At this first meeting, Hen could not see me, but I could see her, literally, psychically, and ethically speaking. She could not suspect that at that very moment a place had been made in me for her: a matricial space. I "perceived" a call for help. I decided to take Hen into analysis. Her face "turned towards me", interpellated me. Hen had not been desired. She had been rejected for a long time. At that moment, I knew nothing of this.

I pointed out earlier that the psychic material is nothing without a place that is offered to it (Kulka, 1998), and the one who offers this place/this space is the analyst.

When I say, "her face turned towards me" [*son visage m'a visée*], I am alluding to the infinite dimension of the face and not to what it looks like or to what it evokes in me. The face calls me, interpellates me. I answer; I am answerable for it. This response is made of this call that has been heard. Answering means being responsible, capable of answering for it. Once again, it is not a question here of a literal answer, but of a responsive, available and malleable position. This position will be all the more effective if, in due course, the literalness of the response is declined. It will be all the more transformative to the extent that the moment when its benevolently enigmatic power can be received as such is patiently awaited.

I can also say that there was a strong and immediate cathexis of Hen on my part. Years ago, we had already discussed in Nice (Chetrit-Vatine, 2002), during a panel on child psychoanalysis at the IPA Conference, the importance of the cathexis of affects in psychoanalysis.

At the time, I proposed the idea that it was first a question of the analyst *cathecting*, that is to say investing his/her patients emotionally. I was speaking above of the analyst's passion, referring to passion in the Bionian sense of the term, defined thus: passion is the product of three emotions: love, hate, and knowledge (in the sense of curiosity; thus, in the sense of an urge for knowledge and not in the sense of established knowledge), and Bion adds, as I have already pointed out (see Part II), each of them is devoid of any trace of violence. Even if I think it is more correct to speak here of affects, Bion uses the term emotions, taking into account the etymology of the word. In the term *emotion*, we find the root *motion*. Vincent (1986) points out in his book, *Biologie des passions*, that Descartes himself sees *movement* as a primordial criterion of passion. In this concept of passion, there is the designation of an intense state that carries us towards another person. For Vincent, passion "constitutes the basis of the experience of being; it is at the source of communication between beings" (p. 16, translated for this edition). For Bion, a true thought is emotion, in the sense that it is emotionally engaged. (I have already referred to Ferenczi's (1933) article on the "Confusion of tongues . . .". He speaks of passion as an adult language in contrast to tenderness, which is the language of the child. He refers to a traumatic seduction of a frankly paedophile type in which the child was used purely for the ends of an adult devoid of any capacity for showing ethical responsibility towards him. It is clear that it is not this sort of passion that I am speaking about. But, as I said earlier, I insist on the term *passion* because its connotation of excess clearly indicates its role in primal seduction.)

The analyst's passion, like parental passion at the beginning of life, is that which affects, when everything goes as well as possible, what is sensed, seen, and heard. At the beginning of life, passion constitutes the affectively engaged part of the enigmatic messages that provoke primal seduction. In analysis, the analyst's passion is what permits her listening, her saying, and her silences to be "affected" (*affectés*). It is passion that will infiltrate and give flesh to the evocation of the primal seduction in analysis, that is, to the transference of primal seduction.

It is also passion that will give flesh to the ethical interpellation that is deepening in the analyst in the encounter with the patient. There is no ethical interpellation that does not arise from a breach or intrusion, which is necessarily felt. It is because the encounter with the other does me violence and is intrusive that I find I am interpellated from the outset. Levinas speaks of ethical passion. Just as this interpellation permitted the parental subject to assist the infant's psyche in its processes of translation (or should have permitted this), so, too, in analysis, it is the analyst's ethical passion that permits the patient to achieve the subjective appropriation based on symbolisation. This passion will give rise to the matricial space transference.

On the analysand's side

I took Hen into analysis. During our first meeting, Hen seemed anxious and embarrassed; she did not want to "let go" of her mother. I invited Hen's mother into the room, too. While commenting on Hen's anxiety, I offered her a comfortable seat. She was very surprised by Hen's behaviour and said, "Hen asked me, 'When are we going to Viviane's?' At the other appointments with the psychologist who made her do some tests, she didn't make such a fuss."

I said, "This time it's not the same. Hen knows now that she has to make a long journey." Hen slipped behind the puppet theatre and made a witch appear and disappear again, before banging it with all her strength on the theatre floor.

I said, "Today I am like that witch for you; yes, she deserves it, she deserves it." She dropped the witch and picked up the little mouse, placing it on the curtain rail. I thought to myself, she has picked up a cushion, put it on the theatre floor, and placed the mouse on it, as she did during the consultation.

I said, "Perhaps the little mouse is alive? Dead? Anyway, it has found a soft place where it can 'rest'."

Hen came out from behind the theatre and turned quietly towards the puppet house. She put the boy dolls in the pram. Then she put the girl dolls and the boy dolls on the potty, in a sitting position. She stopped when she noticed a piece of brown modelling clay in the potty.

I said, "Like a poo." She looked at me, obviously happy, and continued her manoeuvres.

I said, "There, there's no difference, everyone does poo in the same way." I was alluding to the reason for the request to be taken into treatment, expressing the possibility of Hen's "solution": erasing the difference between the sexes. (Remember that Hen had been referred to the clinic because she used the masculine gender when speaking and, according to her mother "took herself for a boy".)

Hen smiled, the atmosphere was relaxed; I looked at the mother, prompting her to leave us.

I said, "Your mummy is going to leave the room." Hen said nothing, and her mother said in a voice lacking energy, "I'm going . . ."

Hen began rolling balls of clay between her fingers. I helped her soften the clay and she began throwing the balls at the ceiling, at first calmly, then more and more violently.

I said, "Your mummy has gone out now and you feel like throwing everything around, like getting rid of everything, you are feeling very angry, Hen." I tried to set some limits: "I am here to protect us and to protect the objects in the room." But the balls, getting bigger and bigger now, were becoming dangerous for the lamps and for us. Hen did not take any notice of what I had said. Alone with me, Hen felt in danger and was putting us both in danger; there was no protection. I myself felt caught on the hop. Suddenly a lump of clay remained stuck to the ceiling; Hen was shocked and worried, and so was I. Then the lump fell off the ceiling and we were both very happy to be able to recover it.

I said, "There you are, she has come back," alluding to her mother, who had rejoined us, and to the fact that we had recovered. At the end of the hour, Hen left, sliding lightly and nimbly down the banister.

At the end of his book *Aux origines féminines de la sexualité*, André (1995) writes,

It was only several weeks after the beginning of an analysis [that the patient] was able to evoke the images that had assailed her during our first interview: the sense of being somewhere illegal, a cross between an agency for clandestine abortion and a dark room in a police station, with the disturbing man sitting in front of her evoking in the confusion both the abortionist and the rapist cop . . . The brutality of this way of beginning is not common; a point she has in common,

however, with other patients who are worried without being
terrorised to this point is that she associates the opening of the process
of the treatment with representations of effraction or intrusion. (p. 159,
translated for this edition)

With Hen, too, the first meeting with the analyst aroused very
strong levels of anxiety. From the beginning I was a witch with
destructive powers (transference of traumatic seduction) and there
was almost immediately an evocation of intrusion, through her own
action (the balls of modelling clay thrown into the air with increasing
violence), following the separation from her mother, which was
experienced by Hen, in this context, as a breach or intrusion of her
psychic envelope.

Following the first interview, Eynat, who was in her thirties,
brought a dream to do with an anxious border crossing. She was
nude, wrapped in a red cape offered to her by her much-loved grand-
mother, but she knew that she was carrying a dose of drugs secretly
hidden on her. There were some dogs and policemen.

Likewise, Tamar, thirty-five years old, was obviously worried
during her first session on the couch. She shared her fantasy with me:
she had the feeling that she was on a hospital bed. She had to undergo
an operation on her right ear. I reminded her of an ear, nose, and
throat specialist whom she had consulted for her young daughter a
few years before, when the latter had almost choked to death after
swallowing a bay leaf.

And Yossi, forty, who had been in face-to-face psychotherapy for
a while, and whom I recommended to do an analysis, associated to the
following fantasy: *once he was lying down, without any control, he would
become the victim of his analyst, who could hit him over the head with a
hammer from behind and at any moment.*

André writes,

The infant's helplessness in relation to the adult, the opening of the
internal world to the other who is necessarily seductive, and the
requirement to "say everything", likens the establishment of the
analytic situation to the inaugural conditions of the psychogenesis of
femininity. (1995, p. 160, translated for this edition)

And he adds that "between the intromitted child (through the
gestures of care and love) and the penetrated woman, between the

superposition of these two figures, there is the traumatic distance of an effect of 'afterwardsness' (*Nachträglichkeit*)" (1995, p. 161, translated for this edition). The same effect of afterwardsness is met with on entering analysis:

> In the absence of an inaugural trauma, in the absence of that moment in which the defences vacillate, it may be doubted whether an analysis, properly speaking, can begin . . . The repudiation of femininity can thus be understood as the rejection of openness to the internal world, to the unconscious, in short, as the rejection of the analysis. (1995, p. 161, translated for this edition)

(See Part IV.)

Yet, for another patient to whom, after a few exploratory sessions, I proposed an analysis, this offer was experienced as a gesture of love, a real gift. *"I can do an analysis! What a stroke of good luck!"*

Intrusion, seduction, to be sure, but also an offer to take her on, the offer of a place there, for her; the offer of an analyst who is ready to be "used", a sublimatory object, a potential transformational object, a symbol-generating object, an object permitting subjectivisation.

The analyst's passion and the analytic process

For a long time, Hen would rage, swear, break, or try to break, toys, throwing them on the floor; she was exasperated by the "state" of the feeding-bottles that she found in the consulting room. These bottles were always unsatisfactory. At a certain moment, I sat down, exhausted, and started, "without thinking about it", to make a baby bottle out of modelling clay. Hen calmed down immediately. "Don't forget the nipple," she said, and, at the end of the hour, she took the bottle I had modelled for her.

This iniative of mine was a leap with regard to the line of intervention that I had taken up until then. I no longer sought to reflect or interpret her violence as I had tried to do previously, even if it was only to myself. I had exhausted my hypotheses concerning the actual origin of her behaviour. It was an intuitive leap out of the chaos in which I had become embroiled, the chaos that I understood retrospectively to be the very chaos with which Hen was struggling, the chaos of her creation and arrival in the world. Hen's demands found expression in her need for ethics as responsibility for the other, a need I had finally met. She was able to take part in a playful manner in the work of symbolisation I had initiated by saying "Don't forget the nipple". By taking the bottle I had modelled away with her, she was taking with her the manifestaion of the existence in me of a matricial space for her. I found myself in a position beyond any form of knowing or knowledge concerning her dynamics or those of our transference or countertransference relationship. Elsewhere (Chetrit-Vatine, 2004b), I have written that if the transference of primal seduction, the "hollowed-out" transference in Laplanche's terminology, allows the psychoanalytic process to follow its course; the matricial space transference is what helps the process get going again when a movement of "counter-processuality" or "anti-processuality" has occurred. It appears in the form of a "subjectal moment" (*moment subjectal*), a specific moment when a matricial space is there, ready to "be used" by the patient. In her book, *Le dialogue psychanalytique*, Amado-Levy-Valensi (1962) has proposed that in the relationship that is created between the analyst and the patient, there is a moment of emergence that occurs beyond the countertransference, which, for her, is of the order of subjectality: "Subjectality," she argues, "is a synthesis of subjectivity and transcendentality" (Éliane Amado, a philosopher and psychoanalyst trained by Lagache, was undoubtedly the first analyst to refer to Levinas's thought and the light it throws on psychoanalytic practice; see, particularly, pp. 117–118. She was also a pioneer in being the first to propose the French terms *subjectal* and *subjectalité*.)

"There can be no subjective appropriation," Roussillon (2001a) writes, "without a work of representation and symbolisation" (p. 8). With Hen, I had been dealing in the last sessions with a form of "paradoxical aggravation, a paradoxical confirmation of the pertinence of the work in process". In Roussillon's words, "The presence of certain forms of negativity is indispensable for the progress of the treatment; it is a prerequisite for a non-alienated subjective appropriation" (2001a, p. 8). I would emphasise that if it is to bear witness to a work of non-alienated subjective appropriation, construction must be generative, "it must open up new questions, new intrapsychic spaces of tension; it must produce new objects, and a new metaphorising generativity" (2001a, p. 8). While I was making that feeding bottle, I was reconstructing, literally and symbolically. Now, construction is the essential operator of subjective appropriation, but, for this construction to take place, a certain mode of presence on the analyst's part is necessary. When the object is neither intrusive nor disinvested, and, thus, for me, in both cases, not traumatically seductive, "the patient can make use of it when he or she has difficulty in metaphorising his or her drives; the object serves as an object of recourse" (Roussillon, 1995b, pp. 50–51)—ethically speaking, an object of assistance. So, the mother, the adult world, and, later, the analyst, will not simply be objects to be symbolised but, first and foremost, objects for symbolising.

During the period of the Purim festival (equivalent of Shrove Tuesday), Hen was excited and finding it difficult to stay in the room. Outside, she was trying to climb up on to the banister, putting herself in danger. I told her that she must get off it, and that I did not want her to hurt herself. I understood her running away from the clinic as re-enactments of her tendency to run off in her infancy. (When she was barely ten and a half months old, Hen, who had learnt to walk even before she was able to sit, would leave the house when her mother was busy with something and was picked up on several occasions by the neighbours.)

In one of the following sessions, she went downstairs to join her mother and placed a chair in front of the door, behind which her mother was involved in a conversation with her own psychotherapist. She took hold of her mother's glasses, licking them, sniffing them, and looking through them.

I said, "Like that, you have the feeling your mummy is very close to you. You really need to smell the taste of her skin, to breathe in her smell, don't you? It comforts you when she's busy elsewhere." Hen did not react. I felt rejected and tired; I would just have to get by alone, cast out like Hen.

When Hen agreed to stay alone with me in the room, what interested her were close physical games, violent at first, then more playful; I spoke again and again about the possibility of being both a girl and strong at the same time.

At the end of one of the sessions, Hen found it difficult to leave. She climbed up on to the roof of the marionette theatre, drew some arrows and a heart on the wall, which I understood as a declaration of love for me. I gave her a piece of cardboard to draw on instead of the wall. She then drew a little man who was standing and having a wee, wrote my first name above it, and added, "Hen did that". In Hebrew, I could see that she had used the feminine form. In this way Hen was proposing that I assume her masculine part, allowing her to speak in the feminine, albeit still in the third person.

At home, she had begun playing secretly with dolls, something she had never done before. (Playing with dolls, an activity that usually appears around the age of eighteen months, has been linked to the development of feminine identity in as much as it affects the crystallisation of the maternal role.)

After the celebration at school of the Purim festival, Hen arrived at her session in a costume disguise I could not identify. She looked tired in her faded make-up and reminded me of a sad little boy. She asked me to guess what she was disguised as, but I was not sure. She said nothing, but during that session and the following ones she spread sand and water all over the room. Once again Hen was in a chaotic state.

I told her that she was probably very disappointed because I could not guess what she was disguised as, that she was probably angry with me as if had not paid enough attention to her, and that she was now making a mess and trying to break everything. Nothing would calm her down. She continued behaving in the same way and I was simply concerned with surviving. Finally, she relaxed and suddenly said to me, scowling, "You said I was dressed up like a boy, but I was disguised as a troll doll; neither boy nor girl."

I said, "It must have been terrible for you that I wasn't able to tell you who you were; I disappointed you. I should have guessed." She then told me that she had been given some hiking boots, like her brother's, and that her ears had been pierced so she could "put on even bigger earrings" than mine. I understood from this that she now had what boys have and what girls have.

When I could not identify Hen's costume, this meant I did not identify her, I did not recognise her, and I threw her into a state of confusion. When I acknowledged the legitimacy of her hurt and disappointment, when I recognised my responsibility, she was then able to feel strong and to see herself as having what boys have and what girls have.

Before coming up for the following session, she asked her mother, "Mummy, haven't you got anything to eat? I'm hungry!" (In Hebrew, one can hear the use of the feminine gender.) This was the first time I had heard Hen using the feminine gender in the first person, and it was to express the lack of something! In the room, Hen wrote her name in Latin letters. She wanted us to make a *méguila* (roll of parchment) on which all the letters of the alphabet—"the Hebrew alphabet, then the Latin alphabet, in upper and lower case letters"—would figure. She rolled up her *méguila*, sealed it, and then, on leaving, let it unroll all the way down the stairs, where she rolled it up again and put it in her pocket. I understood that together we had created something of Viviane and Hen that formed a link between us and that she could keep even if we separated (not for too long), something that spoke of big and small (our difference), of her identity (her first name), and of the questions she had about mine (the use of Latin letters).

After feeling "identified", Hen was able to begin to use the first-person feminine and a transitional space surfaced. At that moment, a linking object made of papers stuck together became a symbol.

The translation of enigmatic messages from the mother and the father can only take place within a process in which the child is seeking support from them, in that part of them that recognises him or her as a subject, as a subject with a sexual identity. For this to happen, a matricial space of asymmetrical and emotionally cathected responsibility for the child must exist in them, ready to be used. The terms "containing", "maternal reverie" (Bion), "holding" (Winnicott) bypass the ethical dimension of such maternal positioning. It is not a matter of indifference, I think, to formulate this dimension as such. It has the advantage of denaturalising this maternal or parental devotion, which soon transpires to be nothing less than biological (see Part IV).

In fact, when Hen's mother asked for a consultation for her daughter, Hen was suffering from a severe confusion about her sense of gender identity. While I was taking notes on her history, it appeared that the first experiences were ones of a non-affective response on the part of the object. The child had not been desired by her mother, whose attention was claimed by the other children, the last of whom, a boy, had worrying difficulties connected with his psychomotor development. At her birth, Hen had encountered a depressed mother who received very little support from her husband. To put it in Roussillon's terms, this non-response of the object-mother-environment, this lack of space in the parental psyche, cancels out the spontaneous psychic movement of the subject, and, eventually, after movements of protest, primary rage, and abjection, leads him, after he has perhaps turned this rage back upon himself, to cease any form of spontaneous movement. With Hen, as with other patients suffering from difficulties of identity, these movements of protest are the result of a primary impossibility of translating enigmatic messages. They cannot be translated owing to their content of non-metabolisable traumatic seduction. A depressed mother, an inadequate father, parents who quarrel violently, a lack of investment from primary objects is always too much for a child's developing psyche. The messages of adults, inevitably compromised by their unconscious, will be experienced as traumatic. Whether the parental difficulties have been decisive or whether the subject has come into the world with constitutional difficulties,

> the child's movements of protest, twisted, disqualified, focalised and perverted by adult messages, will go into reversal, becomed twisted, and will make any further attempt at translation that is required by the constant and inevitable arrival of new messages from the adult world even more impossible (Roussillon, 1995b, p. 136, translated for this edition)

These messages will remain floating, just beneath consciousness, split off for the time being, but might appear in all their intensity at the inciting invitation of the analyst and of the analytic situation.

An exciting or persecuting response from the patient—such as the one I met with repeatedly during a large part of the analysis with Hen, or such as Ireni's response in the analytic sequence that I shall present further on—does not only bear witness to an inadequate parental presence that is barely capable of meeting the ethical exigencies of the child. This exciting or persecuting response itself produces an increase of the excitation needing to be bound, an internal amplification of the subject's instinctual impulses: "the internal traces of the parental messages, the perceptual memory traces", writes Roussillon, "will tend to be reinforced" (Roussillon, 1995b, p. 136). As the qualities required of the object for facilitating symbolisation, reflexivity, the capacity for appropriating subjective experience, and, thus, the child's health, have been lacking since the very beginning of life, the work the analyst must do on himself will necessarily be greatly increased.

If, to use the terms of Vincent (2005, p. 364), "for there to be psyche, there must be the other, an 'affected' other (*un autre affecté*)", I have in turn proposed that for there to be psyche, there must *first* be the other; the primacy of an "affected" other.

In analysis, understood also as permitting the realisation of what has not always been realised in the life of a subject, and which has prevented (and still prevents) him or her from feeling alive, thus at the origin of subjective appropriation based on symbolisation, we must take into consideration the analyst's passion and the ethical seduction of the analytic situation. As I have already pointed out, the analyst's passion, his or her "affected" presence, the implicated analyst, the "touched" (*entamé*) psychotherapist (Bokanowski, 2004), his living presence, his "human presence" (Fédida, 2002), have become an inescapable necessity. As a consequence of such a perspective, I propose that the "benevolent neutrality" of the analyst should be envisaged correlatively as "affected" (emotionally engaged) responsibility for the other".

Boris, a man in his fifties, was worried. His wife was due to undergo open-heart surgery in the near future. The doctor might be in a bad mood. He was worried about the scar she would have between her breasts, and also worried that she might die during the operation. He brought associations related to his own circumcision, which he had decided to have during his first love affair with a young Jewish girl because it was supposed to correct a tendency to premature ejaculation. But he wanted to talk to me about a film he had seen recently: in the film , a father, who was crazy about religion and obsessionally devoted to his God, was not paying attention to his young son, who drowned just a few steps away from him. This led him to think about the sacrifice of Isaac and about the crazy God who requires the man of faith to sacrifice his son. "How absurd," he said, "it makes me really angry!" He was wondering about his associations, and about the fact that in the previous session I had drawn attention to the distant relationship that he had maintained with me throughout the years of his analysis; this was due, I thought, to a fear of too much closeness and also to the absence of the precise idea of a third term. He returned to his comparison between the Christianity in which he had been brought up and Judaism, that terrible religion that demands the sacrifice of a child. He came back to the circumcision and its sacrificial aspect, and to the fact that he was unable to convert at the time "because he didn't have faith". He linked his refusal to convert to his fear of rituals of an obsessional kind, rituals from which he had suffered terribly during his adolescence. He spoke of his "attachment, in spite of everything, to Christianity, a religion of love". I pointed out that Jesus, who had not confronted his father, was sanctified by the crucifixion. This made him think of his stepfather and his drunkenness, which was "equivalent to every kind of crazy mystic position", of the father who was incapable of seeing his child although the mother, however good she was, was not up to the task. The child dies in both scenarios.

I spoke to him about infanticidal impulses of every parent and the difficulties he had faced a few years ago with his eldest son. He told me that, as a matter of fact, he was having difficulties currently with his second son. We parted, and he thanked me.

At the time, I had the feeling that it had been a good session. I later thought that he was also telling me about his feelings of solitude with me. His mother and his wife were perhaps going to die; part of himself was in danger. How sufficient was I in those circumstances? The doctor could very well be in a bad mood on the day. It was a question of putting oneself in human hands, in my hands, which are, by definition, faillible.

In fact, was I sufficiently attentive to his distress, the distress of the child, of an unknown father, who could potentially be abandoned? I found myself in a sacrificial paternal position, the position of the analytic Law, instead of permitting him to appropriate my position of responsibility for him.

The analyst in the setting and other "subjectal moments"

Freud did not think of theorising the setting, even if he wrote, "The patient's falling in love is induced by the analytic situation" (1915a, pp. 160–161), the situation in which the analyst places the patient and which "provokes" this love. But, for him, the setting was an empirically constructed means to help the patient, as much as the analyst, carry out the treatment. This lack of theorisation was perhaps consistent with the fact that the caring environment was taken for granted. Ferenczi remained much more in touch with Freud's first hypothesis—apparently soon abandoned—of the potentially traumatic impact of the first environment. Consequently, he suggested that an "elasticity of analytic technique" (1955) was necessary. He was, thereby, laying down the foundations for a theorisation of the setting. Winnicott (1954) was subsequently to give the "setting" an intrinsic importance in the treatment. In his wake, Bleger (1967) suggested applying the term "psychoanalytic situation" to the totality of phenomena included in the therapeutic relationship between the analyst and the patient. "This situation," he writes, "is studied, analysed, and interpreted" (p. 511). It also includes the frame. The frame, for Bleger, is non-processual. Indeed, he insists on its constancy. On the other hand, he includes the role of the analyst in the analytic frame. Bleger considers the frame as "the repository of the psychotic part of the personality" (1967, p. 513), but does not seem to think that it plays an active role in the process of recovery, as Winnicott believed. "The setting is much more than the metaphor of maternal care," Green (1979), writes, "it is a symbolic matrix, a container that is itself contained, a condition of meaning which depends on another meaning" (p. 370, translated for this edition).

For Green, as for Quinodoz (2002, p. 134), the setting is the instrument of the containing function of the analytic situation; it is the very organ of this containing. For Laplanche, the setting refers to self-preservative needs. These needs are separate from the sexual drives. In this conception, the setting becomes tangential to the analytic situation. Containing, constancy, respect for the patient's basic needs, the analyst's benevolent attention, and even his attentions, make analysis possible. However, as I have already noted, Laplanche does not consider them from the angle of their transformative power. In line with the approach of Winnicott, Bleger, Green, and Roussillon (1995a), I am wondering: is there a separation, other than rhetorical, between the setting and the analytic situation? Is the setting not the product of the analyst himself, no less than the analytic process? To put things simply, does not each analyst organise a space–time that bears the marks of his or her own particular psychic organisation, as well as his or her personal and analytic heritage? Hence, the physical and temporal arrangements will vary from one analyst to another. I want to go further.

Our living presence is significant for all our patients. They need to feel that they have an impact on us, just as much as they need to be able to "use" us and to experience our capacity to survive their attacks, to allow ourselves to be "taken hostage" while recognising their need to experience us as a "malleable medium" (Roussillon, 2005).

For me, the person of the analyst as an ethical subject who is asymmetrically responsible for his or her patient is a finding that is central and not tangential to the analytic process, and no less intrinsic to the setting. In this sense, with each patient the analyst *is* the setting, and the setting *is* the analyst himself.

> Soon it would be the Passover (spring) holidays. I spoke to Hen about our forthcoming separation; she decided to prepare the coloured pieces of cardboard, which, in the course of the following sessions, would prove to be the components of a box that we "were to make together" (I could hear the plural feminine). "Catch! Hold it firmly! Watch out! Don't drop it!" (in Hebrew, *faire tomber* also means to abort). I spoke of a forthcoming separation, and I repeated her injunctions. I had to "hold her firmly, to watch over her carefully, and not let her fall". She would not let me speak. "Stick, and hold tight," she said.
>
> At the penultimate session before the holidays, Hen refused to enter the clinic. She was sitting on the stone ledge at the entrance to the clinic with her back to me, in a dark mood. When I approached her, she tried to kick me.
>
> I said, "You hate me; you are terribly angry with me because of the coming holidays." She curled up into a foetal position. Then, she began rummaging in her pocket and pulled out the *méguila*, the "parchment" roll, which she tore up into small pieces. She threw everything on the floor.
>
> "You will rip up Viviane and Hen together if we don't see each other," I said to her. She remained inaccessible. I reminded her that her box was upstairs and waiting for her, that we could put whatever she wanted in it for memory's sake and that she would find it again after the holidays.
>
> "The box will be there," I said, "and me too." She sat up, but then immediately curled herself up again and dropped to the ground, falling on her feet.
>
> I said, "It's as if I was dropping you completely, as if I were no longer there to hold you; but you are also telling me that you are capable of falling on your feet and picking yourself up again." Was Hen alluding once again to her mother's wish to have an abortion, on the eve of this new separation?
>
> The day before the Easter holidays, Hen arrived, sporting a ponytail. She walked up the stairs with me calmly and then began filling her box with semi-liquid paints, bits of modelling clay, glue, paper, and sand.
>
> I said, "All kinds of liquid raw materials, of all colours, everything that we have done together here, something of you, Hen." On leaving, Hen

showed the box to her mother and said to her, "This is the treasure chest; we'll take it with us at the end."

*   *   *

During the 65th Congress for French-speaking analysts, the theme of which was sublimation, Sechaud and Baldacci presented vignettes illustrating what they described as "fertile moments" of analysis (Baldacci, 2005; Sechaud, 2005). As we saw earlier, such moments can be encountered in every analysis. After Amado-Levy-Valensi, I have defined them as "subjectal moments" (*moments subjectaux*) (see also Chetrit-Vatine, 2005a). I maintain that these moments originate asymmetrically, in the analyst himself, even if they might appear superficially to be the product of the patient or of the analytic couple, the analytic third (Ogden, 1994) or the chimera (de M'Uzan, 1994).

In the examples brought by Sechaud and Baldacci, each analyst proposes to the patient an association coming from his or her own cultural world. What interested me in particular was the fact that in each case the analyst wonders anxiously if he or she has not seduced the patient or has not been seduced by him or her. For these analysts, these moments seemed to result from the fact that they had been seduced by their patients and that they had responded to this seduction. However, Baldacci, following Milner, who spoke of aesthetic seduction, has proposed the term "gift of feelings". In fact, in each case, these associations and their expression, combined with the analyst's anxiety about the potentially seductive aspect of this offer, of this address, even in its ethical dimension, had the effect of getting the process going again, whereas just before the analyst had found him or herself in an impasse. So, it was through thinking of the analytic situation and the analyst as prompting transferences that I came to propose the term "ethical seduction", while insisting on its asymmetry (Chetrit-Vatine, 2005a). Stern and colleagues (1998), for their part, have suggested that it is the mutuality between analyst and patient that allows such moments to emerge, moments that they describe as "now moments". Stern, and in his wake those analysts belonging to the trend currently in vogue in the analytic world (Blass, 2009), do not take into account the fact that these moments occur in a doubly asymmetrical situation, and that it is precisely this asymmetry of the ethical seduction of the analytic situation which bestows on them their transformative power.

André (2002) reports the case of a female patient suffering from a lack of seduction. Like Hen, she had had a depressed mother and a father who was absent most of the time. For André, and I agree with him entirely, there is nothing like a deficit: a lack for a child "is always too much, always traumatic" (p. 14, translated for this edition). In the case he presents, "the scene of seduction was without substance, as empty as the mother's eyes" (translated for this edition). I would say that, paradoxically, this so-called lack of seduction was experienced by the child as a traumatic seduction. The parental messages (however much they were characterised by an absence of affect) could neither be sufficiently translated nor metabolised. As such, they provoked an experience of flooding, of excess. They did not allow for the construction of a psyche endowed with a sufficiently structured unconscious. André's patient wanted to turn her back to the world. "She threatened," he writes, "not to stop the analysis but to disappear as if nothing had happened; or as if what had happened amounted to nothing" (2002, p. 22, translated for this edition). Yet, this patient continued her analysis. In my view, what held her back was the fact that on each occasion her analyst prevented her from leaving. "Each time," writes André, "I held her back" (2002, p. 12, translated for this edition). He insists on the seductive aspect of the analytic situation, as much as on the analyst's listening and interpretations, each of these parameters playing a key role in the analytic process.

In these cases, as in the earlier situations, the analyst's passion was profoundly active in these processes and particularly exposed during these different critical moments. The analyst manifested himself as an ethical seducer, a seducer to life. A matricial space imbued with passion was there, offered to be used by the patient. In other words, on each occasion the patients took with them the woven fabric of the analyst's asymmetrical responsibility for them, and the equally asymmetrical seduction of the analytic situation, both intertwined with the analyst's passion (Chetrit-Vatine, 2008b).

But let us return now to the question of the setting.

When the setting trembles

In the absence of a matricial space, of an "affected" (i.e., emotionally cathected) capacity for asymmetrical responsibility for the other on the analyst's part, the primal seduction provoked by the analytic situation, owing to the very fact of the offer of analysis and to the analyst's passion throughout the whole analysis, may eventually give way to a narcissistic seduction, or, at worst, a traumatic seduction. The analytic situation then risks being perverted by the new edition of early traumatic experiences. Instead of being healing and transformative, it could become iatrogenic.

Taking into consideration the analyst's asymmetrical responsibility is all the more central when the impact of his "affected" presence is recognised. His capacity for self-analysis, for self-reflection, potentially requiring the help of a colleague, will be particularly necessary. Remembering that the analyst's listening and suddenly his or her saying are not only an expression of the matricial space, of proximity, but potentially a manifestation of our voyeurism, our cannabilism, our sadism, and our masochism, and "knowing that psychoanalytic interpretation is an act of cruelty leads us to accomplish it with as much benevolence and tact as possible" (Kristeva, 2005, p. 313) is also important.

It is obviously in situations where the setting is either being attacked by patients (arriving late, unarranged absences, suddenly getting up or leaving, sandwiches or drinks already opened and brought to the session (I'll say no more!), endlessly prolonged silences, falling asleep, direct questions, systematic use of toilets, etc.), or when it is destabilised by the analyst (analyst's vacation, weekends), that his or her active role in the analysis and his or her function as a repository of ethical seduction will be more closely circumscribed.

*　　*　　*

Ireni had been in analysis for more than five years. At that time, I was personally preoccupied by the health problems of one of my children. The matricial space I had available for my patients was thus reduced. Furthermore, my consulting room had just been repainted; it was winter, and very cold outside.

> It was the first session after the weekend. Right away, Ireni, who was somewhat out of breath, asked me in a rather sharp tone of voice to open the window, which I did. She lay down on the couch and remained silent. I was wondering about her breathlessness. Was it her asthma again? I thought, though, that she had got over that!

I said, "You are silent."

She continued, "There's nothing new, my thoughts come and go. I am wondering if the analysis has come to an end. I don't know if I can go any further. In fact, I think I can cope now with whatever happens to me; I can tolerate the painful moments more easily; I can stay silent calmly."

For my part, I was experiencing a slight sense of anxiety.

Ireni said, "I could tell you about what has happened or has not happened during the last few days . . . at work, with painting, and what that evokes for me . . . but I'm fed up with all this talk . . . In class, we drew a model, a woman sitting . . . I wanted to get the whole of her into my drawing."

I thought to myself that she might have noticed that recently I had not been listening to her with as much attention as usual, that she was telling me that she needed me to be more emotionally present, and that the separation at the weekend had once again created a sense of disconnection.

She continued, "I don't think there is much more to repair. Either the analysis ends or I will go and see someone else. As a matter of fact, I'm very often absent from work because I paint all night and then lie in until quite late . . ."

I noticed that she was touching her lips with a finger, and then that she tore off a little bit of skin—a means of discharge that she used from time to time when she was very tense. I remembered that the month before, for the first time, I had decided to say something about it. She had been very touched by my intervention, taking it as a sign of my attention to her.

I said gently, "You are hurting your lip."

She reacted violently, saying, "Mind your own business!"

This time, Ireni experienced my intervention as intrusive, as a traumatic seduction. Indeed, I had intervened on the basis of the recollection of a past intervention, being too concerned with defending myself against what I had perceived as a potential attack on the analysis and on the analyst, that is, her thoughts of breaking it off. In any case, it was a traumatic seduction.

With hindsight, I realised that Ireni had been tense and uneasy from the beginning of the session: the setting had really been destabilised by the smell of fresh paint, and I had not immediately realised the impact that this had had on her.

She arrived for the following session twelve minutes late.

Stopping abruptly at the door, she said, "Open the window!"

So I opened the window.

"This smell is impossible!" Ireni said. "Nothing extraordinary has happened during the last few sessions that would compensate for the nausea that I feel. There are times when analysis goes beyond the concrete level, it can mean something else . . . but this smell of paint is terrible; it's really excessive. This time, it's just the smell. I really feel like throwing up."

I recalled her past reminiscences concerning the unbearable smell of her mother's breath, concerning the nudity that this young woman would expose unabashedly in front of her little girl; I recalled her disgust and her desire to vomit at the smell of sperm. But I was troubled; she put one foot on the ground as if she was on the point of getting up and leaving.

Ireni: "If you were a Lacanian, you would've stopped the session immediately, as a mark of respect!"

Astounded, I asked, "Are you staying here out of respect?!"

Ireni replied, "No, it's the law!"

I said, very practically, "You can use the blanket and I can open the window (*fenêtre*) a bit more."

Ireni: "What did you say? That I've got it coming to me??? (*Que ça va être ma fête???*)

I realised that Ireni felt physically threatened, persecuted, and abused. I was tense and felt a sense of urgency. I was thinking to myself: telling her to leave will be interpreted as a rejection; but if I don't tell her to leave I am not respecting her.

I chose to say to her, "If I don't tell you to leave, I'm not respecting you."

I felt that she was calming down. She seemed more relaxed on the couch. After a few minutes of silence, she said: "My parents never respected me . . . even so, you could have told me not to come; or rather, you should have done something to make sure things didn't happen like that."

I said, "I shouldn't have put you in a situation where you had no other choice than to transgress the law in order to protect yourself." Here I was making an interpretation in the transference, alluding to the history of her violent adolescence, which we had already worked over quite a lot, to her subjective experience at that time, and to her delinquent behaviour.

"I am making you ill," I said.

She replied, smiling, "In a moment you're going to tell me that you are making me ill like my mother made me ill! Actually, I smoked a huge amount last night."

The next session, the last before the weekend break, unfolded in a more organised way. Before separating, I told her that it was possible that there would still be a smell of paint next time. She replied, "It doesn't matter; we'll see and decide when the time comes."

Before the session, the first of the new week, I was careful to warm up the room properly and I left the window wide open.

She glanced towards the window and smiled broadly.

Ireni: "The smells are really something! They definitely come from very far away! My childhood, my adolescence, my parents' house. At home, I paint. It disturbs me a bit, but not as much as all that. Yes, smells, they're exciting . . . sex . . . But the smell of milk, I've never been able to bear that."

She brought associations to a radio programme; it was a course on Jewish philosophy and the subject of the debate was: Does evil begin with conception or with the beginning of life? The answer proposed had been that evil begins with life, but that there is, none the less, free will.

Ireni: "I don't understand what sort of free will this is. Does anyone choose their parents? Is it the soul that chooses? It's too much for me. What? Did anyone choose the Shoah?"

Me: "Good smells and bad smells; good and evil . . ."

She said, "These subjects drive me crazy. What is good, and what is evil? I was thinking about the end of the analysis. First, I must put an end to this relationship with Eli. It would be better if I was still with you when I do that. And then I will begin an analysis with someone else . . . or perhaps it's better to continue with someone I know really well and whom I really trust."

I asked her, "Did you choose me or not? Would you choose me again or not? To what extent are you free or trapped? Good smell or bad smell?"

Ireni: "This story of smells, I'm really ashamed. There's no doubt that that took me back directly to my mother. With her, I didn't react; I kept everything inside. And yet I fought against my parents' perverted values: lies, the supreme value of money, making a good impression on others, etc. When you asked me why I didn't leave, it was because of limits. I have known all my life that I didn't respect them; and I have also always known that no one around me respects them. I knew that when I was very small."

I said, "You knew the difference between truth and lies, between what is just and what is unjust."

Ireni: "Yes, but it hurts so much. And after, one repeats over and over again."

She was silent now. Her silence was calm. Quiet.

Ireni: "Did you heat up the room before opening the window?"

"Yes," I said.

She smiled and passed one of her fingers lightly over her sternum. "It was hurting here last month," she said; "but now the pain has gone."

"You are breathing deeply," I said.

"Yes," she replied.

*   *   *

In this sequence, we can see how, initially, a transference of traumatic seduction was provoked. The destabilised setting relates, in the transference of traumatic seduction, to the body of the analyst/of the mother, an excessively sexualised body owing to the lack of, inadequacy of, or insufficient response to the ethical exigency at the beginning of life.

Subsequently, we can see the ethical seduction of the analytic situation rehabilitated in a process brought about by the weaving of the transference of primal seduction and the matricial space transference. The analytic situation and I myself could once again be experienced by the patient as ethically seductive.

By virtue of a "detour via the other", a detour via an emotionally engaged and passionate analyst, meaning could now be given to material that was initially unbound, allowing for the emergence of what I call a "subjectal moment" as well as a movement of transformation. A renewed capacity for symbolisation and, thus, for subjective appropriation was noticeable, and consequently the analytic process was set in motion again.

We can also see how the primal ethical exigency is evoked in a particularly articulate way by the patient.

We saw above that if, for Sechaud (1999),

interpretation facilitates the emergence of meaning . . . it excites and liberates the sexual, whereas construction soothes; it binds . . . leads to understanding . . . If interpretation is in the service of the sexual, construction is in the service of life, of love, in its function of binding and integrating larger and larger unities. (p. 149, translated for this edition)

I would like to add: if interpretation is given from a matricial position, if it is the product of ethical seduction, it can create a momentary but non-traumatic unbinding; constructing or interpreting is a matter of tact, in other words, of a capacity for empathy. Empathy, considered as foundational to the analytic encounter, has always been central in Israeli psychoanalysis, which is very strongly influenced by Anglo-American analysis. It is true that it has been decried in France owing to the pathos of the "affected" participation that it implies. Yet, there is a whole trend of practice today that includes empathy in analytic work. Widlöcher (1996) has proposed the concept of "co-thinking":

There comes a moment in the psychoanalytic treatment when the patient's internal scenario takes possession of the psychoanalyst's mind; not only can he (or she) not help participating emotionally, but the scenario activates in him associative ideas that are his own and that belong to his personal history, to his own subjectivity. It is through this experience induced by the patient's mind that listening and psychoanalytic understanding is created. (p. 169, translated for this edition)

Widlöcher speaks of an experience induced by the patient's mind, but he slips a bit too quickly, perhaps, no doubt out of a fear of pathos, towards the notion that the patient's internal scenario takes possession of the analyst's mind.

I referred earlier to the demolition or, at least, the taking hostage of the analyst in order to allow for a transformation. The analyst offers him or herself to be used by the patient just as, at the beginning of life, the parent is a presence to be used by the infant, and later by the growing child. Widlöcher evokes a co-production. I would add that for there to be a shared production, the conditions of this production are no less the asymmetry itself of the analytic encounter and, in particular, of ethical seduction (Chetrit-Vatine, 2007). Likewise, when de M'Uzan writes

> The analyst is not only the dedicatee and *agent provocateur* of the trans-ference neurosis, but an organic element of its elaboration, since it is in him, as if he were the analysand himself, that an important part of the work is carried out. (1994, p. 41, translated for this edition)

he is indicating, without insisting on the point—but it is what I want to emphasise—that he is the one who will have to emerge first from the joint "chimera" thus created. He is the one who will first have to rediscover the boundaries of his identity and, thereby, those of his patient. Ogden (1994) speaks of the same phenomenon in his paper "The analytic third". He notes that it is incumbent on the analyst to become absorbed in the transference situation and then, having metabolised it, to be the first to disentangle himself from it.

Thus, de M'Uzan and Ogden echo the work of transformation to which Bion turned his attention, a transformative work carried out first by the mother and later by the analyst. For me, it is essential to consider the ethical dimension of this work. For Laplanche, the analyst guarantees constancy and is benevolently neutral. As I pointed out earlier, for him, the analyst's function is tangential to the analytic process; by respecting the primary needs of the patient, the analyst makes the analytic process possible. Respecting basic needs participates in the self-preservative line, which is distinct, in his conception, from that of the sexual drives, the latter constituting for him the specific field of psychoanalysis. This brings me back once again to the question I have already raised: does Laplanche reduce assisting the newborn baby in distress to a purely biological maternal instinct, which is itself extensively self-preservative?

I propose instead to see in this capacity for responsibility for the other a mark that is just as specific to our humanity as primal seduction. The final part of this book is concerned with developing the question of the origins of this capacity.

PART IV

A NEW PSYCHOANALYTIC STATUS FOR ETHICS? THE FEMININE–MATERNAL ORIGINS OF THE CAPACITY FOR RESPONSIBILITY FOR THE OTHER

Introduction to Part IV

Throughout this work of research which I have been giving an account of in the preceding chapters, I have been wondering, in a sort of parallel process, as it were, about the validity of a hypothesis that is complementary to the classical Freudian, Kleinian, or Winnicottian theses concerning the origins of "ethics", of "reparation", or of the "capacity to be concerned". I have been reflecting on the origin of the human capacity to give the other priority over oneself, on the origin of this human capacity for responsibility for the other.

It became increasingly clear to me that the area of convergence I had identified between Levinas and Laplanche was not articulated solely around the question of the assymetry of the encounter (with the other for whom I am asymmetrically responsible, for Levinas; between the adult and the child, owing to primal seduction and its unconscious origin in the adult, for Laplanche).

For both of them, the other comes first. For each of them this other is intrusive, and the encounter is traumatising. The other does violence to the subject, who is overwhelmed in all his or her passivity.

Furthermore, Levinas and Laplanche alike speak "in the masculine". At the beginning of his work, Levinas (1948) is interpellated by the alterity either of the woman or the son, and even though he finally made the link himself between ethics as responsibility for the other and the maternal (1974a, p. 111), he did not pursue this theme in greater depth. (It was subsequently explored by Lichtenberg-Ettinger (1999).)

As for Laplanche, by proposing the idea of a fundamental anthropological situation, he has, in a sense, neutralised the adult in charge, even if he stresses that the mother is the first seductress. Thereby, he paved the way for the theoretical developments of André, who, conscious of speaking as a male rather than a female author, was to slip, in spite of himself, into phallic logic, according to which every breach or intrusion is by definition of phallic origin, the intrusion (*effraction*) creating what is intruded upon (*effracté*) and, consequently, the feminine.

Yet, it was in learning of the existence of this book by André (1995), whose title, *Aux origines féminines de la sexualité*, had particular resonance for me (!), that I realised how much I myself was concerned by the idea of the feminine–maternal origins of responsibility.

It was, thus, through contact with the parallel work of these two authors that the hypothesis of an origin of the capacity for responsibility for the other in the feminine–maternal dimension of the human being took shape, a hypothesis that resonates in an apparently contradictory way with their respective views. (For supplementary considerations on the "lack of influence" of Levinas's work on that of Laplanche, see Appendix 3.)

My father's death and the process of mourning that followed enabled me initially to make a link, at both an intellectual and emotional level, between *responsibility for the other* and *seduction*. I realised that with his passing I had lost not only the person who represented traditionally and consciously, both for himself and for those around him, the Law, the paternal superego, and the ego ideal, but also, and in a much less obvious way which he openly denied, the incarnation of the feminine–maternal dimension at the origin, as I see it, of his capacity for responsibility for the other, and no less for his seductive capacity. His identification with his mother was, on this point, perfectly evident for me. So, I am obviously not taking issue with the identificatory dimension or my father's internalisation of the maternal superego and ego ideal, but, having been inspired during the course of my research by Laplanche's theory of generalised seduction and by his hypotheses concerning the formation of the unconscious, in its various terms, I have come to consider this identification, this very internalisation, as secondary to a more primary phenomenon that is common to each human being—a phenomenon that functions according to Laplanchian propositions: the proffering of enigmatic messages by the adult world, their translation by the child's psyche, which is all the more partial in that the child is a newborn baby, and the inscription of traces forming the unconscious.

I suggest that if the breach of the psyche provoked by primal seduction and by the implanted and/or intromitted messages coming from the adult does indeed create the feminine dimension in the human being, this does not necessarily mean that the author of this breach is phallic. To put it simply, the adult in charge, paradigmatically the mother, through her seductive, maternal/matricial femininity, is at the origin of the first traces of this feminine–maternal/matricial dimension in the child's psyche. We shall see how.

In the analytic situation, this feminine–maternal dimension is mobilised just as much in the analyst whether the latter is a woman or a man; further, it is what creates the transferences in the offer of analysis, in the analytic process. In other words, as I tried to show in Part III, it is this feminine–maternal dimension that is at the foundation of the ethical seduction of the analytic situation.

The fourth part of this book seeks to account for this parallel process of "thought-emotion" and for its outcomes. Thus, it opens out on to other paths, envisaging another origin, or, rather, another foundation for ethics than that developed by Freud; in so doing, a new psychoanalytic status for the human capacity for responsibility for the other is created.

I shall begin by recalling succinctly the known psychoanalytic hypotheses concerning the possible foundations of this human capacity for being responsible for the other, and then I will develop my own personal hypothesis. Then, retracing my footsteps, I shall return to the approach that I have pursued and that led me to these formulations. I drew on the propositions of André, which I was following closely, to help me think not only about the feminine dimension in the human being, but also about how this feminine dimension interacts with the maternal. I have made some of Levinas's affirmations resonate, in alternation, with André propositions, even if it has been necessary to indicate Levinas's own negations concerning such a highly virtual articulation, if one sees things from what was probably his point of view. Finally, I have sought to find support for this conception of a feminine–maternal dimension in the work of a certain number of contemporary authors who have turned their attention to the question.

CHAPTER EIGHT

Psychoanalytic hypotheses

Generally speaking, and in the wake of Freud, we understand the capacity for responsibility for the other, let us say, concern for the other, as deriving from guilt, itself the heir of the oedipal complex. Furthermore, as we saw at the outset, in Part I, the word "narcissism" attached to "ethics" seems, for Freud, to have a pejorative connotation, and from time to time he regards ethics as illusory. Would it be true to say that such narcissism takes over from the sadistic injunctions of a persecuting superego?

For Klein, this capacity for responsibility is the fruit of innate maturity, aided by a favourable environment. It results from the infant's gaining access to the *depressive position*, thus allowing for the transformation of an early, cruel superego, present from birth, into a less sadistic and less persecuting superego. It can be understood as the capacity to repair the potential harm done to the object, an object that is not only hated but ultimately loved as well.

For Winnicott, building on Kleinian hypotheses, the capacity to be "concerned" results from a transformation, brought about by a "good enough mother", of the child's primary and innate guilt. This capacity, the *capacity for concern*, develops from the infant's "unexperienced, yet very present sense of guilt". However, he posits that the mother, as an environmental object, contains, handles, and holds this sense of guilt. In so doing, she enables the infant to "contribute"; she gives him or her the possibility of making reparation. For Winnicott, the infant, owing to his natural lack of respect, his *ruthlessness* (and not because he is endowed with primary hate), is capable of attacking the mother, of ill-treating her. However, it is not the infant's task to *contain* the guilt thus activated. It is for the mother to fulfil this function, at least partially. In this sense, she is the one who helps the infant "contribute something to making reparation". It is this internalised contribution that will help the child achieve a sense of responsibility. In Winnicott's terms (1963), the mother enables the child to use her. Winnicott developed his concept of "the use of an object" further. (I referred to this in Part II; see Winnicott's (1964) article, "The use of an object, and relating through identifications".) With this use of the object and with his concept of "primary maternal preoccupation", he is referring to a natural maternal order. For me, this maternal order (in the human being), which I have designated by the term "matricial space", is aroused by the child's exigency for an adult world that assumes a position of asymmetrical and ethical responsibility for him. In other words, it is not natural. But let us not get ahead of ourselves.

The Kleinian and Winnicottian propositions developed in a chain reaction. Klein elaborated her theory on the basis of Freud's hypotheses, and notably after he had put forward the idea of two drives (the life drive and the death drive) and the second topography (*topique*). Winnicott developed his theory from Klein's work, even if he was soon to distance himself from it. In this sense, his article, the "The development of the capacity for concern" (1963), to which I have referred above, is indicative of an important turning-point, if not a quantum leap in Winnicott's thought. I would say—with all due respect—that the liberty Winnicott took opened up a space of creativity for the following generations.

In the wake of Freud, and in the light of his reading of Winnicott, Kohut (1970) took up the idea of ethical narcissism from a non-pejorative perspective; indeed, it underlies his conception of moral courage. This conception offers a supplementary alternative to an understanding of the origins of responsibility.

After Bion, Symington (1990) (who makes particular reference to Bion's thought) speaks of an act of freedom, an act of moral courage represented by the mother's holding capacity (interpretation, in the case of the analyst).

But we would have to see to what extent there is a drift in both Kohut and Freud towards a widely shared phallocentrism, while with Symington, as with many authors inspired by the object relations movement, the absence of any reference to infantile sexuality is noticeable.

What I am interested in here is what might constitute the foundations, at the beginning of life, of the human being's capacity for responsibility for the other, foundations that are combined from the outset with the formation of a sexual unconscious. In this sense, I am placing myself downstream from the above propositions. As I pointed out at the beginning of this book, in the *Project* (1895), Freud had initiated a movement in this direction, which I am going to take up. That is to say, he positioned himself right at the beginning of life, at the moment when the newborn baby encounters the *Nebenmensch*. He made an allusion to the *possible origin of moral motivations*. However, he abandoned this path and subsequently proposed an alternative that I have already mentioned in passing. As I have already had occasion to note, the articulation between the feminine and maternal dimensions raises the question of the difficulties that Freud came up against, and which perhaps acted as a *gag* for the feminine–maternal dimension in him. (See also Brun's (1990d) reflections on Schneider's book, *Freud et le plaisir* (1980).) Yet, shortly after his publication on Dora, Freud, whose difficulties linked to the feminine–maternal order have often been noted, published his text on *Gradiva* (1907a). Here, the figure of the analyst is evoked through the heroine, with whom Freud seemed to identify: Zoë, life, a helpful feminine figure. In this text, he touched on an alternative conception to the more familiar split: either feminine or maternal. (See Ashur, 2009; Brun, 1990c, pp. 229–230.)

As I mentioned earlier, I will deal with the question of the foundations of ethics as responsibility for the other in conjunction with the question of the feminine–maternal dimension in the human being, with which it has common cause.

First, however, I would like to return—albeit at the risk of repeating myself—to a certain number of formulations that have emerged in the course of this study.

The first idea is a classical one: the capacity for matricial space is formed through identification with the mother/adult in charge and in possession of such a space. It becomes the manifestation of the ego ideal.

The second idea is that it could constitute itself by means of introjection, starting with the primary experience of a loving and caring adult, with a mother and her responsibility for her child, a mother who is already interpellated during the phase of gestation and herself transported back into a state of "primordial passivity".

The third idea is that the capacity for responsibility for the other—the capacity for matricial space—could be the product of enigmatic messages containing, along with their sexual burden, the prohibition "Thou shall not kill". In this case, it would be the product of the adult, parental superego, itself established, during the generation before, from "unjustifiable and enigmatic" messages that could not be translated. For Laplanche (1987), "categorical imperatives cannot be justified; they are certainly enigmatic in the same way that other adult messages are enigmatic" (p. 139). The origin of ethics as the capacity for responsibility for the other could, thus, be considered as resulting from the internalisation of the "enigm(atic)-ethical" messages of parents who are capable of going beyond their own primary self-preservative needs and of "finding reassurance about their humanity" in this capacity to give to the other, at the risk of their own lives. The problem is that Laplanche understands this superego as Freud or, perhaps, Klein did. He speaks of the ferocity of the superego. In this sense, the capacity for responsibility for the other would be the product of messages proferred from a position of moral, feminine, and erotogenic masochism on the part of the adults in charge.

One could, like Chabert (2006), envisage the superego

> less in terms of its Oedipal inauguration than in terms of its other source, which anchors it in the ego's distress and helplessness – that is to say, the superego as the memorial of the weakness and dependence that once characterised the ego, the superego being understood here from the standpoint of its benevolent and protective function, as dispensing the minimum self-love required for survival. (p. 137, translated for this edition)

It would, thus, be possible to conceive of another origin than that of the enigmatic messages coming from a superego in the Freudian or Kleinian sense of the term, a superego engendering feelings and fantasies associated with guilt. We could imagine a breach that is not linked initially to a prohibition imposed by the superego in the classical sense of the term, but to the mother's experience of being shaken up by the interpellation of her infant's distress, which, when everything goes as well as possible, is followed immediately by the welcoming reception she gives to the infant.

Finally, the idea emerged of an origin for the human capacity for responsibility for the other that would not reside in tamed guilt or in masochism; neither would it be of masculine–paternal origin, but rather of feminine–maternal origin, the feminine–maternal order present in each human being.

A more personal hypothesis began to take shape, for, however internalised and fantasmatic this process might be according to Kleinian or Winnicottian assumptions, it raises questions for me. We know how frequently a mother who receives a blow, albeit quite unintentionally, from her infant, might automatically feel like hitting the infant in return, but she restrains or contains herself, telling herself that he or she is only an infant. However, she also thinks that she would have felt guilty if she had been in the infant's position. She also thinks that it is important for him to become aware of the hurt he has caused the other person, and to apologise or make amends. I understand this commonplace sequence as follows: the mother "takes upon herself" her own hatred that has thus been triggered, and, by containing it, leaves the door open for the child's own role.

Something of this containing capacity, as well as of the underlying conflict, will be communicated to her child in the form of an enigmatic message implanted in his psyche. I consider that enigmatic messages are at the origin of this human capacity for responsibility for the other. They are proffered by the mother to her infant as a consequence of both the violence of the encounter with the infant and the interpellation of what she interprets as an ethical exigency. These messages will be implanted/intromitted in the infant's developing psyche. A part of these messages will be translated and the other part will remain as raw traces.

So, from this point of view, the origin of the capacity for responsibility for the other lies in enigmatic messages that are are proffered by the mother and the parental environment; and the majority of these messages have their origin in ethical seduction itself, the same ethical seduction that we encounter in the very first analytic interview. If Laplanche is interested in the impact of the sexual on the formation of the unconscious of the little human being, for my part I propose to reflect on the combined impact of the sexual and ethics, understood as responsibility for the other, and the role it plays asymmetrically and unconsciously on his humanisation and, consequently, on the formation of his unconscious. This would imply, in Levinas's view (see Critchley, 1998), the existence of a preconscious, or, more precisely, from a psychoanalytic perspective, of a subconscious in the Laplanchian sense of the term. Alternatively, linking up the intuitions of these two authors, it could be said that this subconscious is the product of untranslatable messages proffered by the adult psyche which has been breached by coming into contact with the proximity and vulnerability of the newborn infant.

The mother is intruded upon first of all by the violence of the interpellation resulting from the presence of a living human being growing within her. At the moment of birth, this intrusion will be repeated for the mother on account of the violence of her feelings towards this infant who is absolutely helpless and totally dependent on her. She will experience this helplessness as distress, as an ethical exigency.

For the father, or any adult who happens to be in charge, this intrusion will also be repeated in the sense that these two phases (for the mother), or this first phase (for other adults) could be conceived of as retroactive effects (*après-coups*) of the primal trace inscribed in their body/psyche, perhaps during their own gestation (see Golse, 2006b), and more certainly—which is what interests me here—during their birth and early childhood. (I agree with Dejours, who insists that every enigmatic message is first inscribed *in the body*. In my view, he thereby attributes a more precise role to the affective charge that is necessarily linked to the messages. During the translation process, a certain degree of mentalization takes place. The untranslated remainder will form the unconscious; its affective charge will remain alive, inscribed in the body. In the case of traumatic messages, whose affective charge is more violent, the *inscription under the skin* will not be only metaphorical, and it will be possible to speak of a proscribed unconscious (see Dejours, 2001).)

Freud had an intuition of the "origin of moral motives", but did not develop it further. He did not have at his disposal the means offered later by Laplanche, via the detour of Lacan, such as the question of the Other (*Autre*) or the other (*autre*). The question of alterity was not sufficiently explored in Freud. Equally, the generalised role of seduction in the formation of the unconscious did not find its place either in a theorisation that was capable of sustaining both the impact of enigmatic signifiers and the centrality of translation by the infantile psyche.

My hypothesis is close to Winnicott's, when he reflects on the origin of the capacity for concern, but he seems to create a split between the good enough mother and the woman that she is just as much.

For me, the good enough mother, who is destabilised through the encounter with the infant whose distress she experiences instantaneously as an ethical exigency, transmits (as a result of this destabilisation) enigmatic messages consisting of ethical seduction, messages that will break into, or breach, her child's psyche while structuring it at the same time. Indeed, it is because maternal seduction (when everything goes well) is infiltrated by her capacity for responsibility for her child that it will play a constitutive role in the child's unconscious. It is because this capacity for responsibility for the other will be combined with originary seduction that the enigmatic messages proffered to the child will be partially translated by the infant's psyche. The residues will result from repression owing to the incapacity of the infant's psyche to metabolise the felicitous affective excess of maternal passion.

I would say now that maternal passion results from the trauma provoked by the encounter with the distress of the infant (an encounter understood in the terms developed above), combined with the excitation, the awakening, during this very encounter, of the mother's infantile sexuality.

This mother/this helping adult is only able to receive and welcome her infant after this momentary experience of destabilisation has been overcome.

*   *   *

To resume, I want to advance the following hypothesis with regard to what happens to the adult in the encounter with the newborn infant. While Laplanche (2007b; see Part II in this book) has proposed three meanings for the word "unconscious", what interests me here is the concept of the "enclaved unconscious".

My hypothesis combines two aspects from the outset: an ethical aspect and a seductive aspect. We are dealing with a process in three stages.

On the ethical side

- First stage: evocation of the primal or originary trauma for the parent which has left its traces, devoid of representation, in the infant's psyche. These traces are the product of unmetabolised enigmatic signifiers carrying an ethical charge, and have remained in the "enclaved unconscious".
- Second stage: destabilisation of the mother's/father's psyche, breached/interpellated by what they interpret retrospectively as an ethical exigency of the human infant; at the same time, ethically charged enigmatic signifiers are proferred to the child which will constitute the enclaved unconscious in him.
- Third stage: taking care of and welcoming the infant spontaneously and consciously, and proferring messages that for the most part are translatable, the remainder of which will constitute the repressed unconscious.

On the seductive side

- First stage: evocation of the trauma of primal seduction.
- Second stage: evocation of infantile sexuality and proferring of enigmatic messages to the child which are translatable to a large extent.
- Third stage: tender maternal passion.

We may suppose that this unconscious, whether it is the product of repression, whether it is enclaved or proscribed, and even though it is constituted, according to Laplanche, by the deposits, waste, rejects, and untranslatable remainders of the enigmatic messages, can equally contain the traces of partial perceptions of positive quality, sparks of light, sounds, colours, and smells: the contact of a caress, a sense of well-being, the light of an illuminating smile, the sound of a soothing voice, or, later, the malaise of words that have never been heard and that are still waiting to be heard, an expectation that has itself remained "un-known". The question arises: why have these messages not been translated; why have they been proscribed? I have given consideration here to the insufficient neurological means available to the infant at the moment of their emission. This proscription is not the consequence of the excess, that is, the traumatic excess, of the messages as such, but, rather, may be seen as the result of messages addressed to an organism that is still too limited in its capacities for metabolisation, for translation.

It is my contention, then, that these traces in the unconscious enrich the psyche of the adult when he or she takes charge of the newborn baby and that they also colour the messages proferred to the child. At the same time, they participate in the origin of the potential capacity for responsibility for the other.

The hypothesis I am putting forward thus enlarges Winnicott's (1956) notion of *primary maternal preoccupation*. I am assuming here that this preoccupation, determined by the eventual influence of an influx of oxytocin at the moment of giving birth (Vincent, 2005), is also the product of the repression, the negation or denial of stages 1 and 2 set out above. Consequently, we can envisage scenarios where the destabilisation of the adult psyche will result in hallucinatory formations (psychoses of the post-partum) or a more or less invasive affective misappropriation of the child.

So, to recapitulate: the ethical exigency as responsibility for the other has its origin in the self-preservative needs of the little human being. Its aim is the constitution of his identity. This exigency destabilises the adult who is interpellated by this very exigency, precisely because of the unavoidable violence of this interpellation, of this breach. This destabilisation of the adult in charge occurs retroactively (*après-coup*), for the violence of the interpellation coming from the newborn awakens the traces left in the adult's psyche, from the beginning of his or her own life, of the encounter with the adult world interpellated by his or her own arrival in the world. The traumatic effect of this interpellation will be inscribed, in turn, in the developing psyche of the human infant in the form of traces resulting from enigmatic signifiers, whose translation is impossible. This inscription will be at the origin in the human being of the feminine–maternal dimension and, therefore, of the potential capacity for responsibility for the other.

CHAPTER NINE

The feminine–maternal origins of ethics

I am now going to consider the question of the foundations of ethics as responsibility for the other, in as much as it is bound up with the question of the feminine–maternal dimension in the human being.

I shall begin by making three assertions, which I shall come back to:

- to this day, no human being has developed elsewhere than in a uterus, in a human matrix;
- every adult in charge of a child is reminded of his or her own originary encounter with the feminine–maternal dimension of his or her first objects;
- this encounter, in the modalities set out above, is at the origin of the human being's capacity for responsibility for the other.

In order to reflect on the feminine–maternal origins of the human capacity for responsibility for the other, it is necessary to conceive of the feminine as going hand in hand with the maternal instead of falling into the classical alternative (maternal or feminine).

The feminine origins of sexuality, according to André's primacy of the phallus?

When I discovered this work, entitled *Aux origines féminines de la sexualité* (André, 1995), I was already familiar with André's work and I knew that it was deeply inspired by Laplanche's thought. I thought I would find elements in it corroborating my own propositions. From the title alone, I imagined that the following thesis would be developed: at the beginning there is the woman, the mother, who proffers enigmatic messages to her child and who thus finds herself at the origin of his unconscious and, consequently, of his psycho-sexuality. (Aulagnier (1975) alludes to this thesis in her major work *The Violence of Interpretation*.) For my part, I already wanted, at that stage in my research, to insist on the no less ethical content of these messages and to propose the complementary hypothesis of the "feminine origins of responsibility for the other".

André's thesis is indeed based on Laplanchian thought. The parental other is quite systematically designated as the adult other, without specifying the gender. I had expected to discover a thesis specifying the importance of the feminine dimension of the other, the seductive other who proffers such messages.

However, that is not his thesis; what interests him is the feminisation of the little human being, boy or girl, resulting from the *primal breach* originating in the messages compromised by the unconscious of the adult who is caring for the child.

Finally, this thesis, which I am taking up, enabled me to envisage the idea of a dual primal breach (*effraction*), consisting as much of the feminine as the maternal/matricial dimension of the adult caretaker.

For André, this primal breach is of a phallic order. He refers (1995, pp. 10–23, 45), in fact, to the *case of Dora* and to Freud's (1919e) article "'A child is being beaten'". For him, an adult intervenes in his or her phallic dimension—phallic, because it is penetrating, "'intromitting". (We have seen that Laplanche differentiates between intromission and implantation. André only uses the term "intromission", thereby indicating, perhaps, that he is interested in the enigmatic messages that cannot be translated, but it is certainly also because this term is associated quite automatically with the hypothesis of a phallic quality to primal seduction.)

However, he criticises the way Freud and Lacan cling to the primacy of the phallus, along with their obliteration of the existence of the vagina as well as the uterus, which is even less visible than the vagina but obviously part of feminine sexuality and the vehicle of a considerable amount of fantasy activity in both men and women (Guignard, 1999). I would also add here the role of the breasts as significant erogenous zones as such, and hugely significant objects of fantasy (Parat, 2006), along with the vulva, which is "particularly unrepresentable" (Schaeffer, 2008). André points out that Freud himself situated the mother at the origin of infantile sexuality in the *Three Essays* (1905d) as well as in his text on Leonardo da Vinci (1910c).

Yet, in his writings, as if by an automatic reflex, the father returns in force. He acknowledges this himself in his introduction: as a male author he emphasises, he says, "the instinctual aspect of the feminisation of each human infant and not its identificatory aspect", which, in his view, might more naturally be the theoretical interest of a female author. Thus, it seems that the instinctual aspect of feminisation is of phallic origin. It is in so far as the seductive other is phallic that he or she creates the feminisation of the little human being, whether the latter is born male or female. In the end, if André accords decisive importance to the intersubjective situation of seduction in the constitution of primitive femininity, the key role is attributed to the father's penetrating desire (1995, p. 113). In my opinion, this is to bypass rather too quickly the mother's desire, awakened through her contact with the infant, in particular during breast-feeding. This desire is no less penetrating and, in my view, eminently feminine. Indeed, he comes back to this point when he writes, "But before the mouth, there is the breast, the breast of the mother, of a sexually mature adult, of a woman whose sexuality, essentially unconscious, is dominated by genitality" (André, 1995, p. 114, translated for this edition).

The phallic nature of the breast has been stressed (Lanouzière, 1992, cited in André, 1995, p. 114), coinciding with traditional Jewish perspectives attaching masculine attributes to a woman's breasts as well as to her hair. It is true, that hair and breasts are located, like the penis, in a visible space. Is it justified, however, to "reduce" them to phallic symbols?

Levinas did not avoid the drift of phallic primacy either. As Coblence (1994) has rightly noted, "By reducing alterity too swiftly to difference, and consequently to femininity, since 'femininity is the very quality of difference' (Levinas, 1948, p. 36), there is a risk of the feminine being dissolved in the categories of phallic logic" (cited in André, 1995, p. 10, n. 7, translated for this edition).

Coblence (1994) reports the following proposition of Levinas: "To love is to fear for the other, to assist him in his weakness, even prior to meeting him" (p. 175, translated for this edition). But she rightly emphasises that he closes his proposition again by passing from the loved woman to the relation with the same, since it is the relation between the father and the son. "For the Levinas of *Time and the Other*," she writes, "the passivity linked to Eros, that which is bound up with ambiguity, cannot be contained." She observes shrewdly how a shift occurs in Levinas's work: she writes,

> Maternity is distanced from fecundity, and thus from Eros. He sepa-
> rates ethical fragility and feminine fragility, fecundity and love, the
> mother and the lover ... The encounter with alterity leads to an
> impasse; a woman does not have the "height" or distance (*hauteur*)
> required for ethics; a woman is "one who contemplates with ethics in
> view" [here Coblence is citing Chalier, 1982, p. 92]. (Coblence, 1994,
> pp. 175–176, translated for this edition)

Levinas returns to the all too familiar division between the private sphere as feminine and ethics as masculine! And though, as I pointed out earlier, maternity assumes its full rights again in *Otherwise than Being*, as exposure to the other, as risk, as hospitality (the "psyche as the maternal body") (1974a, p. 67), this body, according to Coblence, is devoid of all femininity.

Here, Lichtenberg-Ettinger introduces some contradictory ele-
ments into the discussion. In an interview with Levinas (1997b, p. 214, 219–220), we can find the following dialogue, which she cites as evidence of an evolution in Levinas' thought.

> *Levinas (EL):* Woman is the category, the ecstasy of the future. It is
> the possibility which consists in saying that the life of another human
> being is more important than my own; that the death of the other is
> more important to me than my own death; that the Other comes
> before me; that the Other counts more than I do; that the value of the
> other is asserted before my own. In the future there is what might
> happen to me; and there is also my death.

Lichtenberg-Ettinger (L-E):   So could we say that the depths of the feminine are the ultimate measure of responsibility? Or the ultimate measure of the ethical relation?

EL: Yes, that is *Keduscha*. [Hebrew for Holiness] (translated for this edition)

Here, the feminine–maternal order is definitely present, but nothing indicates that Levinas has abandoned the sexual/maternal split; woman seems to be nothing but maternity.

Phallic primacy, which is no doubt linked to the "necessity" of maintaining a strict separation between the sexual and the maternal, is a common and widespread "symptom". André speaks of a human phenomenon that he regards as unavoidable: the castration anxiety aroused in a man by the feminine in the other and in himself. However, if "fellation succeeds a feed in fantasy, because it preceded it in the fantasies of the caring adult" (André, 1995, p. 114, translated for this edition), is it not possible that in the fantasies of the caring adult, of the one giving the breast, another scenario might be at the origin of a fantasy giving shape to the responsibility for the other, a fantasy, for instance, proceeding from the feminine/matricial order in her? Could this be the fantasy of offering herself as pasture, "a passivity more passive than all passivity", which could be regarded either as the height of indecency or the summum of self-giving? For this to be considered as a pure act of self-giving, it would first have to be divested of any sexual connotations, of any form of eroticism, for the combination of this offer with the sexual is prone to arouse fears of incest and to be intrusive for the psyche. Is there not a sexual pleasure involved in this gift of the breast which is all the greater in that it is strengthened by the narcissistic pleasure of being able to help the infant grow, of giving a surplus of life?

Primacy of passivity?

For Freud, it is not the fear of castration that is the cause of anxiety in a woman, but, rather, the fear of "losing the love of the object". However, clinical experience does not always confirm such a division. André's answer is that the feminine is common to both boys and girls. He writes,

The fear of losing the object's love, which is a primitive form of anxiety, is common to the infant – regardless of its gender – and to the feminine; which means we have to think about how the latter overlaps with the infantile, well before the construction of the oedipal complex. (1995, p. 2. translated for this edition)

In opposition, then, to Freud's hypotheses culminating in the idea of a little girl, initially masculine in character, who merely lacks a penis to feel happy, André puts forward his own conception of a primary feminine dimension in infants of both sexes, writing

Freud's formulation, 'fear of losing the object's love', however laborious it may be, contains two precious indications. Constructed in the third person, it underscores simultaneously the primacy of the other and the passivity that results from it ... The first lived sexual experiences, those that combine once and for all human sexuality and infantile life and which colour the first maternal ministrations, are *'naturally of a passive character'* (Freud, 1931b, p. 236). . . . First, it is a question of passivity. The little human discovers that the experience of passivity and submission to the goodwill of the other are at the origins of sexuality, even if the identification with the seducer is as hasty as possible. (André, 1995, p. 2, translated for this edition)

Further on, he adds, "passivity enters psychoanalysis with the theory of seduction" (1995, p. 4, translated for this edition).

Thus, I posit at the origins of the maternal/matricial order, at the origins of ethics, this same experience of passivity and interpellation by the fragility of the other, even if retroactively (*après-coup*), in relation to primal passivity, it may be experienced in a regressive situation as a submission to the goodwill of the other, the persecuting baby. In keeping with the hypotheses formulated above, my conception of ethical seduction entails the following question: could it be that this deep anxiety in man also stems from the fact that, as an infant, he or she was breached not only by messages compromised by the adult unconscious, and particularly by the unconscious of the woman and mother who, quite apart from being seductive and nourishing, also had unlimited responsibility for him or her? For she herself was breached, intruded upon, by the interpellation of her child's fragility, by his total dependence, and was not always in a condition to respond to this interpellation. (We can see the outlines here of the hypothesis according to which a sense of guilt results from this imposed responsibility which cannot always be assumed, but from which it is equally impossible to escape.)

Drawing on the first Freudian developments and the traces that bear witness to them, Laplanche proposed a thorough recasting of the theory of seduction, generalising it to the situation (at once anthropological and empirical) in which, in the first moments of life, an unbalanced psycho-sexual encounter takes place between an infant and an adult whose ministrations and love, without their realising it, necessarily communicate the sexual unconscious. Taking this recasting as his starting point, André would propose the hypothesis "of a continuity between the position of the child, who is inevitably seduced, and the feminine position" (1995, p. 5, translated for this edition).

After Laplanche, he takes up a citation from Freud, which formulates with the requisite force the inevitable combination of maternal love, with its seductive components, both passionate and ethical, with the "necessary confusion between primary love, maternal care, and the most incompatible sexuality":

> A mother's love for the infant she suckles and cares for is something far more profound than her later affection for the growing child. It is in the nature of a completely satisfying love-relation, which not only fulfils every mental wish but also every physical need; and if it represents one of the forms of attainable human happiness, that is in no little measure due to the possibility it offers of satisfying, without reproach, wishful impulses which have long been repressed and which must be called perverse. (Freud, 1910c, p. 117)

I am wondering about "the long repressed impulses" in the case of mothers/women who are satisfied by their husbands/lovers, and I want to consider the projective effect of a Freud who was himself rather frustrated and certainly very excited by the situation just mentioned. I retain the idea, however, of an infant who is penetrated by the intrusion of maternal messages, and follow André's hypothesis of a primitive femininity "which is already a form of psychic processing, an elaboration, while remaining very close to the primary intrusion" (1995, p. 5, translated for this edition).

Strangely enough, Levinas speaks the same language:

> The I (*Je*) – or me (*moi*) – approached as responsibility is stripped bare, exposed to being affected, more open than any opening, that is, not

open to the world which is always proportionate to consciousness, but open to the other that it does not contain. (1993, p. 159)

Later, he writes,

The ethical relationship is not a disclosure of something given, but an exposure of the "me" [moi] to another, prior to any decision . . . Here a sort of violence is undergone, a trauma at the heart of myself [moi-même], a claiming of this Same by the Other, a backwards movement of intentionality. The extreme tension of the command pressed upon me by another; a command prior to any opening on my part; a traumatic hold of the Other upon the same. This is a hold I discover in the extreme urgency that calls for my help, to the point where I always come too late, for there is no time to wait for me. We can call this way of laying claim to me, of stirring within me *animation* (which is not a metaphor; I am animated by the other), or again, *inspiration*. And it is in the ethical situation that the latter word receives its proper sense; it is when one uses it to speak of a poet that it is metaphorical. In our sense, it is an *alteration without alienation*. The psyche is that animation and inspiration of the Same by the Other. It is translated into a fission of the core of the subject's interiority by way of its assignation to respond, which leaves no refuge and authorises no escape . . . If this alteration is the psyche, then the psyche is a seed of madness . . . (Levinas, 1993, pp. 187–188)

To return to André's book, there is, therefore, an intrinsic connection between seduction and femininity, one that can be elucidated in the light of Laplanche's hypothesis of primal seduction. There is an equally important link with passivity. "Understanding what necessarily articulates the seduced and the feminine," writes André, "presupposes that we leave the register of psychopathology for one of the widest generality, namely, that of the human being" (1995, p. 109, translated for this edition). By passing from the perverse father to the mother of primary care and of the first important moments of excitation, Freud made a step in this direction. As we saw earlier (see Part II), it was Laplanche who took up Freud's first intuitions in the *Project* (1895), and of the infant in a state of helplessness (Fr. *dés-aide*; G.W., *Hilflosigkeit*), necessarily in distress at the beginning of life, and compared these intuitions with the encounter between a mother/woman, an adult mother endowed with adult sexuality and a sexual unconscious.

Laplanche emphasises that the position of the infant's primal/ originary passivity is inherent to the infant–adult situation. To show the general aspect of passivity, Laplanche refers to Leibnitz (1714), who writes in his *Monadology*: "The creature is said to act outwardly insofar as it has perfection, and to be acted upon insofar as it is imperfect" (§ 49, 50, cited in André, 1995, p. 109, n. 10). Passivity is, thus, held to be of the order of imperfection. André proposes that activity should be seen as a defence in relation to passivity. Originary passivity, on the side of the infant, he adds, is that which characterises the general situation of seduction, that which unites the newborn infant in distress and the caring adult. Consequently, he proposes that

> If the girl owes nothing in terms of activity to the boy, it is not because she is a little man (as Freud (1933, p. 118) maintained). Rather, it is because identification with the active pole allows her, like the boy, to master, to bind, that which is excessive in the passive position, that which overwhelms the integrative capacities of the ego. This excess resides in the conjunction of instinctual passivity and of the "seduced". (André, 1995, p. 120, translated for this edition)

The idea of instinctual passivity then appears, which he formulates positively in these terms: *"Enjoy what happens (to you)*; participate with enjoyment in what penetrates you, intrudes upon you, that is to say the link between passivity and *the inside*". Additionally, he proposes that "Passivity as an instinctual aim 'takes over from' the ego's passivity in the face of an instinctual attack, which itself succeeds the traumatic passivity of the newborn child faced with the adult world" (1995, p. 122, translated for this edition).

Is this not what is reactualised in the mother during her pregnancy, and later in the relation at the breast with her infant, who is as much penetrated as penetrating?

If, for André, this is what makes it possible to understand the repudiation of femininity in both men and women, paradoxically it is perhaps also what makes it possible to understand the seductive nature of Levinasian philosophy. In effect, it offers a reconciliation with this first feminine dimension in so far as it is linked—quite unconsciously for the philosopher and certainly for many of his readers—with that of the giving mother; a mother giving herself, in all her unconscious immodesty, the summmum of seduction in her conscious dis-inter-ested love, for the other. It was not Levinas who would lend support to these considerations, for he wrote, "There is no libido in the relationship with the other; it is the anti-erotic relationship *par excellence*" (1993, p. 174).

Commenting on Levinas's text, Rolland offers the following reflection:

> Is the transcendence of the desirable – beyond interestedness and the eroticism in which the beloved stands – possible? . . . In order for disinterestedness to be possible in desire, in order for the desire, beyond being, not to be an absorption, the desirable must remain separated within desire: near, yet different – which is, moreover, the very meaning of the word 'saint'. [This is only possible if the desirable] commands me to the undesirable *par excellence*: to the other person (ibid., pp. 222–223). (The undesirable other is the other person received "not in the appeal of his face, but in the nakedness and misery of his flesh!"). (2000[1993], p. 303 n. 12)

Here, we have the notion of love without Eros: Levinas makes a split between God as Other, as a desirable, lovable Good, and the other, the undesirable other person. In so doing, he justifies the split between ethics and responsibility for the other on the one hand and the erotic, the desirable, the loved one, thus the site of my concupiscence, on the other.

However, I draw on Levinas (1993) to express in his terms what takes place, in my view, in the mother, in her relation with her child, and which is at the basis of responsibility for the other. He writes,

> 'Finite freedom' is neither first or initial for the willing that it animates *wills* on the ground of a passivity more passive than any passivity, on the ground of a passivity that cannot be taken charge of. This freedom is finite because it is a relationship with another. It remains freedom because this other is another person [*cet autre est autrui*]. Finite freedom consists in doing what is our vocation, that is, in doing what no one other than myself can do. Limited in this way by the other, it remains freedom. It comes from a heteronomy that is inspiration—an inspiration that is the very pneuma of psychic life. The subject's for-the-other, which is this finite freedom, cannot be interpreted as a guilt complex, or as natural goodwill . . . nor again as a tendency to sacrifice. (pp. 178–179)

The point I want to emphasise here is: neither guilt nor natural goodwill, nor a tendency to sacrifice.

Neither guilt nor natural goodwill nor a tendency to sacrifice

André positions himself differently to Freud with respect to masochism. As far as an examination of the question in Freud is concerned, I refer the reader to André's critical recapitulation of it (1995, pp. 124–126). As for his own thesis, André upholds "both the necessary and primitive character of the relations between masochism and femininity". However, this masochism is not linked to the "castrated" condition of the woman, but to his hypothesis of a psychogenesis of femininity as an elaboration of the intromitted and naturally passive position of the child in relation to the intrusion of the sexual adult. Thus, this hypothesis associates jouissance and penetration/intrusion. It upholds both the necessary and primitive character of the relations between masochism and femininity. André writes,

> At the time of the beginnings the most elementary level in which the pair masochism–femininity is rooted resides in the constitution of the unconscious itself and concerns masochism before femininity is associated with it. 1995, p. 127, translated for this edition)

So, in the beginning, there is pain! It is true that jouissance can be derived from co-libidinal excitation linked to pain. It will enable the suffering person to survive the pain. This pain can even, in the case of a perverse organisation, become the condition of this pleasure, at the risk of life itself (see Faure-Pragier, 2000).

Are we obliged, though, to uphold the primary character of masochism? If Laplanchian theory, which accords an "inaugural and founding" dimension to seduction, makes it possible to conceive of masochism as lying at the basis of every perverse organisation, does that necessarily imply that masochism is at the foundations of all human organisation? André writes,

> Such masochism lies in the split generating the unconscious itself, in the return of the repressed in as much as it mingles intrusion and excitation. Pain begins with an excess of pleasure, with the powerlessness

of the infant to metabolise the immoderate nature of fantasy. (1995, p. 129, translated for this edition)

At what point is this return of the repressed, which cannot be metabolised sufficiently, linked to an adult world that is not loving enough, not "binding" enough (Bion, 1962b)? An adult world that is itself overtaken, invaded, by its fantasmatic world, which is constantly experienced as excessive or denied as such? I nevertheless want to propose the idea that intrusion is not necessarily pain. It can be combined from the outset with a position of welcome - a position that is as much conscious as preconscious or unconscious on the mother's part.

For André, Schaeffer evokes "an extremely close relation, a relation of quasi-structural superposition between masochism and femininity", while insisting on the proximity between "the experience of jouissance and the welling up of anxiety". Citing her, he writes,

Everything that is intolerable for the ego: passivity, loss of control, the erasure of limits, the intrusion of penetration, the abuse of power, depossession, is precisely what contributes to sexual jouissance ... defeat, in all the senses of the word, is the condition of feminine jouissance. (1995, p. 130 and n. 56, translated for this edition)

But Schaeffer makes an important distinction between feminine erotic masochism and moral masochism, sacrificial masochism. Psychical erotic masochism is, in her view, neither perverse nor acted; it counter-cathects moral masochism. "In un-binding," Schaeffer (1999) writes, "it ensures the binding necessary for the cohesion of the ego so that it can undo itself and allow for very strong quantities of unbound libidinal excitation" (p. 34, translated for this edition). In this view, then, the ego has to suffer so that jouissance can occur, and this suffering is the condition of the binding necessary for its cohesion. Now, none of this seems at all evident to me. In fact, Schaeffer adds, "Jouissance does violence to the ego, but if the ego welcomes it, it will be enlarged; it will enrich itself with a pleasure of greater intensity" (p. 35, translated for this edition). Here, I am in agreement with Heenen-Wolff (2003) who affirms that feminine jouissance is not necessarily linked to pain, and that it can be linked to welcoming. This is also true of maternity and the capacity for responsibility for the other. So, with Faure-Pragier (1999, pp. 41–55), I wish to question the idea of primary masochism, whether feminine or moral.

Feminine–maternal and narcissism

I should like to take this line of thinking further with some suggestions relating to the articulation between femininity and narcissism. They emphasise the factor of binding represented by Eros and, without proclaiming it openly, they temper André's affirmations above, allowing me to concur with him more easily.

André writes,

> The presentation of the psychogenesis of femininity has led us hitherto to place the accent, from breach (*effraction*) to intrusion, from intromission to penetration, on the opening up of the psycho-soma of the infant by the sexual adult. If this were the only aspect, it is not femininity that would result but, depending on the case, perversion or psychosis. Access to femininity presupposes that the penetration of the internal body is not the equivalent of evisceration or fragmentation. The gap between a seduction that is (also) structuring and psychoticising intrusion with acts of care does not lie only in the fact that the intrication of the sexual remains unconscious for the adult – if it is true that in reality the unconscious is always kept tightly sealed and out of reach of the conscious. It also lies in this . . . that with the turning away which, strictly speaking, constitutes seduction, are intertwined acts of binding contributed by Eros. (1995, p. 150, translated for this edition)

He cites Laplanche, who proposes that caresses and "other forms of cuddling (also) permit the constitution and the confirmation of the total form, of the limit, of the closed envelope constituted by the skin's surface" (p. 150 and n. 3, translated for this edition). And I agree with him when he writes, "Narcissistic pathologies are in fact pathologies of narcissism, whose source is located as much in the failures as in the excess, in the deficiencies as much as in the invasion by the (maternal) adult unconscious" (p. 150, translated for this edition). You will have noted the return to the specification—maternal—of the caring adult, which had disappeared in the course of the text. (I should like to point out that in Parts II and III of this book, I attempted to amplify these suggestions, knowing how much these "affected" (*affectés*) looks, caresses, sayings, if they are indeed linked to a capacity for responsibility for the child respecting his requirement for ethics, are at the origin of his subjectivisation, his creativity and curiosity, the richness of his psychic life, and the realisation of his potentialities.)

* * *

Mary, who was told about her husband's homosexual activities shortly before the birth of their fourth and last child, brought me a poem that she had finally managed to write after a long period of labour, entitled "Weaving love around the well". This theme of the well from which a woman draws water to quench a man's thirst is recurrent in biblical narratives. Mary would elaborate on this theme for several years in her psychotherapy, which she had entered after having a psychotic breakdown of the depressive type. This psychotherapy, in conjunction with neuroleptics, had avoided hospitalisation and allowed her to face the pain of betrayal, her initial blindness, and the fear of separating from a man she loved but whom she was beginning to hate without realising it, other than through hating herself.

Weaving . . . commenting on Freud's paper on femininity, Coblence (2003) writes, "By intertwining or by separating the threads of beauty and excitation, the work of women is to weave a modest canvas aimed essentially at masking the 'defect' of their genital organ" (p. 27, translated for this edition). The defect of their sex?!

Towards the feminine–maternal origins of ethics and a plea for a non-masochistic passivity

I propose, then, to consider the human capacity for responsibility for the other as emanating from the feminine–maternal order in the human being.

Brun, for whom "seduction is maternal in essence", insists on "the woman in the mother". When I questioned her about her position, she told me in 2009,

> The relationship of a daughter to her mother is based on the emergence of hatred towards the woman who is the mother as an object of desire of the man who is the father. This precocious hatred, nourished

with love, will permit the development of the desire to become pregnant, the desire for a child, and the desire for maternity. The desire for
a child emerges, in my view, at an extremely early stage, and has its
origin in this trace of movements of hate and love. Added to this is an
early identification with the father of prehistory (mother and father
are undifferentiated) which paves the way for an unconscious sense of
guilt which itself inaugurates the stages of separation with the first
love-object, who is the mother, and identification with the lost
object/refound in maternity, in the attraction for boys and in rivalry
for men. There can be no deep analysis of women without approach-
ing this early hatred for the woman who was the mother. The ties and
identifications with the father are inherent to these processes. Where I
feel very Freudian is in the role that must be attributed to early hatred
in the necessity of separating from the first love-object, who is the
mother, via the construction of the woman that she is or was. (1990b,
p. 198)

I wish to emphasise here, "Precocious hatred, nourished with love,
will allow for the development of the desire to become pregnant, the
desire for a child, and the desire for maternity". For Brun, the desire
for a child originates in this trace of movements of hate and love.

From my point of view, this desire for a child is no less correlated
with the human being's feminine–maternal capacity to be responsible
for this child. It is true that when this desire exists, it might serve as a
support for this capacity, but not necessarily. It is worth asking
ourselves if we should not make a difference between a conscious and
an unconscious desire for a child. The conscious desire is often linked
to a need for narcissistic reassurance, allowing for the illusion of an
expansion of the self and/or the expression of an ego-ideal, sustained
by a collective ego-ideal. (Evidence of this may be found in contemporary families in religious Jewish circles, the *Haridim*, which have an
impressive number of children.) It might also be combined with the
unconscious or conscious wish for reparation transmitted from generation to generation. This wish might be completely disconnected from
the wish to care for a child. For some who have recently become mothers or fathers, the encounter with the actual newborn baby, the
responsibility and the care that it requires, can provoke not only feelings of being destabilised, of being breached/intruded upon (*effraction*) after the event, to which I referred earlier, but also a real
inflagration of overwhelming feelings of hatred. It is certainly anxiety

about this potential hatred, insufficiently mingled with love, and perhaps inscribed during their own birth and childhood, which is at the origin of this lack of desire for a child. I am thinking here of two cases, one of a woman and the other of a man, neither of whom had any wish to have a child. The first, whose relationship with her mother was full of conscious feelings of hatred, hatred that had systematically been analysed, found herself, as a result of life's circumstances, with parental responsibility for her nephew and niece, and to this day she has brought them up remarkably well. It was only subsequently that she was finally able to express her own wish to have a child. In this case, the lack of desire to have a child stayed with her for a long time, whereas her capacity for emotionally invested responsibility for the other found its expression further downstream, as it were, in relation to this lack of desire.

The second case is of a patient who would begin to have suicidal thoughts as soon as his partner of the moment expressed the wish to have a child. Today, he is the responsible and emotionally invested (*affecté*) father of several children, and soon to be the father of another one, but, once again, without any conscious desire for this new paternity. The expression of his death wishes, of his hatred towards the foetus, within the setting of a long-term psychotherapy with an analyst in a setting that is a repository of ethical seduction will perhaps help, as with the first children, to liberate his capacity to be emotionally responsible for the child to be born. I will not go any further into the question of the "desire for a child" as such; I would just like to say that, in the above cases, the question of a non-masochistic feminine–maternal order has been raised.

I pointed out earlier that Faure-Pragier (1999) has developed a theory that specifically backs up the hypothesis of a non-masochistic feminine–maternal order. She writes,

> When feminine identification is possible, thanks to the support represented by a mother who recognises the active role of the father, passivity can be integrated successfully. On the other hand, if the father is not recognised and does not validate his daughter as a woman for the future, the passivity becomes threatening, for it delivers her over to the mother and then masochism becomes the obligatory path to jouissance. The third object, the father, is present from the outset in the mother's desire, which is focused on someone other than the child. (p. 52, translated for this edition)

In the two cases above, feminine identification was practically impossible. Not only did the mother not recognise the father's active role but the father did not validate his daughter as a woman, or his son as a man, for the future. In fact, the encounter with the parental figures caused a traumatic breach (*effraction*), without there being any possibility for the enigmatic messages from both parents to be metabolised. Analytic work made it possible for the masochistic passivity—thus, for me, pathological passivity—in each of these patients to be transformed into non-masochistic passivity, into a passivity of welcome, into a capacity for pleasure devoid of pain.

So, to return to my preliminary question concerning the maternal–feminine origins of responsibility for the other and the classically related question of primary masochism, I share the position that masochism is not an unavoidable source of jouissance. By the same token, I agree with the affirmation that "masochism, as an obligatory path to jouissance, is directly linked to the invasion of the child by the maternal sexual messages which have not been sufficiently deflected onto the other, the father, the lover" (Faure-Pragier, 1999, translated for this edition).

If the feminine–maternal messages can be envisaged as being deflected on to the father, the lover, and, in the man, on to the mother, the mistress, or any other libidinal investment, I would add that it is precisely because they contain in them this ethical aspect of responsibility for the child, a responsibility that is devoid as far as possible of guilt. Faure-Pragier considers that "the swing" between the mother's investment of the maternal dimension and her investment of the feminine dimension only seems to take account of a conscious movement. "Certainly," she writes,

> there is an alternation between the investments of night time and day time; the censorship of the woman-as-lover (*censure de l'amante*) is keeping watch, but is it linked to mechanisms of repression, of splitting? Or is the maternal a form of drive inhibited in its aim, which allows many sexual messages to persist? (Faure-Pragier, 1999, p. 52, translated for this edition)

As far as I am concerned, I would prefer to speak of a feminine–maternal dimension constituted from the outset by the ethical seduction of the adult, which is at the foundations, in the woman, of the censorship of the woman-as-lover, and, in the man, of the censorship of the man-as-lover.

We have seen that the enigmatic messages addressed to the child become for him or her a primal seduction, and are at the foundations of the formation of his or her unconscious. "The mother's sexuality," Faure-Pragier writes, "plays an active role here but unconsciously, partly involving the fantasies forged by her infantile sexuality", and she continues,

> The guilt that obliges the mother to operate a repression is not oblig-atory, but depends on the quality of the movements of integration and symbolisation which continue throughout life; they are once again particularly necessary during the disturbance created in the mother by the experience of pregnancy and giving birth. Denying the powerful maternal libidinal current and evoking the importance of masochism seem to me to be the expression of the persistence of an infantile sexual theory, the denial of the mother's sexuality, which implies that she cannot be seductive other than mechanically, by means of the ministrations she provides. On the contrary, the mother will – fortu-nately – invest in her child all her narcissistic and libidinal expecta-tions, without there being any reason in general to fear the perversion that haunts the theoreticians, at least as long as a third party is invested. (1999, p. 53, translated for this edition)

Here, I should like to add that the mother will invest in her child all her narcissistic and libidinal expectations, without fearing perver-sion, provided that, while making these indispensable investments, which tend to reduce her child to the same, she remains interpellated in her responsibility for him by his face and his alterity.

So, I do not see any incompatibility between the feminine and the maternal. They go together. The maternal consists at once of narcis-sistic investments, of libidinal investments, and of responsibility that takes into account the child's alterity.

When the love of the woman-as-lover leads to the desire for a child, when having descendents becomes proof of love, love appears as the capacity to make room in oneself for the other, as responsibil-ity. The mother, the father, the parental environment will then be said to be in a matricial position, ethical seducers of their child.

CHAPTER TEN

Conclusions

A certain number of rapprochements and hypotheses have been put forward in the course of this work. I would like to return to a few of them now in order to offer them for discussion.

1. I have been interested in an encounter between Levinas and Laplanche. For each of them, primacy is attached to the other. For each of them, this primacy marks the asymmetry of the encounter. For Laplanche, this encounter is between a newborn infant and an adult world in an asymmetrical relationship owing to the primal or originary seduction coming from the messages of the adult world caring for the child. For Levinas, this encounter is that of the face of the other interpellating me, immediately inciting my asymmetrical responsibility for him.

2. The translation of enigmatic messages, a central notion for Laplanche, whether they come from the mother or the father, can only take place within a movement in which the infant seeks support from them, from that, in them, which recognises him as subject, as a gendered or "sexed" subject (*sujet sexué*). For a child to be able to appropriate subjectively the symbol-generating function of the parents, or other significant adults, they must address themselves to him from a matricial position that meets his "ethical exigency", combined with primal seduction and its affective expression: parental passion. He must encounter an ethically

seductive environment. For this to happen, there must exist in them, ready to be used, a matricial space of asymmetrical, emotionally cathected (*affectée*) responsibility for him. The terms "containing", "maternal reverie" (Bion), and "holding" (Winnicott), bypass the ethical dimension of such maternal positioning. It does not seem to me to be a matter of indifference to formulate this dimension as such. It plays a role in the denaturalisation of maternal or even parental devotion. So, I have sought to differentiate the self-preservative from the ethical. Although, following Freud, Laplanche differentiates between the self-preservative and the sexual, a strange amalgam occurs between the capacity for responsibility for the other, permitting the satisfaction of the child's self-preservative needs, and the self-preservative order as such. If the sexual (*le sexuel*), for Laplanche, is of adult parental origin, the "containing" capacity of the breast is not examined. Although he has shown clearly how the the desire for a child has to pass along complex paths in order to arrive at what, in animals, is given instinctually, he seems to assume, like Freud or Winnicott, that a mother has natural capacities for devotion, unless her nature is perverted. But the capacity for responsibility for the other is a human acquisition and the capacity to be a mother must be differentiated from the desire to be one. (See Brun (1991, p. 13), who differentiates precisely between "the representation of maternity, the aspiration for maternity, and the accomplishment of maternity in giving birth".) Maternal devotion steeped in a woman's unconscious, consisting of her sexual drives and her infantile sexuality depends very little on instinct.

3.   At the beginning of life, as at the beginning of each analysis and throughout the analytic process, in a relation that is sustaining and, thus, creative, "being open [will mean] precisely: being available [in my analytic function] to the other who comes to surprise me" (Laplanche, 1999c, p. 47, translated for this edition). I have insisted, then, on the fact that the analyst is an integral part of the setting, just as the adult environment in charge of the child also belongs to the child's psychic development. I have argued, with Roussillon, that meaning cannot be considered to be always *already there*, deposited in some recess of the subject's unconscious. The unconscious is constituted by unmetabolised remainders of the translation of compromised messages from the adult world. But, as far as the messages are concerned, messages

that are both provoking and provoked at the beginning of life by a traumatic seduction, the intervention of the other is required. So, and particularly in the difficult cases that we increasingly have to deal with today in our daily practice, the capacity for symbolisation, which is necessary for all psychic life, proves to be less something that is given from the outset than the emergence of a process involving two people. In analysis, meaning will gradually be constructed, found, and created at the heart of the analytic process with the help of the emotionally cathected participation of the analyst. I have proposed a different formulation: *by virtue of the analyst's passion*. The analyst is necessarily engaged. To the analysis of the transference must be added not only the analysis of the countertransference, but also that of the ferment constituted by the "affected" or emotionally cathected presence, listening, and saying of the analyst.

4. In other words, when everything goes as well as possible, the analytic situation is a space–time of seduction and an ethical space–time. It is a space–time of ethical seduction in so far as every encounter between a patient and an analyst immediately evokes/reactualises in this same patient the primal seduction encountered in his first contact with the adult world, and in so far as it evokes from the outset the fundamental exigency/need for ethics which should have been satisfied at the beginning of life; if it was not, it still remains to be satisfied. It is in this sense that the analytic relationship is fundamentally asymmetrical.

5. I have argued that the origin of ethics as responsibility for the other resides in the feminine–maternal dimension of the adult, in his or her potential capacity to let him or herself be touched, penetrated, taken hostage, interpellated by the other's fragility. This feminine–maternal order is equally at the origin of primal or originary seduction. This feminine–maternal order in the adult, whether a man or a woman, makes him capable of being receptive, capable of emotionally cathected listening (*écoute affecté*), of recognising alterity, of respecting the limits of this other and, therefore, of affirming him. Thus, I hold that its seductive and ethical combination is at work at the very beginning of life: it impregnates the remainder of the untranslated messages with its homeopathic traces, it participates in primal repression, and, in the child's psyche, it favours the formation of an unconscious, which, although it is sexual, is no less ethical.

Levinas had an intuition of this in *Totality and Infinity*, where he writes (and I am paraphrasing him here), "(Love) is passion and trouble, a constant *initiation* into a mystery rather than *initiative*; the capacity for transfiguration depends, then, on the essential passivity of the subject . . . on his being moved, on his effemination" (1961, p. 270). We have seen that Levinas seems subsequently to have drifted away from this position in order to give primacy again to the phallic, even if he seemed to return to it partially by interposing maternity and the primary metaphor of ethics as hospitality. I have proposed to go further along this path that was traced out before being abandoned by the author. Coblence (1994) writes,

> The great originality of Levinas' thought was that he tried to give prominence to the encounter with the other not only in the experience of love but also at the basis of ethical relations; and, consequently, to raise in all its pertinence the question of the relations between the two, when love is not reduced to the meeting of eyes but constitutes a shared voluptuousness. (p. 167, translated for this edition)

Let me point out once again that in the *Project* (1895), Freud alluded to the first origin of ethics:

> At first the human organism is incapable of bringing about the specific action. It takes place by *extraneous help*, when the attention of an experienced person is drawn to the child's state by discharge along the path of internal change [by its screams for example]. In this way, this path of discharge acquires a secondary function of the highest importance, that of *communication*. The initial helplessness of human beings is the *primal source of all moral motives*. (p. 318, original emphasis)

Freud posits the little human being as being helpless from the outset. Without an object who is there to help him, without an object he can turn to, he cannot survive. Here, the issue is either helping him to live or of letting him die. First interpellation: someone is there, responsible for him or her, and I have proposed that the origin of the capacity to be responsible for the other lies in the violence of this interpellation, in the parental messages that it provokes, and in the inscriptions and traces that they leave in the infantile psyche.

At the same time, I hope that it will be possible to envisage an ethic for the analyst, an ethic in contemporary psychoanalysis, which has responsibility for the other as its axis, an ethic without naivety and yet free of all cynicism. It is in this sense that the question of the analyst as an ethical subject must be posed over and over again.

The analyst's anxiety or ethical awakening

"I slept, but my heart was awake"

(Song of Solomon, 5, 2)

"He who keeps Israel will neither slumber nor sleep"

(Psalms, 121)

Sonia is soon going to give birth to her first child; there are three more sessions to go. She said that she had had difficulty waking up, in spite of the fact that her husband was already wanting to talk to her. But she was still in her dream. At this point, she said to her analyst, "You're not going to fall asleep, are you?" She continued, saying that her husband was not sufficiently available for her: he would come back home after work and immediately start telling her about the content of a book he was reading . . .

Who is available for whom? Which of them is not preoccupied with themselves? The dream, the guardian of sleep, impedes waking. Yet, the analyst's wakefulness, her vigilance, is a fundamental *need* of every patient. It harks back to the ethical need of each newborn baby. The anxious state of wakefulness or alertness of the new, good enough

mother, although it is the source of the development in herself of feelings of hatred that are not solely "objective", is, none the less, the
space–time of her unlimited responsibility for her child, the space–
time for surpassing the violence inflicted by the infant's sometimes
shrieking interpellation—that is to say, a *matricial space*.

In analysis, ethically speaking, this state of wakefulness of the
analyst, which might involve an element of anxiety, becomes the
guardian of his or her responsibility for the patient. "Man is defined
by what worries him, not by what reassures him," writes Wiesel
(1966) in *Le chant des morts*, p. 125). Uncertainty characterises openness
to the other.

Insomnia is conceived by Levinas as the very awakening of the ego
to others, its *animation* or its *inspiration* by the other, the impossibility
of not being attentive to the other (in Hebrew, being attentive is
expressed by *lassim lev* (lit. "put heart"), to put one's heart into something). Insomnia is the awakening of the ethical subject, an awakening
that is never sufficiently awake and that always needs reawakening, a
responsible wakefulness that is an incessant reawakening.

In putting forward another anti-concept of Levinas, and associat-
ing it with a quotation from Wiesel, I am proposing—as part of a
constant process of reappraisal in which something said needs unsay-
ing over and over again—to reconsider the propositions that I have
advanced so far from a different perspective. As I suggested in my
introduction, it is a question of *rethinking analytic practice while taking
into account the world after the Shoah, "a world turned upside down,
whether it wants to recognise it or prefers to ignore it, by the Nazi disaster"*.

My interest in Levinas's thought was undoubtedly influenced by
my own personal heritage. The philosopher developed his thinking
while he was a prisoner, before being shaken up by deportation and
the disappearance of his loved ones. Furthermore, he was involved for
many long years in his job as the head of a boarding school that took
in many young orphans whose own families had been devastated. It
seems to me today that the formulation *psychic suffering and psychopathology are intimately connected with the encounter with a world that is
incapable of responding to our ethical exigency* is clearly underpinned by
the impact of the Shoah on my personal history.

In the third part, when I spoke of clinical experience, I was interested, among other things, in the effects of the *setting*, but I did not
insist on the impact of the setting, of the biological, sociological,

geographical, historical, and political context in which I work and within which I was writing. My interest for the analytic setting is not unconnected with the particularities of this very context.

I would simply say that the subject of this work has been elaborated consciously over the past ten years. During this time I have renewed contact with French psychoanalytic culture after almost twenty-five years of isolation; twenty-five years during which I was occupied, among other things, with trying to get to grips with the local psychoanalytic culture. The latter was influenced at the outset by the context in which the Israeli Institute of Psychoanalysis was founded. Max Eitingon, its founder, and his fellow travellers had been obliged to emigrate to Palestine due to their Jewishness and the rising threat from Nazism. This culture, which is at the basis of the entire Israeli system of "psychology", was soon enriched by the cultural heritages of analysts from Europe, then from North and South America. Finally, this culture and the practices following from it were, and still are, necessarily influenced by the wider socio-political context.

At a more personal level, I should stress that choosing a life companion who was profoundly wounded by his experience of being a hidden child during the Second World War, emigrating with him to Israel forty years ago, learning the Hebrew language, founding a family there, continuing to live there through wars and iterated, albeit quickly forgotten, threats of annihilation, being obsessed by the malaise generated by the mirror effects of the violent experience of living side by side with the suffering, no less vain, of the Palestinians, amounted, in fact, under the cover of a conscious identification with my father's desire (that of seeing in the construction of the State of Israel the end of the persecution of the Jewish people), to a personal enactment in a collective context equally permeated by the Shoah, an enactment of the effects of this disaster.

So, the experience of working with Israeli patients in Israel was, and is, one of an infinite encounter with multiple aspects of the "radioactive" effects of this transmission, the radioactive effects of the identifications that it triggered and continues to trigger (Gampel, 2005, pp. 80–81). Yet, though, outside Israel, it is easier to understand that "people don't like hearing about all that", strangely enough the same difficulty can still be encountered in Israel itself. As for me, this violent return led to the elaboration of this book and the parallel frequentation of Laplanche and Levinas.

From this perspective, each of them operates a reversal in his own way.

Levinas denudes the face of the other and, interpellated by the other and his distress, positions himself as the one who "will not kill" the other man. The question arises: is not this other man who threatens me from the outset precisely, for Levinas, the one who exterminated his father, his mother, and his sister after having taken their clothes off, starved them, gassed them, and reduced their corpses to smoke? For them, he calls for justice. As for him, he is commanded, interpellated in his sense of responsibility: this Nazi is the human, the other, my close relation, the potential Nazi in myself . . .

Laplanche seeks again and again to differentiate himself from Levinas, even though he often speaks the same language, and even thoug,h without realising it, the latter was a source of inspiration for him. Laplanche (2007b, p. 211) speculated on intergenerational transmissions, as such, without any metabolisation. Furthermore, he understands sublimation, or, rather, inspiration, as resulting from the transformation of the sexual death drives into sexual life drives (1999c). This idea echoed for me with the biblical injunction: "I have given you the choice between life and death . . . O that you would choose life" (Deuteronomy 30: 19).

The question I am asking is: how can psychoanalysis still allow itself not to give the dimension of the interhuman encounter its full place and not to give serious consideration to the fact that it is at the heart of this encounter that it is practised?

If Nazism was characterised by the negation of the singularity of the individual, reduced to nothing more than an example of the species (Adorno, cited in Villa, 2011), or worse, a number, stripped of all subjectivity, then, since the analyst is necessarily involved, implicated in the treatment, the question of psychopathological labelling must be reconsidered and the singularity of the patient emphasised over and over again. In a world increasingly devoid of safeguards, the unknowability of the other must be proclaimed and, with it, insistence must be placed on the private and secret space of each one of us. I think that the interest for subjectivisation and the phenomena of subjective appropriation in the treatment may be linked to the fact that more than half a century after the Shoah, many are still barely able to grapple with it consciously. How can we analyse without taking into account the effects, expressions, and manifestations, in both our patients' psyche and our own, of the impact of this disaster? We owe it to ourselves to give consideration to "the return of something which, hitherto, had never existed" (Villa, 2011).

If fear of *passivity* is indeed the rock which psychoanalysis has to contend with, the patients we encounter today, who are often living and surviving in an existential state of stress, need all the more, if they are to be able to make inroads into this rock, to encounter our own passivity—"more passive than all passivity". Scarfone (2011), who is also interested in the relations between the work of Levinas and Laplanche, proposes, following Lyotard, the use of the term "passibility" (*passibilité*), a neologism which I understand as a capacity, aptitude for passivity. Admittedly, in Laplanche's conception, we are dealing with the analyst's activity. This activity consists in the very offer of analysis as much as in the analyst's refusals (*refusements*) combined with the help he gives through his interventions, with a renewed translation of the messages of yesteryear (reactualised eventually in the transference on to the enigma re-presented by the analyst and the analytic situation). But, as I have pointed out on several occasions, from the point of view of his responsibility for the other, the analyst is simultaneously "besieged, persecuted, taken hostage by the other", offered to be possessed, an "actualisation, for the benefit of the analysis, of the fundamental passivity–possibility of every human being faced with the other" (Scarfone, 2011, p. 153, translated for this edition). According to Laplanche, the analyst offers a hollow, a container, as Bion would say. I have tried to show that the analysand finds this hollow, this matricial space, due to the fact that the analyst depositions—in the sense of dispossessing himself of—his own ego in order to rediscover, in Scarfone's terms, "a primordial disposition which, in everyday life, generally passes unnoticed, but which the disposition to listen analytically draws on in an exquisite manner" (p. 156, translated for this edition). I am in complete agreement with him when he writes,

> It could be said that the opening created by the inauguration and re-inauguration of the analytic situation presents itself as a philosophy in action, or rather, the actualisation methodically brought about by an ethical attitude which is called psychoanalysis. (Scarfone, 2011, p. 156, translated for this edition)

And, again,

> If the provocation of the transference by the analyst does not prove to
> be traumatic, it is to the extent that, in contradistinction to what
> happens in ordinary seduction . . . the active role of the analyst in
> provoking the transference is combined with the hollow that he offers
> to receive the transference . . . Without conceding primacy to this
> passivity–passibility, without offering himself as a real hostage of the
> transferential hold, the analyst can only *understand* and not *hear*.
> (p. 156, translated for this edition)

This is why I have spoken of the ethical seduction of the analyst and,
furthermore, why I have tried to show the importance of an emotionally cathected passibility, which, in the analyst's offer, signifies to his
patient, addresses to his patient, a *saying* going beyond the *said*. In so
doing, it is a mark of his responsibility for him. "Presence is only
possible as an incessant renewal of presence," suggests Levinas, "as
an incessant re-presentation" (1974a, p. 59).

For Levinas, *inspiration*, understood in terms of ethics, is a mark of
the combined autonomy and heteronomy of the responsible subject.
"Inspiration can be understood", Calin and Sebbah (2002) write,

> as a non-Kantian response to the Kantian problem of knowing how
> the moral subject becomes the author of the obligation to which he
> submits. Obedience to the obligation which emanates from the infinite
> cannot proceed, as in Kant, from the representation by the subject of
> this obligation thanks to which the will itself establishes the law and
> becomes its author. (p. 39, translated for this edition)

For Levinas (1974a), "I am obliged without this obligation having
begun in me" (p. 13). The obligation by which I am ordered to turn
toward the neighbour is unrepresentable. Thus, Levinasian ethics are
radically heteronomous, but because "obedience precedes any hearing of the command" (p. 148), and because the order is only
announced by the voice that responds to it, "it is the possibility of
being the author of what had been breathed in unbeknownst to me"
(p. 148). Heteronomy, thus, reverts back into autonomy. It is in the
mode of inspiration and not of representation that I become the author
of the obligation. The inspiration of the ego by the other is its animation by the other, in other words, its respiration: "Inspiration is the
very pneuma of the psyche" (p. 124).

I will take up again here, in echo, Laplanche's (1999c) words: "No doubt research, like creation, comes from the individual, and in this sense, it is centrifugal. But what calls it and orientates it is a vector coming from the other" (p. 331, translated for this edition). He adds,

> All the subject can do is to remain open to the trauma and through the trauma. This trauma of the enigma is not acquired or opened once and for all; it comes and goes. Openness is precisely being available for the other who will take me by surprise. (p. 331, translated for this edition)

Laplanche shies away from adopting "any sort of mystic tone", adding:

> I by no means support the idea of Levinas that the enigma of the other is always mediated directed by the vector of the gaze. But on the other hand, I am convinced that it is the enigma of the other—the human adult other—which is the vehicle for other enigmas that are called primary. (1999c, p. 48)

And, speaking, not without reticence, he says, of "the enigma of being", he adopts the formulation of Bonnefoy (1991, p. 365) concerning Alberto Giacometti: "There can be no thought of being except in the encounter with beings" (cited by Laplanche, 1999c, p. 48). Here, we can hear a certain sense of unease in Laplanche regarding his attraction to a discourse which might have mystic resonances. Yet, it is at this very moment that he chooses to introduce the term "inspiration". He says, precisely, inspiration, unlike sublimation "combines into other".

Certainly, for Levinas,

> the *enigma* is the way transcendence, which is non-phenomenal as such, announces itself in phenomenality, and thus opens up the dimension of signification or signifyingness between phenomena; while it leaves its trace among them, it is not, however, captured by them. (Calin & Sebbah, 2002, pp. 20–21, translated for this edition)

By refusing to play the game of the thematising discourse, the enigma opens up the dimension of ethical language, of the language that commands. The enigma is the interruption of all ontology, of all phenomenology; it is pure disorder of being, rupture, interruption of the concept, and, at the same time, the enigma is the site of *significa-tion*. Thus, it must disturb order without causing it to explode. The impact of the interruption can, therefore, be realised only in the subtlety of an insinuation. This double dimension of interruption and insinuation is rendered possible "by the extraordinary nature of the trace left by a past that has never been present" (Calin & Sebbah, 2002, p. 21, translated for this edition). The impact of the interruption is only accomplished in its echo or its trace. Ambiguity is the very work of the enigma.

How can one fail to see a resonance between such a definition of the enigma and the Laplanchian definition apropos of messages compromised by the sexual unconscious?

One last clinical vignette.

Ytsick, a single man in his forties, is the oldest son of a mother who had survived the death camps, after being in the hands of Mengele, and of a father who was tortured by the Nazis and who, without knowing how, had survived the bullets of a firing squad. Having been either in analysis or psychotherapy for years, just surviving, on borrowed time, he had turned to a new analyst.

In a total state of disarray, this analyst had come to consult me. Ytsick was less and less capable of creating, even though he was gifted with extremely high intelligence, and, possessing a rich/heavy psychotherapeutic experience, he was skilful at repeatedly thwarting every interpretative attempt. He expressed his discontent, his disappointment, and his despair that he would never see any transformation occur. He could easily fill the space–time of the sessions, without leaving any opening. After each session he felt "even more desperate" he said; yet, he added, "there must be some reason why I continue to come". His analyst, though, was not taken in by his enacting. According to Ytsick, the other analysts were nothing but superficiality and vague support. His various psychotherapists, all women, had always been full of admiration for him; this time it was no longer working . . . he was enraged. And the analyst was feeling increasingly dispossessed of his means: whereas, a few months before, he too had been under the patient's spell, he was now feeling a mixture of irritation and increasing indifference during and after each encounter. In fact, he felt that he had less and less sympathy for him; he did not recognise himself. And he reproached him with being cold and mechanical. During the last session, the hour preceding the consultation, Ytsick had reported his impressions of the evening before, which he had spent with long-standing acquaintances "for whom he felt nothing". Cynical and disenchanted, he was juggling with the souls of one or the other of them. As I was listening, in my role as consultant, a picture formed in me of an icy landscape, a white expanse, a frozen lake on which Ytsick was dancing at once an aesthetic and mad dance; at any moment the ice might give way and Ytsick would be swallowed up for ever. I shared this vision with the analyst. He was at last able to formulate his combined feelings of hatred and shame, his despair and his fear of losing control and of making him lose control with each intervention. His eyes filled with tears; he feared his patient might have a psychotic breakdown, and said he did not know what to do any more to survive this. It was either a question of playing at cynical clowns or of letting himself be engulfed . . . it was dreadful! The analyst was now coming out of his emotionally frozen state; he was moved and beginning to feel again. A moment of silence followed. I recommended waiting, vigilance, and patience. I said, "He knows that you have not been taken in . . . he knows and will continue to know that he has a violent impact on you, but that you will survive." The analyst thanked me and left, visibly troubled.

I subsequently learnt that, during the next session, Ytsick had been able to speak about his hatred and his anxieties in social life, and that in the following session he had said that he felt lighter and less oppressed. This was a new feeling, one he was not familiar with.

Both Levinasian philosophy and Laplanchian thought take very serious account of the fact that man is capable of conducting himself in the most atrocious ways imaginable. Man can be much worse than a wolf for his fellow man. But *my* underlying proposition has been that he is equally capable of surpassing himself for this other and of finding within himself the resources for taking responsibility for this other, beyond considerations for his own life.

The analyst's ethic as responsibility for the other, as it was articulated by Levinas after the Shoah, is a new perspective for our generation.

"The disquieting (*inquiétude*) of the same by the other," writes Levinas (1986), "is the desire that shall be a searching, a questioning, an awaiting: patience and length of time . . ." (p. 81). The dis-quieting of the analyst by the other, his patient, is a desire that is questioning, that is awaiting in proximity. It is the suffering of someone for someone. Here is another Levinasian saying which can hardly fail to strike a chord in us:

> The other, absolutely other, is the Other. It is not because the Other is a novelty that it 'gives rise' to a relationship of transcendence—it is because responsibility for the other is transcendence that there is something new under the sun. (Levinas, 1986, p. 13)

Appendix 1. The case of new parental configurations: new perspectives

In the course of my research I have touched on the issues raised by the current transformations of the family structure, transformations that have already been taken into account for a long time by Laplanche and his proposition of the "fundamental anthropological situation". I have been interested in the legal situation in this domain in Israel, and I have been able to test my proposition of the ethical seduction of this situation. (The text that follows is in part the discussion of a paper given by Tisseron (2004) called "The difficulty of being a parent today".)

These transformations are due to the development of new techniques of procreation as well as to the evolution of our society and its customs, an evolution that influences this development and vice versa. The mother is not always the one who brings up the child; each child can have several mothers and several fathers (a natural or biological mother, a surrogate mother, a social mother, a biological father, a social father, two social mothers, two social fathers, etc.). The

---

* These texts were written while I was elaborating this work (at the risk of some repetition) though the background contexts were different.

results of recent research pertaining to the future development of these children do not seem to be catastrophic, as had been feared twenty years ago (personal communication from Eva Weill). These results tend to confirm the Laplanchian proposition emphasising the fundamental anthropological situation that merely requires that a newborn infant is taken care of by an adult world, irrespective of the organisational structure of this world. For my part, I want to insist on the intrinsic asymmetry of this care, both with regard to its seductive character and to its burden of responsibility for the child. Those authors who have reflected on this question emphasise the cardinal role of the legislator and insist on the unacceptable nature of a situation where the parents have to take full responsibility alone for the eventual difficulties encountered. For Tisseron, "The legislator has an essential role to play in establishing symbolic reference points that are indispensable for the construction of the internal world of each person" (2004, p. 5, translated for this edition). I am in complete agreement with him. That the legislator should reinforce the function of the sublimatory agent is indeed a very important suggestion. Wondering about the impact, particularly in France of an "ethic of the good" (of the parents? of the children?) where decisions are taken with reference to the moral consequences for the actors without leaving much room for the freedom of each person to decide for himself, I have tried to obtain clarifications concerning the complex and sometimes surprising "ethic of the good" operative in Israel.

It seems to me that here we are dealing with a combination of an "ethic respecting individual liberty", emanating from Anglo-Saxon culture, (which can be qualified as secular) and an "ethic of the good" as it is defined according to Hebrew law. What interested me in particular in this latter perspective was the definition of the "good of the child".

It is defined thus: the child's legal status must be guaranteed and the risk of incest avoided at all costs. Consequently, in Israel, in the case of adoption, a precise registration of the identity of the biological parents has been obligatory for a long time, well before legislation of this kind had been passed in Europe and even in the USA. The adopted child, if he or she so wishes, can obtain information about the indentity of his or her biological parents at the age of eighteen. The adoptive parents are prepared and encouraged to make the child aware, at an early stage, of his status as an adopted child. The adoptive parents will define themselves as "parents who help the child to grow up" and will distinguish themselves from the biological parents "who were unable to take care of the child when he or she came into the world". From the standpoint of Hebraic law, the official registration of the biological parents' identity thus guarantees the child that he or she will not be considered as illegitimate—a problematic status in Hebraic law—and that he or she does not run the risk one day of marrying his or her sister or brother. It is worth noting here the connection implied by Hebraic law between respect for a child's need to be aware of his origins and the fundamental importance of respecting the prohibition of incest.

As for artificial insemination using a sperm donor (AID), and ovocyte (egg) donations and/or the use of the services of a surrogate mother (loan of a uterus), Hebraic law appears to be astonishingly open, in particular where egg donations and uterus lending are concerned, contrary to current French legislation.

This openness in Israel towards new modes of parenting, which necessarily stems from the openness itself of Israeli legislation, has its roots in several sources (see Weiler, 2004).

1. In the Talmud Bavli, we can find the following quotation: "Three partners are involved in creating a human infant: God, his father and his mother". In the evocation of the participation of the actors in the conception of the child, we certainly have the premises of openness towards the original father–mother duality.

2. We can also find this citation: "The creator is infinite; he knows what there is in everything". In other words, for some exegetes, if present-day science makes it possible to invent new techniques for creating human infants, not only does God play a part in this, but he gives his benediction.

3. At the foundations of the search for, and the possibility of, such openness is the *mitzvah*, the duty, to "grow and multiply". Every scientific discovery whose goal is the growth and multiplication of humanity, and of the Jewish people in particular, tends to be taken into consideration by the Rabbinic authorities and to receive approbation, after due reflection and consideration of favourable arguments.

4. From the Jewish perspective, the affirmation, "there is only one mother!" is by no means evident. We can find traces of this in the

> Old Testament: when Sarah was sterile, she asked Abraham to conceive a child with Agar, his servant, so that she "could give birth to a son" through her intermediary. By the same token, the wives of Jacob "offered" him their servants. Rachel offered Bilhah to him, saying, "She will give birth on my knees, and so I will have given birth to a son, through her". Leah did likewise with Zilpah: the child is considered as the son of the father's official wife.

It should be pointed out that Leah is the one who gives Zilpah's sons their name. Thus, she becomes their matronymic mother. In this connection, in the Jewish tradition, when people are called to go up and read the Torah, during the blessings, the sons are named after their father: "David, son of so-and-so", and the daughters are named after their mother: "Hava, daughter of so-and-so". (Thus, it seemed increasingly evident to me that the centrality of the name-of-the-father, and with it patronymic parenthood, which are both very much characteristic of Western society, owe a clear influence to Christianity and the Trinity.)

Although Israeli law is firmly based on English law, the influence of Hebraic law is present in it. As far as contracts between parents who seek the services of a surrogate mother and the latter are concerned, Israeli law, to this day, requires the participants in the surrogacy contract to be registered, as it does in the case of adoption. However, from the point of view of the Rabbinic authorities, certain important details are missing in Israeli legislation, which is different from Hebraic law, even if it is influenced by it. Currently, the details of the identity of both the parents requesting the services of a surrogate mother, and of the latter, are registered. When the sperm and the egg belong to the former, there is no problem concerning the child's future status, but when there is an egg or sperm donor, the details of the genetic parents are not registered and they can very easily become inaccessible. From the standpoint of the Rabbinic authorities, this can prove very problematic later on for the child.

As far as the donation of sperm in the case of sterility of the male partner of a married heterosexual couple is concerned, Israeli legislation, influenced this time by Hebraic law and the prohibition of adultery, recognises the paternity of the legally married man as legal paternity, without going into the details any further. In principle, the question of a sperm donor participating in the conception of a child in the case of a woman married to a sterile man is not resolved positively by Jewish law. In fact, though, the means will always be found to justify the practice.

To return to a more global vision of these issues, the new forms of parenthood are troubling. The development of new techniques allows homosexual couples, whether of masculine or feminine gender, to create a family. And, for quite some time already, single women have been able to become mothers, if they so wish, by means of artificial insemination with a donor.

No methodology has yet been developed that is capable of identifying the factors guaranteeing the psychic health of children born and raised in these new familial constellations, and these upheavals sometimes create a considerable amount of anxiety both for families and for consultants.

The anxieties may be verbalised in the following terms by professional therapists. What about the formative primal scene, the formation of gender identity, the sexual orientation of these children? What will become of them? Is it enough simply to put words to all these situations? Are we not simply collaborating with manipulations, which, when all is said and done, are perverse? Is it responsible on the part of those involved, on the part of these parents? Whose needs are being fulfilled? Whose desires are we trying to satisfy? Does anything go? Does this not represent a threat for Freudian theory as a whole?

Other questions might be added to these. In which cases should we pass judgement? Does the novelty of new forms of parenthood allow us to make certain comparisons? Are there grounds for projecting on new situations old concerns in relation to adultery, as the Rabbi do? Should we keep quiet in view of the fact that we have no experience of the consequences of such options, and wait several generations before regretting that we did not issue warnings earlier?

I remember that when the first ultrasound scans were introduced thanks to the new possibilities of establishing the sex of the child well before its birth, the teams of Michel Soulé and Serge Lebovici had spoken of the "voluntary interruption of fantasy", an association linked to the "voluntary interruption of pregnancy".

Thirty years later, this expression seems laughable and translates many of the anxieties of that period. Now, the psychological transformations capable of making it possible to assimilate these new practices are already well under way. Are we analysts not in danger of finding ourselves lagging behind these transformations, attached as we are to our first beliefs and theoretical identifications?

Three-year-old Dana is the younger of two girls born by artificial insemination, each of whom had a different donor. The two half-sisters have been growing up since their birth with their biological mother and her female companion. These two women have been living as a couple for many years and collaborate closely in raising the children.

I would say, using a classification proposed by Tisseron, but one that I have modified, that the two girls have:

- the same maternal genetic filiation;
- the same matronymic genealogical filiation (they have the family name of their biological mother, which is in fact the name of the maternal grandfather—so, in the end, is it a matronymic or patronymic component?);
- the same maternal educative filiation; to be more precise, they have in common a dual maternal educative filiation;
  On the other hand, they have a different masculine genetic filiation (is the term "paternal genetic filiation" really adequate?);
- finally, their filiation, in both cases, is lacking the paternal educative component.

When she was visiting her maternal grandparents, whom she did not know very well, Dana asked her young aunt about the identity of this man and this woman: "Who is she?" she asked. "That's my mummy," replied the aunt. "Who is he?" the little girl then asked about the man. "That's my daddy!" said the aunt. "No! No! No!" little Dana protested gently, "That's not your daddy! No! No! Girls only have mummies!!!"

So, already at the age of three, Dana has constructed her theory; the human being is a self-theorising creature, Laplanche reminds us. But the parents and their messages will permit this potentiality to be realised and, in fact, they will participate fully in the formation of the representations of the child. Dana seems to have a good sense of the difference between the sexes: she and her sister are girls and not boys, her mother and her companion are women–mothers. She is also able to recognise generational difference: there are parents and children.

But she has no idea (or does not formulate the idea) that a man's sperm was necessary for her to be conceived and that, like every human being to this day, she is also the fruit of a masculine genetic filiation.

One year later, Dana began questioning desperately all the men she met, asking over and over again, "Are you my daddy?"

Dana seems to have come to the painful realisation that children, whether boys or girls, generally have a mum and a dad. But would it satisfy her to hear her mother tell her that she also has a masculine genetic filiation?

Several years ago now, we were wondering about what was the appropriate thing to say (*le bien-dire*, lit. the "saying things well") to a little girl, also conceived by artificial insemination by donor (AID) and brought up by a mother living without a companion who had come to consult us at the Maison Verte. Opinions were divided and we could not find any common ground.

Tomorrow, will we come across little girls resembling their mother like two drops of water, who were born by parthenogenesis or other combinations that are unthinkable today? (We have recently learnt, though, that the paternal genome has the effect of activating the formation of the trophoblast, the beginnings of the placenta ... see Soulé, 2006, p. 138.)

Would the idea of a God, who, as some patients believe, is present in all cases at the moment of conception, suffice to introduce a third party? Put more simply, will the triangularity and space that are necessary between the parent and the child be guaranteed by the fact that this parent lives with a partner, of whatever sex, irrespective of whether they have sexual relations or not? Does the existence of a father "in the mother's head" suffice? And what will happen in the second or third generation? Will the existence of a legislator requiring the registration of the identity of the different parental components be sufficient? And what if the legislator, in so doing, were simply the perverse representative of a society that is itself perverse?

In themselves, these new techniques are neither structuring nor destructuring, Tisseron asserts; everything depends on how they are taken up by the familial and social discourse. I propose that the utterances of parents, in the broad sense of the term, accompanying images, and their listening to the utterances of their children will facilitate the translation and metabolisation of the messages because it will also actualise the ethical asymmetry, the "matricial position" from which they address and speak to them. In my view, that is what will reduce the risks of the "pathogenisation" of these images as well as messages of other kinds, and it is what underlies the possibilities of transformation as much in life as in the analytic situation.

To approach this question, then, which aims to distinguish what comes from outside and what comes from inside as far as the origin of the child's representations is concerned, I have proposed to take into account the "primacy of that which comes from the outside" and its ethical implications.

Questions related to the inevitable existence of the emission of "compromised" messages, addressed to children by adults who have them in their care, questions related to the adequacy of the parents' capacity to contain, metabolise, and transform, initially for themselves and then for their child, the shame, the conscious and unconscious guilt, and the suffering to which they have been subjected, the history and the conscious and unconscious motivations of his or her conception, will be raised again and again. Finally, questions will be asked relating to the "good enough response", to the revelation of what is representable and to the "keeping secret" of what is not or cannot be represented yet . . . perhaps. Here, the ethical position will consist in "saying things well" (*bien-dire*) but never in "saying everything". This presupposes the equally inevitable need for a parent who is capable of offering the child the "matricial space" that the latter is fundamentally in need of. A parent who is capable, that is, of "meeting" the needs of this child as a matter of priority over his or her own needs, with another adult who deserves to be designated by the child as his or her father or mother because this adult is recognised as such by the partner: "It is not the one who conceived me that is called father", the Midrash (ancient commentary on part of the Hebrew scriptures) says, "but the one who took care of me, the one who helped me grow up".

Appendix 2. Milena*

In her book, *Milena*, Buber-Neumann (1986) writes:

> The combination of permanent monotony and menace that formed the atmosphere of the camp increased the intensity of the authentic friendships that existed amongst the prisoners; we were abandoned to our fate even more than those who have been shipwrecked are. The SS had the power of life or death over us, and each day could be the last. In this situation (atrociously human), intellectual, spiritual and physical forces developed in us that, in the normal course of existence, remain buried most of the time. In this deadly atmosphere, the feeling of being necessary to another human being was the greatest conceivable happiness and gave a meaning to life; it gave one the strength to survive . . . (p. 209, translated for this edition)

Further on, Anicka Kvapilova, another young Czech inmate from Ravensbruck, writes,

---

* This text was written in August 2004, while I was simultaneously tracing the broad outlines of the project of this book.

I found myself among a group of new Czech arrivals, at the entrance
to the infirmary. We had been sent there to undergo the medical examination required on entering the camp. Demoralised and shaken by
our first impressions of the camp, by the horror that we were discov-
ering, racked by fear, we were waiting for the next torture. And at that
point Milena appeared at the door, at the top of the stairs, and, making
a friendly gesture with her hand, called out to us: "I wish you a warm
welcome, girls!" It came from the bottom of her heart, as if she was
inviting each one of us to her home, like a hostess receiving her friends
. . . It was the first true manifestation of humanity in the middle of all
this inhumanity – (Oh! How human it was, too!) (pp. 209–210, translated for this edition)

For me, Milena's greeting echoes the propositions of Levinas. The
declaration of hospitality, this address to the prisoners speaks for
itself. Anicka could cling to life with all the force of her sexual life
drives that had been buried up until then . . . it was the greatest happiness conceivable, giving meaning to life, giving the strength to survive. Something of this illusion is derived, Freud tells us, from "moral
narcissism". When Milena greets the girls, her life narcissism erupts
and awakens in Anicka the trace of this moment when there was
someone to greet her into the world and to introduce her to her own
humanisation.

The matricial space that infiltrates primal seduction is no less enigmatic.

Ethical asymmetry, transcending oneself for the other, is never
justified by the subject. It is felt to be stronger than him. When parents
are questioned about what often appears to be their "sacrificial"
conduct, or a soldier who risks his life to save another injured soldier
is questioned about the motives of his action, they or he will say, "It's
like that, it's natural; it's instinct!" Now it is this same kind of explanation—which is not an explanation for psychoanalysis—that we
meet with in any individual who displays behaviour of an instinctual
type, acting out, with more or less serious consequences, "It's instinc-
tive, it's human", or, "It's stronger than me."

In neither of these situations does the subject see himself as the
agent of his acts. If these acts are carried out in this way, it is, of
course, because they are the product of the unconscious. The subject
cannot regard himself as the agent of actions that seem alien to him.
Laplanche has argued that this unconscious is sexual and that, as the

other is at the origin of the formation of the unconscious, the manifestations of the unconscious are on this account doubly alien to the subject. "The other . . . is present," Laplanche (1999c) writes, "from the very beginning . . . from the establishment of the psychical apparatus, as both the other of the message and the specular other" (p. 40). Although he is not referring directly to the other of Lacan, perhaps he is thinking of the other in the form of the mother of the Winnicottian gaze / mirror. Why separate a specular other from the other of the message? (This specular other refers, for me, to the ethical aspect of the message.)

Once again, the capacity for responsibility for the other might, of course, be considered as superego-based, narcissistic, and masochistic, but I would argue that it is non-reducible, infiltrating every parental message and ensuring its metabolisation.

If language is given to the child by an adult world and allows for the potentialty of speech (neurologically given) to expose itself (at the risk, in certain cases, of not developing or in a very reduced manner), if the potential for curiosity and creativity exists, just as the potential for symbolisation and self-theorisation exists, then, if this potential is to be realised, primal seduction and an encounter with an adult environment that assumes responsibility for the child is necessary on account of the compromised messages of the adult sexual unconscious. To be satisfied with the position, "all that goes without saying", does not seem to me to be sufficiently demanding, even if attempting to discover the vagaries of it might be pretentious, if not insolent.

But do not these potential judgements concerning the pretentiousness and insolence of this quest not point to that *something more* that we would, none the less, prefer not to classify as belonging to the domain of mysticism? (Unless "the divine proves to be analysable" . . . see Kristeva, 2008).

So, although we are always at risk of sliding back and forth between guilt and responsibility for the other, I think that we can envisage a developmental axis of responsibility which, though it often gets mixed up with guilt and, therefore, with its various masochistic manifestations, does not, however, have a very particular origin and is not, at each instant, conflictual. It is a question of imagining an adult in a position of responsibility for a child who, in order to assume this responsibility, did not only have to overcome a sense of guilt linked to his "potential drive-based madness (*folie pulsionnelle potentielle*)".

Appendix 3.
Responding to (*répondre à*), answering for (*répondre de*): Laplanche and responsibility in Levinas*

In his article entitled "Responsabilité et réponse" (1999b), Laplanche begins by pointing out that Freud, in his paper on telepathy, examines the subject of responsibility in the context of the subject's responsibility for his dreams. He notes that Freud, who is discussing demonic possession on the one hand and telepathy on the other, operates a Ptolemaic reclosure, a self-centring, a recentring on the biological, without taking into consideration what he himself had evoked, that is to say, "the primacy of the other", the first other in relation to the perception of every message—every message being proffered first by this other (p. 160). Then Laplanche emphasises the difficulty, in a "universe which, from Descartes to Kant, to Husserl, to Heidegger, and to Freud, is irremediably Ptolemaic", in perceiving a Copernican approach, as he understands it, that is to say, as operating a decentring of the subject in relation to himself. It is at this point that he refers to "his recent and largely fortuitous encounter with Levinas's thought. It was more of an overlapping" (translated for this edition).

---

* The main part of this text was written in August 2007.

(And yet, in 1990, Laplanche wrote a paper entitled "Le temps et l'autre" (1992b); on p. 255, he notes that this title took up the very title of Levinas's book to which I referred in the first part of my book (see Levinas, *Time and the Other*, 1948).) He recalls that, as a young student in *khâgne* (a two-year preparatory course for the *Ecole Normale Supérieure*), where he was studying philosophy, he had studied Levinas's work, *The Theory of Intuition in Husserl's Phenomenology* (1930). (In fact, Levinas is recognised in the French philosophical world for having introduced it, with this work, to the thinking of Husserl, which was little known in France before then.)

Laplanche recognises in Levinas's work the Copernicism to which he himself is attached. In Levinas and Laplanche alike, primacy comes from the other. Admittedly, as he points out, Levinas' reflections were based on Husserl, who had posited the relationship with the other as an irreducible intentionality of the subject and, consequently, as Ptolemaic. Yet, in the end, Levinas opposes Husserl, for he proposes the idea of a rupture of intentionality (1982b, p. 32). However, Levinas—admittedly, he is not an exception among philosophers, apart perhaps, from Merleau-Ponty—errs on the side of adultocentrism. But the "primacy of childhood", Laplanche (1999b) writes,

> takes us back to a situation that is not one of self-centring, a situation that is not even one of reciprocity (. . . or of interaction), an essentially asymmetrical situation in which I am passive and disarmed in relation to the other's message. It is a situation whose trace we refuse to recognise, in the structure of the alienness or extraneousness of persecution, of revelation or of dreams, but also in the structure of the extraneousness of the analytic session, as and where it was discovered. (p. 164, translated for this edition)

At this point, Laplanche reverses Levinas's "answering for" (*répondre de*) into "responding to" (*répondre à*). He iterates his theory of generalised seduction in these terms, "It begins with the confrontation of the human infant with so-called enigmatic sexual messages – they are enigmatic because they are so [I would add: also] for the other, for the adult who transmits them". The

> treatment of this message by the infant, whose means for doing so are necessarily inadequate . . . is an attempt at translation, a *response* that

is always inadequate because it leaves out what I call 'thing-presenta-tions' which are nothing but unconscious signifiers. Imperfect trans-lation, failure of this translation, it is a matter here of giving a content to what Freud called 'primal repression', that is, the constitution of the unconscious. (Laplanche, 1999b, p. 164, translated for this edition)

We can see clearly here how, for Laplanche, the unconscious has a wholly individual origin and cannot be "reduced to a biological id".

With the notion of "responding to", Laplanche remains preoccu-pied by the messages of the other.

This leaves us with the open question of the "answering for". Unless this "answering for", corresponding to the adult—an uncon-scious seducer but equally in a position of responsibility for the other—is included in this "responding to" of the child *via* his own unconscious activity of repression. In this view, the child might be said to repress because included in the enigma of the message is the very fact of the adult's repression, which itself results from this asym-metrical responsibility for the child. The child would, thus, appropri-ate subjectively the unconscious motive of the adult's activity of repression. (My views were refined subsequently, and after this text had been written (see Part IV).)

Laplanche relates the story of Job, who is interpellated by an enig-matic message following all the misfortunes that suddenly fell upon him (1999b, p. 165): "Job believes that he is being asked to 'answer for' ... What have I done to be treated like this?" (translated for this edition). More than responsibility, it is a question, in my view, of the sadistic work of the superego as described by Freud in *Civilization and its Discontents* (1930a). "He reasons, he justifies himself, when respect would require silence," Laplanche writes (translated for this edition). It seems to me that, in his analysis, Laplanche confuses guilt, which has its origin in the superego, and responsibility.

I would say that Job, at grips with a sadistic superego and inva-ded by persecuting guilt, attributes the cause of the events that are demoralising him to himself. As a result, rather than facing up to his helplessness, to this return to the fundamental state of distress, to the basic state of helplessness (for which Laplanche has coined the term *dés-aide*), he prefers to "tell himself" that he is at the origin of the sufferings that have befallen him. "He answers when respect would require silence" (Laplanche, 1999b, p. 166, translated for this edition).

In fact, he does not answer for anyone; he is only concerned with re-establishing, let us say even with shoring up, in fantasy, his narcissism, which is threatened. He wonders where his guilt lies. There is no question here of responsibility. There is no one else he is concerned about. There is no evidence that he is concerned about his relations or his children as such. He is preoccupied purely with himself.

In fact, Levinas, too, is sometimes confused in his definition of responsibility, slipping himself between guilt and responsibility when he turns to Dostoevsky for help (*Ethics and Infinity*, 1982b, p. 101).

To return to Laplanche: he continues by discussing the origin of cruelty in man, which cannot be found in animals. "One would have to shut one's eyes in order not to recognise in cruelty something quite different from war (albeit closely connected with it) . . . that is, sadism, even *sexual* sadomasochism" (1999b, p. 168, in a footnote, translated for this edition: cf. the term "Shoah", often referred to as the "Holocaust", with a sacrificial meaning, or reduced to a natural catastrophe, with the risk of effacing its constituting dimension of destructivity all too human in origin). For Laplanche, what may be called the sexual death drive is neither biological nor instinctual:

> . . . it is linked to the sexual fantasies which inhabit our unconscious, to which our dreams bear witness each day. I do not see how these cruel fantasies, involving the suffering of the other and the imagination of this suffering, can be situated on the side of nature and the innate. (p. 169, translated for this edition)

And here I am in total agreement with him.

However, by the same token, I do not see how loving fantasies, involving the other's well-being and the imagination of this well-being, can be situated on the side of nature and the innate. "The human infant, who is not in a position to do so, must respond to messages imbued with sexuality", Laplanche writes. I would add, imbued as much by the sexuality of life as of death. When everything goes as well as possible, the sexuality of life dominates; the messages will come from a primal seduction bathed in responsibility for the other. They will be at the foundations of the work of translation that is necessarily partial. "In the primordial communication," Laplanche (2007b) writes,

> the adult message cannot be grasped in its contradictory totality. For example, in the typical model of breast-feeding, there is a mixture of love and hate, appeasement and excitation, milk and breast, the 'containing' breast and the sexually exciting breast. (p. 207)

The innate or acquired codes that the infant makes use of are, therefore, insufficient for coping with these enigmatic messages. "The infant must resort to a new code," Laplanche continues, "at once improvised by him and invoking the schemas furnished by his cultural environment . . . The translation or attempt at translation establishes in the psychical apparatus a preconscious level" (Laplanche, 2007b, pp. 207–208). A process of historicisation will, thus, become possible.

> But because the message is compromised and incoherent, located on two incompatible planes, the translation is always imperfect, with certain residues left aside. These are the remainders that constitute the unconscious in the proper Freudian sense of the term . . . necessarily marked by the sexual, since it owes its origin to the compromising of the adult message by the sexual. (pp. 207–208)

As it is clear that the child will have to completely reorganise the implanted message, the question arises as to what will enable him to do this. To do it, he needs a symbol-generating object. As Laplanche points out in his last proposition of "Three meanings of the term 'Unconscious'", alongside the partial failure of translation one can have a total failure. The intromitted message cannot be translated and will constitute "the enclaved unconscious—without historicisation, it will remain under a thin layer of consciousness" (p. 208). Concerning the causes of such a radical failure of translation, Laplanche opens up a path of investigation: "Can someone be 'possessed' by messages that he has failed to translate?" (p. 211). While the causes are multiple, I am interested in those linked to an exigency or need for ethics as responsibility for the other, a need that is not sufficiently met where the child is concerned. It is when the enigmatic messages are more the product of the sexual life drives of the parents that a translation, necessarily partial, can take place, and with it the constitution of an unconscious. On the other hand when these messages are primarily the product of the sexual death drives, they will be largely untranslatable and enclaved; they will "possess" the child's psyche, and, later, the psyche of the adult who will transmit them to the next generation without any possibility of metabolisation, unless, in the best of cases, it has been possible to do thorough psychoanalytic or psychotherapeutic work.

In his chapter related to the fundamental anthropological situation, Laplanche (2007a) refers once again to Levinas. Discussing alterity, the unconscious, seduction, as well as the seduction of the analytic situation and its irreducibility, he writes,

> There was an extraordinary conjunction of the alterity described in the situation of seduction [he is alluding to the "first theory of seduction", the Freudian theory of seduction] and the double alterity of the experience of the unconscious within us and of the experience of the analytic situation. Freud's stroke of genius is to trace back the alterity of the unconscious and the alterity in the transference to the alterity of the originary situation of seduction. This alterity is a radical asymmetry. (p. 101)

Although, for the philosophers, relations are always adult–adult, the adult other being "reduced" for phenomenologists by the constitution of the other, he writes, "In the post-phenomenology of the Levinasian type, the other is indeed irreducible in the face-to-face relation". But he adds, "Levinas does not take account of what produces the irreducible, that is to say the unconscious, the sexual unconscious, the infantile sexual unconscious." (Laplanche, 2007a, p. 101).

But Levinas touches on this asymmetrical dimension which is just as irreducible as the interpellation by the fragility of the newborn in distress, even if he does not refer to it directly, a task that was taken up by Jonas. This interpellation is formulated by Levinas in the words "Thou shall not kill". Could this be a message enkysted in the mother's psyche that originated in her own mother: "You must because you must"? Or the manifestation of the parental ego ideal, largely made up of translated messages? But, then, does the ego ideal assume a preconscious character? Is it desexualised? Or, alternatively, does it have its origin precisely in largely translatable messages because it is the work of expressions of the sexual life drives of the first generation? This would not imply a radical translation, but always a translation with a remainder.

It might be posited, therefore, that the irreducibility of the other's face, its approach through the caress, through sensibility, through vulnerability, and yet without there being any choice—whether I like it or not—comes from the unconscious, from the untranslatable remainder of these messages that have been implanted (but not intromitted owing to the very fact of this responsibility for the other which shaped them); a remainder that has retained the trace of them. (My positions on this subject have evolved owing to a certain disatisfaction with this hypothesis, and I now envisage a triple inscription in the child's psyche: see Part IV.)

For Laplanche, what is irreducible is the asymmetry between the infant and adult. The adult has a sexual unconscious but, at the beginning of life, the infant does not. With attachment theories, what Laplanche has qualified as the self-preservative, dyadic, and reciprocal dimension in the relations between parents and children has been given a place again. What is lacking, he says, is the need to take asymmetry into account at the unconscious level: the parent–infant dialogue is scrambled and parasited from the beginning by the intervention of the adult unconscious. If the adult–infant situation is one that reactivates the adult's infantile unconcious drives, I would say that the adult–infant situation reactivates just as much the binding aspect of these drives, producing messages that are largely infiltrated by the sexuality of life. The infant is identified by his or her mother as the one for whom she is implacably responsible. "This notion of *identification by*", Laplanche (2007a) writes, "would certainly enrich the question of the ego ideal" (p. 111). (I have tried to take this line of thinking further.)

I will conclude with a final commentary on Laplanche's article "Responsabilité et réponse" (1999b), where he alludes to an earlier article, "Réparation et rétribution pénales, une perspective psychanalytique" (1992). I have myself long considered that every criminal act must be judged, and that an announcement of the sentence linked to the crime and to the prejudice suffered by the victim should in all cases be pronounced. This in no ways implies putting the sentence into effect. Announcing that a murderer has been sentenced to death and carrying out the death penalty are two completely different stages. The first proclaims that there has been an injustice and that it must be denounced. The second is an act of arrogance and a repetition of the injustice itself, betraying the incapacity of the judges to contain their judgement. There is an intrinsic contradiction here, to my mind. Clamouring for someone's death and executing them are two different things. "Someone who thirsts for justice", Laplanche (1999b, p. 175, translated for this edition) writes, "is screaming against the torturer in himself". True enough, but he is screaming, I would add, at the other torturer, so that the victim's (the victim that he was) right to justice, which has been trampled on, is recognised. Space for compassion for the other person can then emerge. As for the torturer in ourselves, he must be recognised and we have to come to terms with the impossibility of appeasing him.

Laplanche insists,

> One of the things that I think I know is that psychoanalysis, the analytic situation, as it was inaugurated by Freud, is the major, if not only site where the human being can try to re-elaborate his response, his responses, to the strangeness of the sexual, first of all within himself, and outside perhaps. (1999b, p. 172, translated for this edition)

My question remains, then, what is it, in this situation, that allows his responses to this strangeness to be re-elaborated if it is not the reactualisation in the analytic encounter of what should have been, and was partially, experienced at the beginning of life, which is the weaving of primal seduction with this responsibility for the other, the work of the ethical seduction of the analytic situation?

Why was Laplanche not interested in this strange human phenomenon of responsibility for the other, regarding it as something that is self-evident? For Wittgenstein (cited in Assoun, 1988, p. 196), ethics commands one to "come onto the stage as a person and to say I" (translated for this edition). He adds, "If a man could write a book on ethics, this book, like an explosion, would destroy all the books in the world" (cited in Assoun, 1988, p. 196, translated for this edition). In other words, ethics frightens us more than the sexual and its manifestations. If ethics designates something as a factuality, and if Freud was able to tell Oskar Pfister that he did not worry much about the subject of good and evil, it seems, none the less, that he had less difficulty with evil than he did with the good. In fact, as Wittgenstein (1939, p. 46, cited by Assoun, 1988, p. 196) writes, "Being psychoanalysed is a bit like eating from the tree of knowledge. The knowledge thus acquired poses new ethical problems for us; but it contributes nothing to their resolution" (translated for this edition). For Wittgenstein, psychoanalysis lacks spirituality.

It is true that psychoanalysis can do good without resolving the question of the good, Assoun reminds us. Freud (1923b) wrote,

> If anyone were inclined to put forward the paradoxical proposition that the normal man is not only far more immoral than he believes, but also far more moral than he knows, psycho-analysis, on whose findings the first half of the assertion rests, would have no objection to raise against the second half. (p. 52)

We can add here his own footnote: "This proposition is only apparently a paradox; it simply states that human nature has a far greater extent, both for good and for evil, than it thinks it has – i.e. than its ego is aware of through conscious perception" (p. 52, fn. 1). If the question of knowledge by the ego (*Pcpt-Cs*) of its limits is specifically indicated here by Freud, and if that of evil and its "unknowability" is effectively the field of psychoanalysis, that of the good, which is also barely knowable by the ego (*Pcpt-Cs*), remains open.

REFERENCES

Akhtar, S. (1999). The distinction between needs and wishes: implications for psychoanalytic theory and technique. *Journal of the American Psychoanalytic Association, 47*(1): 113–145.

Alvarez, A. (1992). *Live Company: Psychoanalytic Therapy with Austistic, Borderline, Deprived and Abused Children.* New York: Taylor & Francis.

Amado-Levi-Valensi, E. (1962). *Le dialague psychanalytique.* Paris: Presses Universitaires de France, 1972.

André, J. (1995). *Aux origines féminines de la sexualité.* Paris: Presses Universitaires de France, 2004.

André, J. (Ed.) (1999). *De la passion.* Paris: Presses Universitaires de France.

André, J. (2002). Borderline transfert. In: *Transfert et états limites* (pp. 11–22). Paris: Presses Universitaires de France.

André, J. (2006). *La folie maternelle ordinaire.* Paris: Presses Universitaires de France.

André, J. (2009). L'évènement et la temporalité. L'après-coup dans la cure. *L'après-coup, Revue Française de Psychanalyse, 73*(5), 1285–1352.

Anzieu, D. (1974). *The Skin Ego.* New Haven, CT: Yale University Press, 1989.

Aron, L. (1996). *A Meeting of Minds: Mutuality in Psychoanalysis.* Hillsdale, NJ: The Analytic Press.

Ashur, D. (2009). The healing power of love: the literary / analytic bond of marriage in Freud's essay on Gradiva. *International Journal of Psychoanalysis, 90*(3): 595–612.

Assoun, P.-L. (1984). *L'entendement freudien. Logos et Ananké.* Paris: Gallimard.

Assoun, P.-L. (1988). *Freud et Wittgenstein.* Paris: Presses Universitaires de France.

Assoun, P.-L. (1993). Le sujet et l'autre chez Levinas et Lacan. *Rue Descartes, Collège de philosophie, Logiques de l'éthique, 7*: 123–145.

Aulagnier, P. (1975). *The Violence of Interpretation. From Pictogram to Statement.* London: Routledge, 2001.

Baldacci, J.-L. (2005). Dès le début, la sublimation. *Revue Française de Psychanalyse, 69*(5): 1405–1474.

Benjamin, J. (1988). The first bond. In: *The Bonds of Love: Psychoanalysis, Feminism and the Problem of Domination* (pp. 11–50). London: Virago, 1993.

Bick, E. (1968). The experience of the skin in early object-relations. *International Journal of Psychoanalysis, 49* (2), pp. 484–486.

Bion, W. R. (1962a). *Learning from Experience.* London: Heinemann.

Bion, W. R. (1962b). *Second Thoughts.* London: Heinemann.

Bion, W. R. (1963). *Elements of Psychoanalysis.* London: Heinemann [reprinted London: Karnac, 1993].

Blass, R. (2009). Psychoanalytic controversies. On the idea that analysts should acknowledge to their patients that they have failed them: a clinical debate. *International Journal of Psychoanalysis, 90*: 437–439.

Bleichmar, S. (1985). *Aux origines du sujet psychique dans la psychanalyse de l'enfant.* Paris: Presses Universitaires de France.

Bleger, J. (1967). Psychoanalysis and the psychoanalytic frame. *International Journal of Psychoanalysis, 48*: 511–519.

Bokanowski, T. (2004). *Le processus psychanalytique.* Paris: Presses Universitaires de France.

Bollas, C. (1978). L'esprit de l'objet et l'épiphanie du sacré. *Nouvelle Revue de Psychanalyse, 18*: 253–262.

Bollas, C. (1987). The transformational object. In: *The Shadow of the Object.* London: Free Association Books

Bonnefoy, Y. (1991). *Giacometti.* Paris: Flammarion.

Brun, D. (1990a). L'énigme de la féminité chez Freud, la théorie en déroute. In: *La maternité et le féminin* (pp. 137–161). Paris: Denoël.

Brun, D. (1990b). Le refus de la féminité, de l'énigme au refus: un trajet réparateur. In: *La maternité et le féminin* (pp. 183–200). Paris: Denoël.

Brun, D. (1990c). Identification inconsciente à la mère. In: *La maternité et le féminin* (pp. 201–209). Paris: Denoël.

Brun, D. (1990d). Les sources infantiles de la théorie chez Freud. In: *La maternité et le feminine* (pp. 211–230). Paris: Denoël.

Brun, D. (1991). La maternité dans les écrits freudiens et post-freudiens. *Etudes freudiennes, 32*: 9–34.

Buber-Neumann, M. (1986). *Milena*. Paris: Seuil.

Calin, R., & Sebbah, F. D. (2002). *Le vocabulaire de Levinas*. Poitiers: Ellipses.

Carhart-Harris R.-L., & Friston K.-J. (2010). The default-mode, ego-functions and free-energy: a neurobiological account of Freudian ideas. *Brain, 133*: 1265–1283.

Chabert, C. (1999). Les voix intérieures. Les enjeux de la passivité. *Revue française de psychanalyse* (Spécial congress), *5*: 1446–1488.

Chabert, C. (2006). Le moi, le soi, et le sujet. In: F. Richard & S. Wainrib (Eds.), *La subjectivation* (pp. 123–138). Paris: Dunod.

Chalier, C. (2002). Désir et appel, Levinas et la psychanalyse. *Le Coq-héron, 171*(4): 13–25.

Chetrit-Vatine, V. (2002). Case study. In: K. Gilmore, Child psychoanalysis: cathecting and verbalizing affects in a new relationship: aspects of the analytic method in work with children (Report to Panel). *International Journal of Psychoanalysis, 83*(2): 473–477.

Chetrit-Vatine, V. (2004a). Primal seduction, matricial space and asymmetry in the psychoanalytic encounter. *International Journal of Psychoanalysis, 85*(4): 841–856.

Chetrit-Vatine, V. (2004b). La personne de l'analyste ou . . . un espace matriciel pour Mr E. *Revue française de psychanalyse* (Le processus psychanalytique), *68*(5): 1751–1757.

Chetrit-Vatine, V. (2005). De l'emprise à la caresse, le temps . . . d'un moment sublimatoire. *La sublimation, Revue Française de Psychanalyse, 69*(5): 1495–1503.

Chetrit-Vatine, V. (2007). Signifiance de la signifiance; ou la dimension éthique de l'écoute et du dire de l'analyste. *La cure de parole, Revue française de psychanalyse, 71*(5): 1497–1502.

Chetrit-Vatine, V. (2008a). Some thoughts related to the ethical seduction of the analytic encounter. *International Journal of Psychoanalysis, 89*: 491–496.

Chetrit-Vatine, V. (2008b). Aux origines de l'appropriation subjective: passion de l'analyste et seduction éthique de la situation analytique. In: F. Rousillon (Ed.), *Affect et symbolisation*. International Colloquium, University of Lyon.

Coblence, F. (1994). Et l'amour, et l'autre. *Nouvelle Revue Française de Psychanalyse, 49*: 165–183.

Coblence, F. (2003). La nature fait bien les choses. *Libres cahiers pour la psychanalyse*, (L'enfance du féminin), *8*: 25–39.

Critchley, S. (1998). Le traumatisme originel. Levinas avec la psychanalyse. *Rue Descartes*, Collège de philosophie, *19*, 165–174.

Danon-Boileau, L. (1999). Affect, éprouvé, émotion, sentiment: notations terminologiques. *Revue française de psychanalyse, 63*(1): 9–12.

De Beauvoir, S. (1949). *Le deuxième sexe*. Paris: Gallimard.

Dejours, C. (2001). *Le corps d'abord. Corps biologique, corps érotique et sens moral*. Paris: Payot, 2003.

De M'Uzan, M. (1994). *La bouche de l'inconscient: essais sur l'interprétation*. Paris: Gallimard.

Denis, P. (2007). L'éthique du psychanalyste. *Nouvelle revue de psychosociologie, 3*: 83–93.

Derrida, J. (1967). *Writing and Difference*, A. Bass (Trans.). London: Routledge & Kegan Paul, 1978.

Desche, Y. (2008). Vivre pour raconter ou raconter pour vivre. Processus psychanalytique avec des patientes ayant subi des sévices sexuels (Lecture given in Hebrew to the Israeli Psychoanalytic Society on 11 November, 2008).

Donnet, J.-L. (1987). L'acte de conscience, le devenir conscient: compte rendu des journées sur la séduction en psychanalyse. *Etudes freudiennes, 29*: 166–167.

Faure-Pragier, S. (1999). Le désir d'enfant comme substitut du pénis manquant: une théorie stérile de la féminité. In: J. Schaeffer, M. Cournut-Janin, S. Faure-Pragier, & F. Guignard, *Clés pour le féminin* (pp. 41–56). Paris: Presses Universitaires de France.

Faure-Pragier, S. (2000). *La perversion ou la vie. Klim, l'homme aux deux noms*. Paris: Presses Universitaires de France

Fédida, P. (2002). Le psychanalyste, un état-limite? In: *Transfert et état-limites* (pp. 59–68). Paris: Presses Universitaires de France.

Ferenczi, S. (1928). The elasticity of psycho-analytic technique. In: *Final Contributions to the Problems and Methods of Psychoanalysis* (pp. 87–101). New York: Basic Books, 1955.

Ferenczi, S. (1932). The confusion of tongues between adult and the child. The language of tenderness and of passion. In: *Final Contributions to the Problems and Methods of Psychoanalysis* (pp. 156–167). New York: Basic Books, 1955.

Ferenczi, S. (1934). Some thoughts on trauma (included in *Notes and Fragments*, 1920–1933). *The Selected Papers of Sandor Ferenczi, vols 2 and 3*. New York: Basic Books, 1955.

Freud, S. (1895). *A Project for a Scientific Psychology. S.E., 1:* 281–397. London: Hogarth.

Freud, S. (1900a). *The Interpretation of Dreams. S.E., 4 & 5.* London: Hogarth.

Freud, S. (1901b). *The Psychopathology of Everyday Life. S.E., 6:* 1–279. London: Hogarth.

Freud, S. (1905d). *Three Essays on the Theory of Sexuality. S.E., 7:* 135–243. London: Hogarth.

Freud, S. (1907a). Delusions and dreams in Jensen's '*Gradiva*'. *S.E., 9:* 1–95. London: Hogarth.

Freud, S. (1908d). "Civilized" sexual morality and modern nervous illness. *S.E., 9:* 179–204. London: Hogarth.

Freud, S. (1910c). *Leonardo da Vinci and a Memory of his Childhood. S.E., 11:* 59–137. London: Hogarth.

Freud, S. (1912–1913). *Totem and Taboo. S.E., 13:* 1–161. London: Hogarth.

Freud, S. (1915a). Observations on transference-love. *S.E., 12:* 159–171. London: Hogarth.

Freud, S. (1919e). 'A child is being beaten'. *S.E., 17:* 179–204. London: Hogarth.

Freud, S. (1923b). *The Ego and the Id. S.E., 19:* 3–66. London: Hogarth.

Freud, S. (1924c). The economic problem of masochism. *S.E., 19:* 157–170. London: Hogarth.

Freud, S. (1925i). Some additional notes on dream-interpretation as a whole. *S.E., 19:* 125–138. London: Hogarth.

Freud, S. (1930a). *Civilization and its Discontents. S.E., 21:* 57–146. London: Hogarth.

Freud, S. (1931b). Female sexuality. *S.E., 21:* 223–243. London: Hogarth.

Gampel, Y. (2005). *Ces parents qui vivent à travers moi, les enfants des guerres.* Paris: Fayard.

Golse, B. (2006a). *L'être-bébé.* Paris: Presses Universitaires de France.

Golse, B. (2006b). Vie foetale, transgénérationnel et après-coup. In: *Anthropologie du fœtus* (pp. 1–9). Paris: Dunod.

Gori, R. (2002). *Logique des passions.* Paris: Flammarion.

Green, A. (1979). Le silence du psychanalyste. In: *La folie privée, psychanalyse des cas-limites* (pp. 365–400). Paris: Gallimard, Folio-essais, 424, 1990.

Green, A. (1980). Passions and their vicissitudes. In: *On Private Madness* (pp. 214–253). London: Karnac, 1997.

Green, A. (1986). *On Private Madness.* London: Hogarth [reprinted London: Karnac, 1997].

Guignard, F. (1999). Maternel ou féminin? Le "roc d'origine" comme gardien du tabou de l'inceste avec la mère. In: J. Schaeffer, M. Cournut-

Janin, S. Faure-Pragier, & F. Guignard, *Clés pour le féminin* (pp. 11–24). Paris: Presses Universitaires de France.

Guillaumin, J. (1999). Transfert et contre-transfert ensemble comme moyen de séduction de la pulsion de mort. *Transferts, Monographie de Psychanalyse*. Paris: Presses Universitaires de France.

Guyomard, P. (1998). *Le désir d'éthique*. Paris: Aubier.

Heenen-Wolff, S. (2003). La première séductrice. L'enfance du féminin. *Libres cahiers pour la psychanalyse*, 2(8): 89–99.

Heimann, P. (1950). On counter-transference. *International Journal of Psychoanalysis*, 31: 9–15.

Hoffman, I. (1998). *Ritual and Spontaneity in the Psychoanalytic Process: A Dialectical Constructivist View*. Hillsdale, NJ: Analytic Press.

Jacobson, E. (1964). *The Self and the Object World*. New York: International Universities Press.

Jonas, H. (1979a). *The Imperative of Responsibility*, H. Jonas & D. Kerr (Trans). Chicago, IL: University of Chicago Press, 1984.

Jonas, H. (1979b). *Le principe responsabilité*, J. Greisch (Trans). Paris: Flammarion, 1998.

Jonas, H. (1984). *Le concept de Dieu après Auschwitz. Une voix juive*. Paris: Rivages poche, Petite Bibliothèque, 1994.

Kemp, P. (1977). *Levinas, une introduction philosophique*. La Versane: Encre Marine.

Killingmo, B. (1995). Affirmation in psychoanalysis. *International Journal of Psychoanalysis*, 76: 503–518.

Kohut, H. (1970). On courage. In: P. Orenstein (Ed.), *Search of the Self*, vol. 3 (pp. 129–182). Madison, CT: International Universities Press.

Kristeva, J. (2005). *La haine et le pardon. Pouvoirs et limites de la psychanalyse*. Paris: Fayard

Kristeva, J. (2007). *Seule, une femme*. Paris: L'Aube.

Kristeva, J. (2008). Cet incroyable besoin de croire: le séculaire et le sacré en début de 21e siècle. First interdisciplinary conference, Psycho-analysis and Other Disciplines: *Mishkenot Shaananim*, Jerusalem, 18–20 November (Acts to be published); see also Google, Julia Kristeva, Forum international des religions, Jerusalem, November 19–24, 2008.

Kulka, R. (1998). Discussion of my scientific presentation at the end of training, Israel Institute of Psychoanalysis, 10 February, in Hebrew.

Kulka, R. (2005). Entre le tragique et la compassion (Introduction to the Hebrew edition of Heinz Kohut's *How Does Analysis Cure*). Tel-Aviv, Am-Oved, "Psycho-analyza", p. 22.

Lacan, J. (1986). *The Ethics of Psychoanalysis, 1959–1960. The Seminar of Jacques Lacan Book VII*, D. Potter (Trans). New York: Norton, 1997.

Lanouzière, J. (1992). De l'allaitement comme séduction originelle et comme scène originaire de seduction. In: *Colloque international de psychanalyse* (pp. 151–168). Paris: Presses Universitaires de France.

Laplanche, J. (1987). *New Foundations for Psychoanalysis*, D. Macey (Trans.). Oxford: Basil Blackwell, 1989.

Laplanche, J. (1992a). Reparation et rétribution pénales, une perspective psychanalytique. In: *La revolution copernicienne inachèvée: travaux 1967–92* (pp. 167–183). Paris: Aubier.

Laplanche, J. (1992b). Time and the other. In: J. Fletcher (Ed.), *Essays on Otherness* (pp. 234–259). London: Routledge, 1999.

Laplanche, J. (1992c). Implantation, intromission. In: J. Fletcher (Ed.), *Essays on Otherness* (pp. 133–137). London: Routledge, 1999.

Laplanche, J. (1992d). Du transfert, sa provocation par l'analyste. *Psychanalyse à l'université*, 17(65): 3–22.

Laplanche, J. (1995). Seduction, persecution, revelation. In: J. Fletcher (Ed.), *Essays on Otherness* (pp. 166–196). London: Routledge, 1999.

Laplanche, J. (1999a). A short treatise on the unconscious. In: J. Fletcher (Ed.), *Essays on Otherness* (pp. 84–116). London: Routledge, 1999.

Laplanche, J. (1999b). Responsabilité et réponse. In: *Entre séduction et inspiration: l'homme* (pp. 147–172). Paris: Presses Universitaires de France.

Laplanche, J. (1999c). Sublimation and/or inspiration, J. Fletcher Y& L. Thurston (Trans.). *New Formations*, 48: 30–50.

Laplanche, J. (2007a). Starting from the fundamental anthropological situation. In: *Freud and the Sexual* (pp. 99–113), J. Fletcher, J. House, & N. Ray (Trans). New York: International Psychoanalytic Books, 2011.

Laplanche, J. (2007b). Three meanings of the term "Unconscious". In: *Freud and the Sexual* (pp. 203–222), J. Fletcher, J. House, & N. Ray (Trans.). New York: International Psychoanalytic Books, 2011.

Leibnitz, G. (1714). *The Monadology*, G. MacDonald Ross (Trans.). Oxford: Oxford University Press, 1999.

Levinas, E. (1930). *The Theory of Intuition in Husserl's Phenomenology*, A. Orianne (Trans). Evanston, IL: Northwestern, 1973.

Levinas, E. (1947). *Existence and Existents*, A. Lingis (Trans.). The Hague: Nijhoff, 1978.

Levinas, E. (1948). *Time and the Other*, R. A. Cohen (Trans.). Pittsburg, PA: Duquesne University Press, 1987.

Levinas, E. (1961). *Totality and Infinity*, A. Lingis (Trans.). Pittsburg, PA: Duquesne University Press, 1969.

Levinas, E. (1972). *Humanisme de l'autre homme*. Montpellier: Fata Morgana.

Levinas, E. (1974a). *Otherwise than Being*, A. Lingis (Trans.). Pittsburgh, PA: Duquesne University Press, 1981.

Levinas, E. (1974b). *En découvrant l'existence avec Husserl et Heidegger*. Paris: Vrin.

Levinas, E. (1982a). *Ethique comme philosophie première*. Paris: Rivages poche, 1998.

Levinas, E. (1982b). *Ethics and Infinity: Conversations with Philippe Nemo*, R. Cohen (Trans.). Pittsburgh, PA: Duquesne University Press, 1985.

Levinas, E. (1985). Violence of the face. In: P. Hayat (Ed.), *Alterity and Transcendence* (pp. 169–182). New York: Columbia University Press, 1999.

Levinas, E. (1986). *Of God Who Comes to Mind*, B. Bergo (Trans.). Stanford, CA: Stanford University Press, 1998.

Levinas, E. (1987). A propos de Buber, quelques notes. In: *Hors sujet* (pp. 60–69). Paris: Fata Morgana.

Levinas, E. (1993). *God, Death and Time*, B. Bergo (Trans.). Stanford, CA: Stanford University Press, 2000.

Lichtenberg-Ettinger, B. (1997a). The feminine/prenatal weaving inter-subjectivity-as-encounter. *Psychanalytic Dialogue, 17*: 367–405.

Lichtenberg-Ettinger, B. (1997b). Que dirait Eurydice? *Barca! Poésie, politique, psychanalyse*. Paris: BLE Atlelier.

Lichtenberg-Ettinger, B. (1999). *Regard et espace-de-bord matrixiels. Essai psychanalytique sur le féminin et le travail de l'art*. Brussels: La lettre volée, "Essais".

Little, M. (1991). *Psychotic Anxieties and Containment: A Personal Account of an Analysis with Winnicott*. New York: Jason Aronson.

Meir, E. (1994). The dimension of the feminine in Levinas' philosophy. *Iyun, 43*, Bar-Ilan University (in Hebrew).

Meltzer, D. (1988). *The Apprehension of Beauty: The Role of Aesthetic Conflict in Development and Art*. Strathtay, Perthshire: Clunie Press.

Meng, H., & Freud, E. L. (Eds.) (1963). *Psychoanalysis and Faith: Letters of Sigmund Freud & Oskar Pfister*, E. Mosbacher (Trans.). New York: Basic Books.

Mi-Kyung Yi (2007). L'enfant impossible. In: J. André & S. Dreyfus-Asséo (Eds.), *La sexualité infantile de la psychanalyse* (pp. 107–127). Paris: Petite Bibliothèque de psychanalyse, Presses Universitaires de France.

Mitchell, S. A. (1997). *Influence and Autonomy in Psychoanalysis*. Hillsdale, NJ: Analytic Press.

Newberg, A., d'Aquili, E., & Rause, V. (Eds.) (2003). *Pourquoi "Dieu" ne disparaîtra pas. Quand la science explique la religion.* Vannes: Sully.

Noy, P. (1984). The three components of empathy: normal and pathological development. In: J. Lichtenberg, M. Bronstein, & D. Silver (Eds.), *Empathy,* vol. 1 (pp. 167–199). Hillsdale, NJ: Analytic Press, 2007.

Ogden, T. (1989). The autistic–contiguous position. In: *The Primitive Edge of Experience* (pp. 47–81). New York: Jason Aronson.

Ogden, T. (1994). The analytic third: working with intersubjective facts. In: *Subjects of Analysis.* New York: Jason Aronson.

Ouaknin, M.-A. (1992). *Méditations érotiques.* Paris: Balland.

Parat, C. (2006). *Sein de femme, sein de mere.* Paris: Presses Universitaires de France.

Pisanté, J. (2002). Levinas–Winnicott, le rendez-vous manqué. *La psychiatrie de l'enfant,* 45(1): 247–260.

Phillips, A. (1993). Playing mothers. In: *On Kissing , Tickling, and Being Bored: Psychoanalytic Essays on the Unexamined Life* (pp. 101–108). Princeton, NJ: Harvard University Press.

Pontalis, J.-B. (1977). A partir du contre-transfert. Le mort et le vif entrelacés. In: *Entre le rêve et la douleur* (pp. 223–240). Paris: Gallimard.

Pontalis, J.–B. (2000). *Fenêtres.* Paris: Gallimard.

Quinodoz, D. (2002). *Des mots qui touchent: une psychanalyste apprend à parler.* Paris: Presses Universitaires de France.

Racker, H. (1953). A contribution to the problem of countertransference. *International Journal of Psychoanalysis,* 34(4): 313–324.

Rosenberg, B. (1991). Masochisme mortifère et masochisme gardien de la vie. *Monographies de psychanalyse.* Paris: Presses Universitaires de France.

Roussillon, R. (1995a). *Logiques at archaeologiques du cadre.* Paris: Presses Universitaires de France.

Roussillon, R. (1995b). La métapsychologie des processus et la transitionnalité. *Revue française de psychanalyse,* 5: 1351–1528..

Roussillon, R. (2000). La capacité d'être seul en présence de l'analyste et l'appropriation subjective. In: J. Cournut & J. Schaeffer (Eds.), *Pratiques de la psychanalyse, Monographie de psychoanalyse* (pp. 37–49). Paris: Presses Universitaires de France.

Roussillon, R. (2001a). L'objet médium malléable et la conscience de soi. *L'Autre,* 2(2): 241–254.

Roussillon, R. (2001b). *Agonie, clivage, symbolisation. Le fait psychanalytique.* Paris: Presses Universitaires de France.

Roussillon, R. (2005). Aménagements du cadre analytique. In: F. Richard & F. Urribarri (Eds.), *Autour de l'œuvre d'André Green* (pp. 53–65). Paris: Presses Universitaires de France.

Roussillon, R. (2006). Pluralité de l'appropriation subjective. In: F. Richard & S. Wainrib (Eds.), *La subjectivation* (pp. 59–80). Paris: Dunod.

Sartre, J.-P. (1938). *La Nausée*. Paris: Gallimard.

Scarfone, D. (1997). *Laplanche*. Paris: Presses Universitaires de France.

Scarfone, D. (2011). Dans le creux du transfert: l'analyste entre activité et passivité. *Libres cahiers pour la psychanalyse*, 23: 149–161.

Schaeffer, J. (1993a). Horror feminae ou les liaisons non dangereuses. *Revue française de psychanalyse* (Spécial Congrès), 57: 1761–1770.

Schaeffer, J. (1993b). Que veut la femme? ou le scandale du féminin. In: J. Schaeffer, M. Cournut-Janin, S. Faure-Pragier, & F. Guignard, *Clés pour le féminin* (pp. 25–40). Paris: Presses Universitaires de France.

Schaeffer, J. (2008). *Le refus du féminin*. Paris: Presses Universitaires de France.

Schneider, M. (1980). *Freud et le plaisir*. Paris: Denoël.

Schneider, M. (1993). La culpabilité et l'éthique originaire. *Trans*, 2: 189–209.

Sechaud, E. (1999). Interpréter le transfert. In: *Transferts* (pp. 131–150). Paris: Presses Universitaires de France.

Sechaud, E. (2005). Perdre, sublimer. *Revue Française de Psychanalyse*, 69(5): 1309–1379.

Smirnoff, V. (1969). Du style dans l'interprétation. In: *Un promeneur analytique* (pp. 169–190) . Paris: Calmann-Lévy.

Soulé, M. (2006). Regards du pédopsychiatrie sur le foetus. In: J. Bergeret, M. Soulé, & B. Golse (Eds.), *Anthropologie du foetus* (pp. 99–148). Paris: Dunod.

Stein, C. (1986). Quest-ce qu'on t'a fait, à toi, pauvre enfant? *Psychanalyse à l'université*, II(42, 43): 175–243.

Stein, C. (1987a). En quel lieu, dans quel cadre, à quelles fins, parler de ses patients? *Etudes freudiennes*, 31: 9–28. 1989

Stein, C. (1987b). *Les Erinyes d'une mère*. Quimper: Calligrammes.

Stein, C. (2011). *L'enfant imaginaire*. Paris: Flamarrion, Champs-essais 1017.

Stein, R. (1997). Analysis as a mutual endeavour—what does it look like? *Psychoanalytic Dialog*, 7: 869–880.

Stern, D., Sander, L. W., Nahum, J. P., Harrison, A. M., Lyons-Ruth, K., Morgan, A. C., Bruschweilerstern, N., & Tronick, E. Z. (1998). Non-interpretive mechanisms in psychoanalytic therapy: the "something more" than interpretation. *International Journal of Psychoanalysis*, 79: 903–921.

Symington, N. (1990). The possibility of human freedom and its transmission. *International Journal of Psychoanalysis*, 71(1): 95–106.

Tisseron, S. (2004). La difficulté d'être parent aujourd'hui. *Les parents,* 7th Meeting of the COPELFI (French-Speaking Conference on Child and Adolescent Psychiatry in Israel), October, Maaleh Ha Hamisha, Israel.

Tustin, F. (1984). Autistic shapes. *International Review of Psychoanalysis, 11:* 279–290.

Villa, F. (2011). Malaise dans la civilisation et desastre totalitaire. In: *Idéal, déception, fiction. Annuel de l'Association Psychanalytique de France* (pp. 73–94). Paris: Presses Universitaires de France.

Vincent, J.-D. (1986). *Biologie des passions.* Paris: Odile Jacob.

Vincent, J.-D. (2005). Biologie du désir et anthropologie de la psyché. In: F. Richard & F. Uribarri (Eds.), *Autour de l'œuvre d'André Green* (pp. 361–383). Paris: Presses Universitaires de France.

Weiler, Y. (2004). La mere porteuse et les changements de conception de la parentalité. (In Hebrew: *Em pundakait ve ha chinouim betfisat ha orout*). Accessed at: www.daat.ac.il/kitveyet/assia/haem.

Widlöcher, D. (1995). Pour une métapsychologie de l'écoute psychanalytique. *Revue française de psychanalyse, 59*(1): 1735–1786.

Widlöcher, D. (1996). *Les nouvelles cartes de la psychanalyse.* Paris: Odile Jacob.

Widlöcher, D. (1999). Affect et empathie. L'affect et sa perversion. *Revue française de psychanalyse, 63*(1): 173–186.

Widlöcher, D. (2007). Dialogue avec Julia Kristeva. *Revue française de psychanalyse, 71*(5): 1503–1507.

Wiesel, E. (1966). *Le chant des morts.* Paris: Seuil.

Winnicott, D. W. (1947). Hate in the counter-transference. In: *Collected Papers: Through Paediatrics to Psychoanalysis* (pp. 194–203). London: Tavistock, 1958.

Winnicott, D. W. (1954). Metapsychological and clinical aspects of regression within the psycho-analytical set-up. In: *Collected Papers: Through Paediatrics to Psychoanalysis* (pp. 278–294). London: Tavistock, 1958.

Winnicott, D. W. (1956). Primary maternal preoccupation. In: *Collected Papers: Through Paediatrics to Psychoanalysis* (pp. 300–305). London: Tavistock, 1958.

Winnicott, D. W. (1963). The development of the capacity for concern. In: *The Maturational Processes and the Facilitating Environment: Studies in the Theory of Emotional Development* (pp. 73–81). London: Hogarth Press, 1976.

Winnicott, D. W. (1964). The use of an object, relating through identifications. In: *Psychoanalytic Explorations* (pp. 218–246) . London: Karnac, 1989.

Wittgenstein, L. (1939). *Remarques mêlées.* Paris: Flammarion.

INDEX